Praise for *A Gathering of Spirits*

Doug Gwyn, a master of deep research and weaving multiple ideas and themes into a coherent whole, sharpens his focus to examine how today's "liberal" Friends evolved. From nineteenth century Hicksites, through the lens of biennial Friends General Conferences, to mid-twentieth century, we see FGC Friends and how they got here. By the beginning of the twentieth century Hicksite Friends mirrored the larger white middle class Protestant culture's focus on "practical Christianity" and "evolutionary progress," including "purity." The biennial Conferences that provide the lens for examining a half century of change, adopted the Chautauqua model of family vacations with uplifting lectures. Friends embraced the AFSC as the embodiment of moral activism. Two world wars and a Depression shook these complacent ethnocentric assumptions, as did the tireless work of individuals including Anna Jackson and Bayard Rustin enlarging Friends' understanding of racial issues, Rufus Jones and Clarence Pickett in emphasizing the importance of God, and a large cohort of Young Friends challenging lengthy vocal ministry, academic lectures, and the old divisions among Friends. Doug Gwyn weaves a variety of strands, inviting productive pondering of where we are and how we got here.

— Martha Paxon Grundy, author of *Tall Poppies: Supporting Gifts of Ministry and Eldering in the Monthly Meeting*

Doug Gwyn is probably contemporary Quakerism's most prolific and wide-ranging author, equally at home in the seventeenth and twenty-first centuries. *A Gathering of Spirits* is an important contribution to understanding recent Quaker history, with implications and insights for historians, not only of Quakerism, but pacifism, social activism, and liberal religion generally.

— Thomas Hamm, Professor of History and Director of Special Collections, Earlham College and author of *The Quakers in America*

Friends General Conference is more than 135 years old. It has helped liberal American Friends get through peace and wars, booms and busts, theological twists and turns, and not a few shocks of recognition. It has been the home and showcase for many important Quakers, most of whose stories and achievements have been sorely neglected. That's because FGC's "progressive" ethos has been resolutely anti-historical. Only now, Doug Gwyn has begun to open the door to seeing and learning from the journeys of FGC Friends. His story goes from its insurgent beginnings in the 1870s to a certified, if characteristically "peculiar" niche in the 1950s Protestant Mainstream. Doug's narrative is gentle but searching, and he deftly puts FGC into a wider historical and religious context. Those who want to understand this major stream of Quakerism, the better to ponder and shape its future, can do no better than to start here.

— Chuck Fager, author of *Remaking Friends: How Progressive Friends Changed Quakerism & Helped Save America*

A Gathering of Spirits

The Friends General Conferences 1896–1950

by Douglas Gwyn

QUAKERPRESS PHILADELPHIA, PA

The inspiration for the title of this book is from a line from Quaker singer-songwriter Carrie Newcomer's "A Gathering of Spirits"

There's a gathering of spirits
There's a festival of friends
And we'll take up where we left off
When we all meet again.

The ideas expressed in her song express beautifully the best of the Friends General Conferences over the years.

Lean more about Carrie at carrienewcomer.com/

Copyright © 2018 by Douglas Gwyn

All rights reserved.

QuakerPress of Friends General Conference
1216 Arch Street, 2B
Philadelphia, PA 19107

Printed in the United States of America

No part of this work may be reproduced or transmitted in any form or by any means, electronic or mechanical, including photocopying and recording, or by any information storage or retrieval system, except as may be expressly permitted by the 1976 Copyright Act or in writing from the publisher. Requests for permission can be addressed to Permissions, Quaker Press of FGC, Friends General Conference, 1216 Arch St, Suite 2B, Philadelphia, PA 19107

Composition and design by David Botwinik
Backcover photograph of Doug Gwyn by John Meyer

ISBN 978-0-9993823-4-9 (paperback)
    978-0-9993823-5-6 (digital)

Library of Congress Cataloging-in-Publication Data
Gwyn, Douglas, 1948-
    A gathering of spirits: the Friends General Conferences 1896-1950 / by Douglas Gwyn
      pages cm
      ISBN 978-0-9993823-4-9(paperback) / ISBN 978-0-9993823-5-6 (digital)
      1. American History—Religious aspects—Society of Friends. 2. Society of Friends—Doctrines. 3. Christian life—Quaker authors. I. Title.
BKR803-76 1-6482010641 2018

To order more copies of this publication or other Quaker titles call 1-800-966-4556 or see the online catalog at www.quakerbooks.org.

CONTENTS

PREFACE
ix

INTRODUCTION
xi

CHAPTER 1
Pilgrims of Progress
Hicksite and Progressive Friends
on Their Way to Friends General Conference
1

CHAPTER 2
A Quaker Chautauqua
FGC's Formation and First Conferences, 1896-1904
35

CHAPTER 3
The New Normal
FGC Conferences 1906-1914
72

CHAPTER 4
Progress Revised
FGC Conferences 1916-1928
100

CHAPTER 5
An Expansive Depression
FGC Conferences 1930-1936
138

A Gathering of Spirits

CHAPTER 6
War Without, Reassessment Within
FGC Conferences 1938–1944
179

CHAPTER 7
Pax Americana and the End of FGC's Heroic Era
FGC Conferences 1946–1950
217

CONCLUSION
253

APPENDIX 1
A Quaker Moral Compass
266

APPENDIX 2
End Notes
270

INDEX
285

SOURCES
292

ACKNOWLEDGEMENTS
293

ABOUT THE AUTHOR
295

PREFACE

I am not a regular attender of Friends General Conference (FGC) Gatherings. I'm an introverted, bookish type who easily feels overwhelmed by the kaleidoscopic profusion of so many people, workshops, interest groups, and spontaneous happenings. I'm also melancholic, a temperament that recoils somewhat from celebration. Besides the jamboree atmospherics, Gatherings are also perennially interested in the new, the now, and the next. I've wondered, is this anything more than *zeitgeist*, the spirit of the times, blowing this way and that through a "Society of Trends" cast loose from the moorings of its tradition? Gathering themes such as 1993's "Riding the Wind of Spirit" seemed to confirm my misgiving. And yet, every time I have attended, I have been energized, inspired, and intrigued. What goes on here? I realized that perhaps I needed to take "zeitgeist" more seriously.

I also reflected that my interest in Quaker history has always been not only to understand what Friends said and did in different times, but to gain some *feeling* for what it was like to have faith and act faithfully in those times. So, the movement of the Spirit amid the "spirit of the times" has always been a keen interest motivating my work, in my several projects researching and writing on early English Friends, and more recently my history of Pendle Hill as a twentieth-century center for American Quaker renewal. This project, following the trajectory of the FGC Gatherings, offers an illuminating parallel to the Pendle Hill story.

I had originally hoped to trace the development of FGC Gatherings throughout the twentieth century, but that proved too large a task. As my research came up to 1950, I realized that the late 1940s were a time of major transition for liberal Quakerism in America, and I already had a good-sized book's worth of story to tell. Along the way, I found affect theory, a recent development in cultural studies, a helpful theoretical discipline for taking zeitgeist seriously. As with every book project I have undertaken, I have learned a great deal from this research and from the reflective and writing processes that it generated. I have grown in my admiration of the modern genius of Friends General Conference and gained greater perspective on my abiding misgivings. After all, the study of history is always an invitation to mixed feelings. I hope readers will find their own inspiration from this bittersweet story.

Douglas Gwyn
Pendle Hill, December 2017

INTRODUCTION

Doesn't a breath of air that pervaded earlier days caress us as well? In the voices we hear, isn't there an echo of now silent ones?... If so, then there is a secret agreement between past generations and the present one. Then our coming was expected on earth. Then, like every generation that preceded us, we have been endowed with a weak messianic power, a power on which the past has a claim. That claim cannot be settled cheaply.

— Walter Benjamin[1]

The Friends General Conference (FGC) was formally organized in 1900 as the culmination of an effort to pool the resources, courage, and vision of seven liberal-progressive yearly meetings of the Religious Society of Friends in North America. Biennial Conferences had begun during the preceding decade on an exploratory basis, with growing momentum. They became annual events in 1963 and were renamed FGC "Gatherings" in 1978. They continue to this day as joyous and ambitious reunions of one to two thousand Friends on various college campuses, mainly in the eastern United States.

This book tells the story of Friends General Conference up to 1950. It is the story of resurgence among liberal Hicksite yearly meetings, which had been in steady numerical decline over the nineteenth century. FGC has pursued a number of programmatic objectives, including religious education, outreach, ecumenical relations, and social action/service. But this story focuses primarily upon the Conferences themselves. These powerful but ephemeral events serve as a "registering instrument" of sorts, allowing us track what has inspired and concerned liberal-progressive Friends over the course of more than fifty years. The Conferences as such were not *actors* in that period of history so much as a kind of *Greek chorus* that registered the affects and reflections upon world events, social dilemmas, and Quaker responses to them. In a sense, the whole gathering of Friends and the busy week of lectures, round-tables, socializing, and recreation served as a collective lens through which each participant viewed afresh him/herself, the Religious Society of Friends, and the world with renewed courage and resolve.

Melancholy, Spleen, and Other Affects

The Conferences were filled with all kinds of informative presentations and critical discussions, but their main function was *affective*. In particular, the Conferences served (and still do today) to transform the affects of melancholy and grief into the affects of joy, celebration, and re-energized commitment. Melancholy is not an affect Americans, including modern Friends, readily recognize in themselves or express to others. We are a "yes we can" nation. Yet as Jonathan Flatley suggests in *Affective Mapping: Melancholia and the Politics of Modernism*,[2] melancholy and grief are the recurrent experiences of modernity, which promises so much advancement in the human condition, but which delivers cataclysmic wars, grinding poverty, systemic racism, and environmental devastation along with genuine progress. Friends probably carry the weight of the world's pain and yearn for a world of peace and justice more than most people. Moreover, their declining numbers and small, struggling local meetings often make the experience of melancholy even more acute.

Melancholy has been viewed in many ways throughout the centuries. Among the ancient Greeks, Hippocrates saw it as arising from an excess of black bile (the literal meaning of "melancholia"), one of the four bodily humors in ancient thought. Aristotle viewed melancholics as the most creative people in politics, literature, and the arts. In Elizabethan England, it was framed as despondency and withdrawal from the world. Later, the Romantics of the early nineteenth century viewed melancholy positively as intensified consciousness, as exemplified in Keats's "Ode to Melancholy." In the twentieth century and up to the present, "depression" replaced "melancholy" and has been viewed as a symptom to be treated and eliminated with the growing pharmacopeia of medical technology.

INTRODUCTION

Certainly, melancholy can descend into depression, numbness, and paralysis. As the cultural Marxist Walter Benjamin advocates in "Left-Wing Melancholy," melancholy must become *splenetic*—angry, energized—and connect with a political concern.[3] (In ancient humoral thought, the spleen was associated with yellow bile and an angry, choleric temperament.) At a workshop I recently attended at Pendle Hill, an FGC Friend and vibrant political activist described the energetic formation of her social witness. She said that rage energizes and sustains her action. Below the rage is sadness and fatigue. "But really, I just want to play."

Accordingly, I would suggest that paradoxically, melancholy—or grief—is the key affect undergirding the energetic activism that is so salient in liberal-progressive Quakerism. Friends spend most of the year in communities and workplaces where most people do not share Quaker faith, values, and hopes for the world. For one week of the year, and for more than a century, FGC Conferences have offered a prime opportunity to transform melancholy into *spleen*, through reunion, confirming speakers and workshops, celebration, and play.

Affects such as these become decisive in a liberal Quaker tradition that has emphasized spiritual experience, while being slowly drained of any particular set of beliefs. Liberal Friends explore a variety of cognitive systems: religious, scientific, psychological, sociological, and so on. But as a group, they identify with none of them in a definite way. One's personal experience remains the authoritative reference point.

But experience is an affective, embodied, precognitive realm that is not entirely a private domain. It partakes of wider affects floating in the culture.[4] Certain affects dominate a particular era and culture. For example, over the nineteenth and well into the twentieth century, the expanding horizons of human knowledge, the advances of science and technology, the broadening of the electoral franchise, the new wealth generated by capitalist expansion, generated in America and Western Europe an air of confidence in almost inevitable human *progress*. This story follows the ways liberal Friends experienced, thought about, and acted upon the pervasive ethos of progress in this period, primarily as it found expression in FGC's biennial Conferences.

xiii

Affects and the Inward Light

It should be clear that the concept of affect has implications for the Quaker understanding of the inward light and how its leadings are discerned, both individually and collectively. How do we differentiate between the light's divine leadings and the affects that blow around and within us? In the case of Friends General Conference, with its confidence in the light's "continuing revelation" and its acute attention to current events, the relationship between cultural affects and a finer discernment of the light's leading becomes crucial. How did the understanding of the light change in the development of liberal Quakerism?

Early and traditional Friends had used the term "inward light" to suggest that the inner, *immanent* revelation derives from a *transcendent* source, a God beyond human nature and the created order. They understood the inward light's divine revelation as intimately intertwined with Scripture's historical revelation. The two forms of revelation interpreted one another. As the nineteenth century progressed, Hicksite and Progressive Friends increasingly wrote in terms of an "inner light." That shift reflected a growing understanding of religious experience in humanistic terms. As we shall see in Chapter 1, this new emphasis was driven in part by the polarization between Hicksites and Orthodox Friends. The latter strongly emphasized the authority of the biblical revelation.

A more one-sidedly humanistic understanding of an "inner light" left the light's transcendent aspect less defined, even optional. We will hear a continued use of Christian, biblical language in the Conferences, but we will also detect a growing religious sensibility that could operate with or without reference to the Bible or God. As we will hear Jesse Holmes suggest, an inner light might simply be human nature at its best, a "best self."

This shift had implications not only for personal and communal discernment of the light's leading but also the way Friends discerned the larger currents of society and history. Early and traditional Friends had followed the Hebrew prophets in a *providential* reading of events. For example, George Fox understood the Quaker movement as the culmination of God's work in history to gather humanity into the light's teaching and to restore the harmony of Eden. Later, John Woolman envisioned a dark cloud of divine judgment to come upon European Americans for the sin of African American enslavement.

By contrast, we will hear among Hicksite and Conference Friends a sustained emphasis upon human *progress*, sometimes predicated upon divine purposes, other times stated in more purely humanistic terms. As the catastrophes of the twentieth century accumulate and Friends struggle to meet them in new forms of service, we will hear some Conference speakers such as Clarence Pickett and Bliss Forbush reassert the need for divine guidance and faith in divine purposes in history.

These are significant trends to note as we try to understand the trajectory of FGC Conferences in the twentieth century. No matter how it is defined, the experience of the light is primarily at the affective level. Human reason frames it with available concepts that seem appropriate to it, whether biblical, humanistic, or scientific. George Fox's counsel to "stand still in the light, out of all thoughts" is an invitation to immerse oneself in the affective level of knowing. While the light should not be simply reduced to affect, the affective level of existence is where it is encountered. Early Friends made this point when they wrote of the light abiding in the human heart or conscience, but not to be identified with heart or conscience as such.

Viewing FGC Conferences within Three Concentric Horizons

The widest horizon, or frame of interpretation, of this book will be the transitions of capitalist political economy, starting with the high-point of the British imperial regime in the latter nineteenth century, followed by the inter-imperialist war (1914-1918) pitting Germany against Britain, France, and eventually the United States. That cataclysm led to the demise of the British regime and the emergence of the American regime as decisive in the global economy. This widest horizon is a "political unconscious" largely outside the FGC conversation.[5]

Cosmopolitanism, a worldly perspective, is the cultural ethos of imperialism at its centers of power. Liberal FGC Friends prided themselves in their cosmopolitan outlook, a worldliness their more sectarian Quaker grandparents decried. Metropolitanism, the privileged vantage-point of a world-city, also informed the FGC perspective, given that nearly half of its members were in the Philadelphia area over the first half of the twentieth century. The eventual choice of Cape May, New Jersey (a short train ride from Philadelphia) as the regular site of biennial Conferences provided a cool respite from the dank heat of the Delaware valley and a liminal (threshold) space for personal refreshment and collective encouragement. As one speaker at Cape May in the 1930s quipped, the Conference was testimony to "the fatherhood of God, the brotherhood of man, and the neighborhood of Philadelphia."

The second horizon is the middle-class moorings of progressive reform politics in this period. More than they cared to admit, FGC Friends were part of a wider Protestant coalition among the growing American middle classes. They were outraged by the arrogant excesses of the rich and equally appalled by the miserable social conditions and degraded morality of poor immigrants and minority races in America. These Friends were leaders in the purity campaigns of the progressive movement, particularly the drive for temperance that eventually led to Prohibition. Chautauqua, the Methodist-founded lakeside resort in western New York State, was the focal point of the Protestant progressive movement. It served as the template for FGC Conferences, combining the middle-class family summer vacation with uplifting, informative lectures and discussion.

Liberal Friends downplayed their commonalities with the larger liberal Protestant consensus, perhaps because Friends had used the wider Church as a rhetorical foil since their beginnings. Quaker sociologist Ben Pink Dandelion has sometimes described liberal Friends as a "liberal sect," implying a group with abiding sectarian sensibilities, while largely sharing the convictions of a wider liberal-progressive consensus.

The third and narrowest horizon is the wider family of Friends. British Friends, who were undergoing their own liberal renewal at the end of the nineteenth century, became important allies to FGC Friends. Their importance loomed especially large owing to the

INTRODUCTION

global dominance of the British Empire and its regime of capitalist expansion. Meanwhile, the long-standing polarization between liberalizing Hicksite Friends and evangelizing Orthodox Friends during the nineteenth century provides the FGC trajectory with a mirror-image where the contrasts between the two also confirm their commonalities. The "twinning" dynamics between the two made this nearest horizon the most conscious for Friends at the time, but also the most mystifying. These two competing versions of Quakerism were in many respects two versions of the same thing, particularly when viewed within the wider horizons.

These are the horizons within which we will follow the trajectory of 27 FGC conferences (1896 to 1950), from their convergence out of nineteenth-century Hicksite Quaker developments, through two world wars and a major depression, to mid-century.

Outline of This Book

In Chapter 1 we will begin by reflecting upon the formation of the early Quaker movement out of two different forms of Seeker expectation in the 1640s and 50s. The seeds of eventual divergence and separation among American Friends in the nineteenth century were contained in the bipolarity of those expectations. The original synthesis of those expectations which energized the early Quaker movement slowly broke down among American Friends, following the defeat of their utopian aims, particularly in Pennsylvania. We will then follow the trajectory of developments among Hicksite and Progressive Friends over the nineteenth century, leading to the first General Conferences of the 1890s. We will also devote some attention to the mirror-image trajectory of Orthodox and Gurneyite Quakerism in the same period.

In Chapter 2, covering 1896 to 1904, we will first set the context of liberal Quakerism in the wider progressive movement and the Chautauqua phenomenon. We will devote special attention to the watershed moment of the 1896 Conference on the Swarthmore College campus. We will note its resonance with the Manchester Conference the preceding year among British Friends and the communicating influence of John William Graham between the two. The decision to create an ongoing Friends General Conference during the 1900 Conference at Chautauqua in western New York State attests to the latter's influence. The aura of confident optimism, boosted by a Eurocentric ideology of evolutionary progress, expanded rapidly from there. We will find Friends to be leaders among progressives working for moral purity, most of all for temperance.

Chapter 3, covering 1906 to 1914, tracks the euphoric affects among FGC Friends, peaking in 1912, the year of progressive triumph with Woodrow Wilson's election as President. The ideology of steady, inexorable evolutionary progress reached its zenith in these years, only to be blind-sided by World War I's devastating impact. The 1914 Conference, held during the first weeks of the war, found Friends in disarray regarding their peace testimony, which had become a "peace principle" or "peace position"—a matter of advocacy rather than an existential commitment for many. But along the way, we will hear urgent calls for more work on behalf of African Americans during these darkest days of segregation, along with a growing sense of imminent triumph among suffragists.

Chapter 4 follows Conferences from 1916 to 1928 alongside the formation of the American Friends Service Committee, which helped refocus FGC's chastened progressivism during and after the war toward more concretely constructive avenues of service. The rise of a mainstream peace movement balanced the decline of the wider progressive movement. New modes of group process began to make slow headway at Conferences with the work of Rachel Davis DuBois. And FGC finally began its long series of Conferences at Cape May. We will finish by noting the importance of the new liberal book culture both in the mainstream and among Friends.

In Chapter 5, Conferences 1930 to 1936 show Friends becoming expansive amid the Great Depression, with the AFSC leading the way. Young Friends began asserting themselves as a generational cohort concerned not only about the growing threat of war but also with the continuing blights of racism and pressing FGC to renew its religious sense of purpose. The "Statement of Economic Objectives" was a high-point of socialist thought among American Friends. Jesse Holmes and Jane Rushmore, leaders of an earlier generational cohort, were at the peak of their leadership and influence.

INTRODUCTION

New independent and united meetings, inspired by the influence of AFSC, appeared increasingly on FGC's horizon.

Chapter 6 follows Conferences 1938 to 1944, when a second world war rallied Friends together in new ways. There were large-scale defections from the peace testimony among draft-age Quaker males in this war as in the preceding one. But a growing high-school-aged cohort of Friends were growing in conviction regarding issues of racial justice. Bayard Rustin, African American Friend and Fellowship of Reconciliation activist, was one important influence. Meanwhile, we will hear more acute questions raised about FGC's religious convictions from Lewis Benson, Bliss Forbush, and Clarence Pickett. The passing of Jesse Holmes in 1942 marks the end of FGC's most ebullient era.

Finally, Chapter 7 finds FGC's initial heroic era ending with the Conferences from 1946 to 1950. The death of Jesse Holmes was followed by that of Rufus Jones and major changes in FGC and AFSC leadership. Friends held deep concerns about the rise of a permanent military establishment, continuing conscription, and the advent of cold war politics in America. The confirmation of FGC's membership in the World Council of Churches, combined with the movement toward "organic union" with Orthodox Friends, continued to press issues of religious identity and purpose as the postwar era began.

A Conclusion will summarize the main findings of the chapters and offer a brief sketch of major trends in FGC Quakerism during the second half of the twentieth century.

Caveats

First, readers may be challenged by the consistently androcentric language, well-intended but paternalistic racial attitudes, Eurocentric cultural assumptions, and Christocentric religious perspectives of the speakers and writers in this period. It is salutary to let these Friends be persons of their times, groping their way as best they knew how, as we do in ours. It brings to mind Tina Fey's wonderful comment when receiving the Mark Twain Award for comedy: "I just hope that a hundred years from now, people will marvel at what a racist *I* was."

Second, it is also important to note that this is more or less a history of FGC Conferences, not an annual catalog. There is no attempt here to give a complete accounting of speakers, round tables, business sessions, or other events at the Conferences, useful as that might be. I have chosen to highlight speakers, addresses, themes, round tables, and some related FGC organizational developments within the context of wider trends among Friends, American society, and world events. As stated earlier, I chose to study the Conferences as a "registering instrument" for the affects of inspiration and concern among American liberal Friends during this period. Other researchers would no doubt find other Conference materials to highlight, according to different interests.

And third, I undertook this study to understand better a major Quaker phenomenon of the twentieth century that has attracted and intrigued me over the years. The resulting book serves as a companion piece to my recent *Personality and Place: The Life and Times of Pendle Hill* (2014). But this is not an uncritical telling of the story. The following chapters pose a number of questions, mostly as they were raised by Friends within or near FGC's orbit. These regard the neglect of intellectual, theological, and spiritual foundations by a liberal-progressive renewal strongly oriented toward outward social issues and activism. The chapters also emphasize wider cultural influences on FGC developments, partly as a corrective to many Quaker histories that are written as if nothing came before Friends and nothing else was going on around Friends. I hope readers will appreciate the occasional references to wider context, even if they make Friends look a little less "special."

I should also acknowledge that I grew up in the Orthodox-Gurneyite stream of American Friends and have continued to devote periods of my ministry in that stream. This no doubt adds a particular perspective to this book. But I have happily spent much of my adult life in FGC circles, always stimulated and challenged among these my Friends. Like Reinhold Niebuhr, I often find myself "theologically to the right and politically to the left of religious liberals." It may be my combination of Christian and Marxist perspectives that makes me suspicious of the "progress" that was such an article of faith among liberal Friends in the period of this book.

CHAPTER 1

Pilgrims of Progress
Hicksite and Progressive Friends on Their Way to Friends General Conference

Progress is the stirring watchword
Cheers them upward to the height:
Canst thou pause and play the laggard,
With its glories full in sight?
— from a Quaker hymn to progress, 1850[6]

Melancholy and Spleen: Early Seekers and Quakers

It can be useful to follow the trajectory of developments that led to a movement or institution, and not simply begin with its founding. In the case of a religious institution like the Friends General Conference, it is revealing to trace the creative interaction of religious ideas with wider social currents and cultural affects. So, this chapter tells the story of Hicksite and Progressive Friends in their progress through the nineteenth century, leading up to the formation of Friends General Conference. But let us begin by looking briefly at the origins of the Quaker movement in the 1650s, which contained the seeds for the bifurcation of American Quakerism in the 1820s.

As I showed in earlier work,[7] the early Friends started out as a nonviolent cultural revolution from the grassroots of English society during the Puritan Commonwealth of the 1650s. They gathered together a variety of religious and social radicals, particularly the thousands of Seekers who had dropped out of all churches during the English Civil War of the 1640s. These Seekers were of two basic orientations.[8] The first still held to the Reformation dream of "primitive Christianity revived." But after so many virulent debates and wars between competing reformations, they no longer believed that the true Church could be reconstructed by chapter and verse of Scripture. They looked for new apostles and a new Pentecost to restore the true, visible Church. These new apostles would offer a correct teaching, beyond the Reformation stalemate over creeds, church government, and sacramental practice. In effect, these Seekers were conservatives driven to radical conclusions. This orientation seems to have predominated in northern England where the Quaker movement took shape and where most of the central leadership was gathered by George Fox.

But a second variety of Seekers, sometimes called Waiters, emerged by 1647. They were probably more numerous in the South and in the Parliamentary Army. They reasoned that God would not restore a New Testament Church that had corrupted so soon after the apostolic generation. God would not take them backward, but was taking them forward, toward a dawning new age of the Spirit. Ancient Israel had lived in the dispensation of the law, then the Church lived in the dispensation of the gospel. But both had fallen into corruption. The new dispensation of the Spirit would produce "spiritual Christians" who would receive the Spirit's teaching and the sacraments as inward experience. They believed that this new age was dawning, and that it would be known beyond the bounds of Christendom, by all who seek the Spirit within. Consequently, they were less interested in restoring a visible Church than in recognizing a universal, invisible Church of all who know the Spirit. These Seekers were *proto-liberals*, anticipating the Enlightenment's emphasis upon universal reason and progressive revelation, each dispensation moving to a higher, clearer vision of truth.

However, by 1650, both kinds of Seekers experienced an eclipse of their hope. They were grieved to see the Puritans in Parliament and its Army settling the nation far short of the kingdom of heaven on earth or even the civil and religious liberties that had been promised. Seekers increasingly called themselves "mourners after Sion." Some despaired and fell into Ranter rage against the new establishment.

The Quaker movement emerged from that twilight of radical hope. Its message and spiritual breakthrough both confirmed and disconfirmed the various expectations of both kinds of Seekers. The central founding figure, George Fox (1624-1691), a Midlander, seemed to be the apostle northern Seekers were looking for, and he galvanized their energies to begin restoring a true, visible Church. But he offered no new creed or sacramental observance. Meanwhile, he confirmed the Waiters' expectations that the Spirit taught directly and the sacraments were inwardly received. Yet he scorned their dispensational schemes of progressive revelations. Fox's apocalyptic message that "Christ is come to teach his people himself" by the light in all human consciences neither turned back toward New Testament times nor strained forward toward a dawning age of the Spirit, but grounded their practice in "waiting upon the Lord," finding Christ present in the present to lead them in fulfillment of their dashed hopes.

Fox's message and spiritual direction transmuted Seeker melancholy into the spleen (righteous anger) of the Lamb's War, a relentless attack upon the established Church of England, various social ills, and moral blights. It was a nonviolent campaign for nothing less than the kingdom of heaven on earth, enacted through concrete peaceful, egalitarian practices. But Quaker nonviolent spleen was quickly answered by violent spleen from the government and hostile mobs weary of years of political and religious upheaval.

Through sustained persecution, first by the Puritans and then after 1660 by the restored monarchy and state church, the Quaker contagion was slowed, its founding prophets imprisoned and dying. Starting in 1666, Fox and other surviving leaders repositioned the movement to become a hedged, trans-Atlantic sect within a secularizing, early modern society. This transformation was so complete that by 1700, new generations of English Friends did not grasp the revolutionary meaning of their sect's beginnings. They believed they had been persecuted for thirty-seven years for their religious beliefs and practices, not for their earlier threat to the entire social order. Still, in terms of collective affects, a certain melancholic sense of defeat and loss remained.

Quaker utopian energies found a second, revised expression in the colonial experiment of William Penn (1644-1718), an upper-class, second-generation convert. As post-revolutionary Friends moved past the apocalyptic moment of a revelatory present, Penn's thought split along the two Seeker trajectories we described above. He could write as a Protestant-style sectarian in books such as *No Cross, No Crown* (1682). But as he wrote political tracts in the 1670s promoting religious toleration, Penn also developed a Quaker version of early liberal social contract theory. Penn's thought has singular relevance for our story.

The first generation of Friends had proclaimed that God's *covenant* was a living light in human conscience. The Old and New Testaments (another word for covenants) were important historic revelations of that living covenant, but they are not the covenant itself, which must be constantly discerned and renewed among people of faith. Similarly, Penn argued that a constitution is a living, evolving reality within and among the people of a given polity. Written constitutions are simply the historic expressions of understandings reached by the people in time and will evolve over time. Perhaps wishing not to equate constitution with covenant, Penn adopted a Platonic term, *synteresis*, for the ongoing process of constitutional discernment within a given polity.[9]

Penn had an astonishing opportunity to test out his political theories when he received a colonial charter from Charles II and founded Pennsylvania in 1682. He drafted successive Frames of Government for his colony, none of which were adopted by the Pennsylvania Assembly. It took a twenty-year process to complete Pennsylvania's constitution. This was a matter of great personal frustration to Penn, but it confirmed his theory of constitution as a process of continuing discernment, or synteresis.

Penn's experiment struggled yet succeeded well for its first fifty years. But Quaker control of the colony proved untenable as it was outflanked by unruly European elements flooding into the colony, violating the friendly agreements Penn had established with native peoples. Finally, Quaker peace policy was overruled by British imperial policy in the French and Indian War of the 1750s. Friends began withdrawing from government. Then, by the time of the American Revolution, they were scapegoated as loyalists for their attempts to mediate the conflict and for their refusal to join the military struggle for independence.

CHAPTER 1   Pilgrims of Progress

In the meantime, Friends were enormously successful on both sides of the Atlantic in business, banking, and advances in science and technology. But socially and religiously, they kept some distance from the mainstream, as Britain expanded its imperial quest and the American colonies ran roughshod over Native American peoples and exploited the slave-labor of African Americans. With the collapse of Penn's utopian experiment, American Friends withdrew further and undertook a major tightening of internal discipline. Large-scale disownments of members ensued during the latter eighteenth-century. By 1800, Friends were diminished in numbers and politically marginalized. But they had also succeeded in renouncing slaveholding and become early leaders in the movement for abolition. They had regained their countercultural edge, even if it came at great cost to their prestige and influence.

A melancholic tone pervades in the published religious journals of this period, written mainly by Quaker ministers. These were the Friends most deeply immersed in traditional Quaker spirituality, and in the arduous practice of a nonprofessional ministry that included considerable travel. That melancholy is sharply etched in the journal of Elizabeth Ashbridge[10] (1713-1755), perhaps because she came to Friends from another background. She grew up in the Church of England, had a free spirit, and was good enough at singing and dancing to be recruited by a stage company. As a teenager, she lived for a while with a Quaker relative, who forbade her to sing and dance. "The great vivacity of my natural disposition would not, in this instance, suffer me to give way to the gloomy sense of sorrow and conviction.... I became more wild and airy than ever."

Ashbridge emigrated to America. She had occasion to visit a Quaker meeting for worship in Boston, where "I heard a woman Friend speak, at which I was a little surprised ... and I looked upon her with pity for her ignorance, and contempt for her practice, saying to myself, 'I'm sure you're a fool, and if ever I turn Quaker, which will never be, I will not be a preacher.'" Over time and through personal trials, however, "I became extremely melancholy, and took no delight in any thing. Had all the world been mine, I would have given it gladly for one glimpse of hope.... My singing was turned into mourning, and my dancing into lamentation."

5

By degrees she became a practicing Friend, for which her husband reviled her. She persisted, however. He eventually relented, saying, "My dear, I have seen the beauty there is in the Truth, and that thou hast followed the right way." She replied that she hoped he too would follow in that way. But he replied, "O, I cannot bear the reproach thou dost, to be called turn-coat, and become a laughing-stock to the world; but I'll no longer hinder thee." Ashbridge eventually became a recorded minister in Burlington (New Jersey) Quarterly Meeting, the same Quarter as the better-known Quaker minister, John Woolman (1720-1772). Both died while traveling abroad in ministry. Ashbridge fell ill among Irish Friends and succumbed at the age of forty-two. Woolman died of smallpox among English Friends at age fifty-two.

Woolman's journal exudes a less acute but pervasive melancholy over the spiritual and social tendencies he witnessed in the American colonies in general and among Friends in particular.[11] Woolman was part of the alliance of ministers and elders that succeeded in tightening Quaker discipline in both Britain and America in the latter eighteenth century. These astringent measures had unintended effects on Quaker faith and practice, however. In terms of practice, the ranks of Friends were closed more tightly against the incursions of "the world."[12] But attention to *practice* led to a neglect of the *faith* that had earlier undergirded and enlivened the practice. The spiritual wine was turning to vinegar. And by the start of the nineteenth century, tensions within the Society were starting to show.

Fault-lines Among Friends

Not surprisingly, given the relative neglect of matters of faith, the flashpoints of controversy developed around points of belief and the Bible. The doctrine of atonement, that most unique and complex core of Christian faith, was a key confusion. Sometime before his death in 1793 (of smallpox at age 42, while traveling in ministry in Ireland), the American Quaker minister Job Scott wrote "Remarks on the Nature of Salvation by Christ" and some related essays,[13] restating the traditional Quaker understanding. He maintained the tragic sense that one is saved by Christ's death only as one *participates*

CHAPTER 1   Pilgrims of Progress

in it, by renouncing self-will and living into the light of God's will and universal love. One is not justified by Christ's death without also being sanctified through a long process of conversion to the way Christ himself lived. But perhaps weary of their melancholic marginalization in American society, Friends were ready to trade this tragic spirituality for a more comic one.

Some Friends, most notably wealthier ones with wider social connections, were attracted by the evident vitality of evangelical Protestants, with their doctrinal clarity, emphasis upon the Holy Spirit, moral rigor, and social reform energies. These Friends looked upon their own implicit faith with alarm and began pressing the importance of Christian doctrines such as the Trinity, the divinity of Christ, the substitutionary atonement of his death (with no need to share in it), even the virgin birth.

Other Friends were scandalized by this doctrinal emphasis, which had never been codified by earlier generations of Friends. They responded not only with objections against doctrinal standards, but also with various skeptical viewpoints about the Bible itself. Two camps began to form in the early years of the century. Those influenced by evangelical doctrine were referred to as the Orthodox, while those who objected were dubbed "Hicksites," as they gathered around the most venerable and articulate critic of Orthodoxy, the Long Island farmer and recorded minister Elias Hicks (1748-1830).[14] While the Orthodox were influenced by evangelicalism, some sectors of the Hicksite faction, particularly wealthier urban Friends, were drawn toward Unitarianism, with its confidence in human progress, liberal attitudes to religion, and its own social reform activities.

The doctrinal controversies that ensued reveal that many Friends had lost the early Quaker sense of Scripture. Both sides argued over the literal, propositional truth or falsehood of biblical texts and the Christian doctrines that churches had derived from them. But the early Quaker breakthrough had been to know the truth of the Bible's stories and teachings *participationally*. For example, the early Quaker leader Richard Hubberthorne in an audience with King Charles II in 1660 was asked, "How did you come to believe that the Scriptures were true?" He answered, "I have believed the Scriptures from a child to be a declaration of truth, when I had but

Elias Hicks. Courtesy of Friends Historical Library of Swarthmore College.

a literal knowledge, natural education and tradition; but now I know the Scriptures to be true by the manifestations and operation of God fulfilling them in me."[15] So, for example, the gospel story of Jesus born of a virgin was a matter to be neither affirmed nor denied as history; but its truth could be discovered in the mystery of Christ formed in a pure heart. Thus, one knew the truth of the Bible only as one participated in its stories, through the enlightening guidance of Christ's Spirit.

    Later in the century, some Hicksite Friends further questioned the Hebrew Bible's description of Israel's wars as divinely sanctioned. Their experience of a God of peace and universal love gave them moral qualms regarding the Old Testament.[16] They viewed the New Testament revelation as a progressive advancement on a primitive Hebrew faith. By contrast, early Friends raised no questions about the holy war traditions of the Bible, but instead quoted from them

CHAPTER 1   Pilgrims of Progress

freely in their nonviolent struggle, the Lamb's War, against religious repression and social injustice. But they also witnessed that as followers of Christ, their weapons were strictly spiritual.

Thus, as both parties lost the deeper, spiritual reading of Scripture, Orthodox Friends resorted to doctrinal affirmations while Hicksites raised moral objections. And as biblical literacy had slowly ebbed from its all-time high at the end of the Reformation, fewer Friends were so immersed in Scripture as to find their way between its lines. Hence, many Orthodox and Hicksite Friends were trapped in the same literalism, albeit coming to opposite conclusions.

This problem was compounded by Hicksite perceptions that the Orthodox aimed to impose their will upon Friends through the select meetings of ministers and elders. These yearly meeting bodies possessed authority to set standards of faith and practice and to discipline Friends at variance with those standards. Hicksite suspicions grew during the 1810s when Philadelphia Yearly Meeting proposed a conference of all American yearly meetings to produce a uniform discipline, a standard for all American Friends to follow.[17]

If we view these developments in light of the Quaker beginnings we briefly described at the start of this chapter, we may see the two Seeker agendas pulling apart. The Orthodox drifted toward the Reformation, by way of its renewed evangelical energies, while Hicksites drifted toward the liberal Enlightenment and its glowing promises of progress.

We have been examining the growing polarization and eventual split among American Friends at the cognitive level of religious ideas. But the deeper motivations of separation took shape on the embodied, *affective* level. We can gain helpful perspective from Sigmund Freud's analysis of melancholy as insufficiently mourned losses. In "Mourning and Melancholy" (1895) Freud viewed mourning as a process in which the shadow of the lost object of desire falls upon ego. Mourning becomes melancholy as "one part of the ego sets itself over against the other, judges it critically, and, as it were, takes it as its object." He clarified this process further, observing that as the shadow of the lost object fell upon the ego, "an object-loss was transformed into an ego-loss and the conflict between the ego and the loved person into a cleavage between the critical activity of the

9

ego and the ego as altered by identification."[18] This is the key point of Freud's theory for our consideration. Let us apply it to the collective affects of the Hicksite controversy.

I would propose that the breakdown in Quaker consciousness derived from the lingering affects of two traumatic losses of utopian desire. The original persecution and defeat of the revolutionary Lamb's War in the seventeenth century was compounded by the defeat of the American Quaker utopian project, Penn's "Holy Experiment" in Pennsylvania, and the further trauma as Friends were stigmatized as loyalists during the American Revolution. There was also a collective guilt for their failure to protect their Native American friends and for their participation in African American slaveholding, which they had completely renounced only by 1800.

The consequent tightening of discipline and self-marginalization of Friends constituted a withdrawal of libidinal-utopian energy into the collective Quaker ego, as intensified self-identification. But an internal division occurred, a split in the collective ego, becoming in this case two altered identifications (one with evangelicalism and the other with Unitarianism) and two judgments, each against the other. The shattered affects of this period are evident in the rampant mutual vilification before, during, and long after the split, and in the impaired powers of discernment among even the most gifted ministers. For example, Joseph Hoag (1762-1846) lost his psychic ability to "discern states" of individuals and meetings during the controversy and schism, and apparently never regained it.[19] The divisions in theology and polity were the semi-conscious outworkings of this deeper affective split.

Thus, melancholy turned into spleen destructively through internal conflict. But it did not end with the Great Separation between Orthodox and Hicksites in 1827-28. Both parties suffered further conflict and schism among themselves. Elias Hicks and most who followed him were conservatives, disturbed by the intake of foreign doctrines by Orthodox Friends. In fact, most Orthodox Friends were similarly conservative. Farmers, artisans, tradespeople, shopkeepers, and other small-business people populated both groups. Meanwhile, the impetus both for evangelical renewal among the Orthodox and for Unitarian revision among Hicksites came primarily from a small sector of wealthier, urban Friends, with wider social connections and intellectual influences.[20]

Separation and Its Discontents

The Great Separation was bruising enough. But both streams experienced further controversy and schism over the next twenty years, as the more provocative minorities on both sides pushed their agendas for renewal and as conservatives drew back. The English Quaker banker and minister Joseph John Gurney (1788-1847) made a major impact on Orthodox Friends during an extended American tour (1837-38). Gurney had been strongly affected by Anglican evangelicals at Cambridge and offered an articulate synthesis of evangelical and Quaker doctrines that inspired many. More conservative Orthodox Friends, led by the New England minister John Wilbur (1774-1856), separated from "Gurneyites" in 1845. Other "Conservative" Quaker departures followed the "Wilburites" over the remainder of the century.

Gurneyite Friends gained in numbers and momentum, eventually adopting revivals, pastoral leadership, and "programmed" meetings for worship after the Civil War. They were the only American Quaker group that experienced growth during the nineteenth century. The largest gains were achieved across the Midwest and West, as Gurneyites hybridized first with evangelical Methodism and then with the Holiness movement in the 1880s.[21] But these developments are not part of our focus here—except as a revealing mirror-image of Hicksite trends.

Among Hicksite Friends, the conservative majority hoped to return to the hedged quiet of traditional Quaker faith and practice. "As the Israel of God, we must dwell alone, and not mix in the popular currents of the world," Amos Peaslee wrote in 1838.[22] But the more articulate and activist minority viewed the Separation as a long-awaited liberation for radical reform, both among Friends and in the wider world. Elias Hicks and other elder leaders of the movement passed from the scene by the early 1830s, clearing space for new leadership with bolder visions. Most notably, Lucretia Mott (1793-1880), Joseph Dugdale (1810-1896), and Jonathan Plummer

(1835-1918) would become influential leaders in the decades to come.

Conservatives and reformers were soon in conflict. Phebe Johnson told Hicksite conservatives in 1831, "Framed within the narrow limits of sectarian feeling, your hearts are forbidden to expand with that universal love which marked the early founders of a society, that owned no other bond of fellowship than unity in the spirit—no other hedge than the circumscribing power of truth."[23] From the conservative side, Richard Price complained in 1845 that "the very people, whose activity was the procuring cause of the Separation—They used Elias as a cloak to get unbounded liberty, & to press upon Society their new Doctrines."[24] Of course, "new doctrines" among the evangelical Orthodox were the very thing that had scandalized Hicks and his followers in the first place. But new doctrines among the Hicksites were coming from very different directions.

The 1830s saw an expansion of the electoral franchise in many states to include all white males, enriching the atmosphere of democratic aspiration. The spread of public education increased literacy in many areas. New paper, printing, and binding technologies—concomitant with the market revolution underway in Britain and America—exerted profound effects upon everyone, including Friends. There were fewer than ten newspapers in America in 1789. There were more than a thousand by 1835. There were no American Quaker periodicals in 1820. There were four by 1830. The Hicksite controversy had generated tract warfare from both sides and the Quaker penchant for publishing only continued to grow.

Reform-minded Hicksites like Phebe Johnson, quoted above, were reading more widely. Their world was opening up to newspapers, magazines, literature, books about scientific discovery, abolition, and other reform causes. Harriet Beecher Stowe's *Uncle Tom's Cabin* (1852) was a watershed event for the abolition movement, an affective synthesis of literary art and social concern that made hearts ache in empathy and burn for justice. Print media affected human consciousness in this period as profoundly as electronic media have impacted our own in the past half-century. By 1855, Wilmington Hicksite Benjamin Ferris remarked, "It seems that the principal channel for the intellectual and spiritual improvement of our race, so far as that improvement depends on man, is through the reading of books. This is emphatically the reading age."[25] All these developments augured against the authority of the select meetings of elders and ministers, to whom Friends were expected to defer in all questions of faith and practice.

So, we can readily recognize the cognitive expansion of the Hicksite worldview, especially among the reform-minded. But it was also an expansion of the affective registers, an attunement to the wider culture, increasingly quickened to the new and the next. The discoveries of science, the innovations of technology, an increasingly optimistic view of human nature and its potential, and a demand for religious and social reform converged into a steady drumbeat that found its name in "progress." A sense of progressive revelation can be heard occasionally from Hicks himself, who wrote in 1823 that "every generation must have more light than the preceding one." His friend and correspondent William Poole (1764-1829) went further to suggest that "we may now be on the verge of a great revolution" and hoped that Friends would "go every length that such a revolution in sentiment may require."[26]

Revolutions usually involve some amount of patricide, literal or figurative. Hicks and Poole were perhaps fortunate to die before the bloodletting began. But there were still plenty of conservative patriarchs left to resist change. Ruth Spencer, a minister from upstate New York, prophesied to the men's business meeting of Baltimore Yearly Meeting in 1832, "A day is coming [that] will try the foundations of this Society more than it has been tried. . . . Nothing but judgment will do for us. . . . Many there are that might have been as Stars of the first magnitude in the firmament of God's power that are falling and have fallen." Progressive reformers in the 1830s were determined to limit the terms of elders, to reduce the authority of select meetings of ministers and elders, or to eliminate them entirely, to "mingle" more freely with "the world's people," particularly in the pursuit of social reform, and generally to introduce more liberty of individual conscience in matters of both faith and practice.[27]

The select meetings insisted that they should control the Quaker message to the wider society on abolition and other social issues. Individual Friends should not speak out. But in some cases, it

Lucretia Mott. Courtesy of Friends Historical Library of Swarthmore College.

appeared that wealthy Quaker elders were not anxious to make official statements detrimental to their investment or trade in cotton and other slave-produced commodities.[28]

In a word, the matter at issue might be called Quaker *deregulation*. No one probably considered the connections at the time, but surely the growth of free-market economics under the Anglo-American regime of capital expansion was one factor in the growing free market of ideas through print media and the free-market spirituality developing among the most advanced Hicksite spirits. The interaction of economic integration, technological innovation, and expansive ideological ferment produced a heady brew of affects in the first half of the nineteenth century.

CHAPTER 1 Pilgrims of Progress

Lucretia Coffin Mott emerged by the 1840s as the most articulate leader among this new generational cohort of leaders. Like George Fox among the first generation of Friends, she became a central figure among progressive reformers, Quaker and beyond, through her ability to synthesize and articulate key innovations, and to discern the tendency of events. Mott read widely (her home was full of books, newspapers, and magazines) and possessed a keen intellect. In an address given in New York to the annual meeting of the American Anti-Slavery Society in 1848, she spoke of a "law of progress" running through human history, from God's command to Abraham to leave his father's house for an unknown land, through the teachings of Jesus, the Reformation, the advent of women ministers, the growth of the temperance and peace movements, and most of all the rising tide of sentiment for the abolition of slavery.[29] That same year, Mott was a key initiator of the first women's rights convention at Seneca Falls, New York. Elizabeth Cady Stanton, another key organizer, recalled her early impressions of Mott:

> It seemed to me like meeting a being from some larger planet, to find a woman who dared to question the opinions of Popes, Kings, Synods, Parliaments, with the same freedom she would criticize an editorial in the *London Times*, recognizing no higher authority than the judgment of a pure-minded, educated woman.
>
> When I first heard from the lips of Lucretia Mott that I had the same right to think for myself that Luther, Calvin, and John Knox had, and the same right to be guided by my own convictions, and would no doubt live a higher, happier life than if guided by theirs, I felt at once a new-born sense of dignity and freedom.[30]

In terms of religious doctrine, Mott had made it clear as early as 1843 that she was happy being called a "heretic." Her husband, James Mott, reported, "Lucretia preaches heresies boldly, to the great annoyance of all orthodox believers."[31] Notwithstanding her prestige as a recorded Friends minister, Mott stood with other Quaker reformers in advocating the abolition of select meetings of ministers and elders. The Orthodox had used the select meetings in trying to corral Hicksites. And now conservative Hicksites aimed to use the same tactic against the reformers. Mott concluded, "While our present Discipline remains as it is, giving power to a few over the ministry, we may expect such results to follow.... A radical change is called for."³²

Progressive-reformers and conservatives found themselves in spiraling conflict during the 1830s, erupting into new separations during the 1840s. The issue of abolition was the flashpoint. As gradualism gave way to "immediatism," a wave of "come-outerism" swept among reformers in many churches. It was time to leave any religious body hesitating to support abolition unambiguously. New separations followed, resulting in Progressive, or Congregational, yearly meetings. Chuck Fager and Thomas Hamm have provided new studies of this phenomenon, important to our understanding of Friends General Conference beginnings.³³

The Spirit of 1848

There seem to be certain years when powerful affects sweep across the land, even around the globe. George Fox recorded quaking erupting in his Midlands network of worship groups in the year 1648. Gerrard Winstanley alluded to it the same year, further south. He started his notorious Digger commune in Surrey early the next year. In my own lifetime, the year 1968 saw revolutionary ferment in the United States and around the world. And 1848 was another such year: revolutionary movements swept across Europe; in the United States anti-slavery momentum surged, utopian communities were founded, and agitation roiled many churches. New schisms among Friends began that year. And like many uprisings, this one began at the margins, among Midwestern Hicksites.

Genesee Yearly Meeting was a Hicksite body formed in 1834, with meetings in Ontario, western New York State, and Michigan. Its Michigan Quarter laid down its select meetings of ministers and elders in 1842. When they refused the Yearly Meeting's command to reinstate them, a separation ensued. Waterloo Yearly Meeting was gathered from the Michigan Quarter and other Genesee reformers "according to the congregational order." They approved a "Basis of Religious Association" that declared:

> Man is made to sustain a relation of an intelligent and accountable agent under the Supreme Intelligence; has the law of God

written on the conscious powers of his soul; stands in such contiguity to Omnipresent God as to have immediately revealed to him God's will regarding him. This is THE FUNDAMENTAL FACT IN RELIGION.[34]

This premise shifted the emphasis of Quaker polity from the collective to the individual. A less structured congregational basis was its logical mode. In correspondence that same year, Lucretia Mott suggested that the decentralized "Congregational form of religious association will ultimately prevail as man comes to understand Christian liberty."[35]

Waterloo was followed later in 1848 by the revolt of Green Plain (Ohio) Quarterly Meeting against the conservative control of Indiana Yearly Meeting. Joseph Dugdale, whose progressivist pilgrimage Chuck Fager has traced,[36] was a key catalyst. When Indiana Yearly Meeting tried to disband them, they left. Green Plain Quarterly Meeting became Green Plain Yearly Meeting, drawing other dissident spirits from elsewhere in Indiana and Ohio. Like Waterloo, they made a statement of their identity and purpose:

> Believing that religious sentiment is deeply laid in man's nature ... man should never concede to any combination or order of men, his *individual freedom* ... we now associate in the capacity of an annual meeting that shall be advisory in its character and designed to aid us in more effectually carrying forward the testimonies of the Gospel.

They testified against slavery and capital punishment and called for state legislatures to repeal all laws discriminating according to race. Such laws "must be superseded by new dispensations."[37] Progressive revelation and liberty of individual conscience were emerging as immutable articles of faith.

We can also hear in the Waterloo and Green Plain statements a shift of religious authority toward human nature itself, realized in individual freedom, to be encouraged and coordinated but never overruled, by religious association. Through such freedom of exploration and expression, the traditional Quaker testimonies would become more progressive. "New dispensations" were understood to work inexorably toward the freedom and rights of all humanity. As Dugdale wrote in 1850, "God moves continually upon the face of the waters . . . a continual everlasting progress in the works of Divinity."[38] The Waterloo Yearly Meeting of 1854 declared its intention to "to call together a true Universal Church, which shall be emphatically the Church of Humanity, open to all who will come, whether Christians, Jews, Mahommedans, or Pagans."[39]

Philadelphia Yearly Meeting Hicksites experienced a split in 1853, producing the Pennsylvania Yearly Meeting of Progressive Friends (with Joseph Dugdale again serving as a key catalyst). They approved that year an "Exposition of Sentiments," the most complete manifesto of progressive Quaker commitments. It defined Quakerism as a religion of action and reform. Within that frame, Friends should no longer consider themselves a "peculiar people." *All* people are chosen for the work of reform. The churches as such are "only human organizations." Jesus left his disciples to organize in whatever ways would "promote the object of their mission." Congregational order was best suited to protecting individual freedom of conscience, which they defined as "the instincts of our moral and social nature." Such freedom leads to the "highest efficiency" in doing God's work and follows the "progressive unfoldings of truth and duty." A truly Christian church should have "unity of purpose, but with the most entire freedom for the individual."[40]

However, unity of purpose and individual freedom were a hard equation to balance. Progressive spirits progressed in many directions at once. A non-Quaker observer at an 1857 Congregational Friends gathering in Salem, Ohio reported with some exasperation,

> They went on for three days, discussing *everything*, without coming to a conclusion on *anything*. How they ever expect to advance the progress of the Human Race without a co-operation of action, or a sympathetic feeling on any one point, may be clear enough to them, but mysterious to those who have *progressed* more slowly.[41]

Similar trends could be found in Hicksite strongholds such as Philadelphia Yearly Meeting. The conservative Joseph Foulke wrote in 1846:

> There is too much sound and too little Silence in our Meetings. There is also a Spirit that is exceedingly busy and is getting into our Meetings and presuming to lecture on what the Itinerant Speakers call Moral

CHAPTER 1   Pilgrims of Progress

Reform. To this, spirit kindred is claimed with Thomsonianism, Phrenology, Abolitionism, Temperance, Nonresistance.[42]

As Hamm summarizes,[43] by 1853 all Hicksite yearly meetings except Baltimore had experienced Congregational/Progressive separations, and Baltimore too had experienced tensions, especially in its central Pennsylvania meetings. Progressive groups were smaller but very articulate. Lucretia Mott remained a member of Philadelphia Yearly Meeting but supported most Progressive/Congregational viewpoints. It is impossible to know how many Progressive reform groups formed in this period. The Pennsylvania Yearly Meeting was the longest lived. Most were ephemeral, some not even Hicksite in origin. Fager has compiled a provisional list from his own and other researches.[44]

Progressive Friends generated many far-sighted visions. They were the clearest of all Friends in their advocacy of women's rights and the most active in the political struggle for the abolition of slavery. Some even recognized the links between women's oppression and slavery. They expressed concerns regarding the market economy, labor relations, and monopolies. They advocated democracy in all forms. But given their wide-ranging concerns and activism, it was easier to make visionary statements than it was to find unity. So, in place of the traditional Quaker practice of reaching decisions by the sense of the meeting, Progressive Friends resorted to voting.[45] Perhaps that was a logical outcome of liberal democracy eclipsing a sectarian focus, and constitutionalism superseding a covenantal identity.

Progressives were also drawn to the spiritualist phenomenon that swept much of America between 1848 and the outbreak of the Civil War. Spiritualism may have served to counterbalance their strong emphasis upon rational inquiry and this-worldly activism. Communication with the spirits of the dead broke out in upstate New York in 1848 with the sensational claims made by three teenage sisters, Margaret, Leah, and Katherine Fox. Progressive Friends Isaac and Amy Post were nearby supporters, and soon Isaac was receiving communications from the dead as well. In 1851, he received George Fox's endorsement of the Progressive cause. The more recently deceased Edward Hicks (cousin of Elias and a recorded minister) expressed regret for his conservatism in this life. Progressives and some Hicksites saw a convergence between spiritualism and progress: the barrier between heaven and earth was breaking down. Lucretia Mott remained skeptical but didn't remark openly against it. The Progressive value on openness to new truths from any quarter made even the doubtful hesitate to scoff.[46]

Reflections on Progressive Friends before the Civil War

From a wider historical perspective, Progressive Quaker interest in spiritualism may be seen in attunement with the larger theological and ideological shifts we have followed. Early Friends were the final flowering of the Spiritualist Reformation in Europe, a small and often persecuted wing of the Radical Reformation that emphasized the indwelling of Christ, the living Word who leads the faithful through direct revelation.[47] The participational reading of Scripture mentioned earlier in this chapter developed from the Spiritualist Reformation's conviction that the Word re-enacts the history of Scripture in the mystery of experience. But two hundred years later, Enlightenment rationalism and skepticism of Scripture reframed human experience as human *per se*, rather than Christ as an emergent humanity from within the old. So, in place of the risen Christ, any dead soul might speak in this new spiritualism. One might call it a democratization of the spirit-world. Hence, within an increasingly secular, rational, scientific world, the new spiritualism was a fresh outbreak of the uncanny, the irrational. It provided a cathartic release from the deepening political stalemate regarding slavery and other issues in the 1850s. The mourning for lost objects of desire, from dead relatives to fading political hopes, received spectral reassurances, if only by way of mysterious raps on the table.[48]

In a related manner, both progressive and evangelical Friends had shifted from tragic to comic modes of narrating their identity and purpose. From being the Quaker Israel dwelling apart from the world and its follies, nobly mourning lost utopian losses, Gurneyites and Progressives alike opened themselves toward an open horizon and a bright future. Gurneyites were gaining in numbers and planting new meetings further westward by hybridizing their traditional

CHAPTER 1   Pilgrims of Progress

Quakerism with evangelical doctrines and practices. For their part, Progressive/Congregational Friends were still declining in numbers but broadening in vision and expanding in their sense of relation to the whole human family. Like the two kinds of pre-Quaker Seekers we briefly described at the start of this chapter, the Reformation-oriented Gurneyites were planting visible churches while the Enlightenment-oriented Progressives embraced a more universal, invisible church. Both groups had "hitched their wagons" to larger driving forces in American culture that took them further afield from each other.

Progressives styled themselves as "practical Christians," freed from the shackles of creeds and pointless wrangling over doctrine, to pursue reform and "practical righteousness." They were concerned to glean truths, especially new discoveries, which could serve the purposes of human progress, social reform, a more inclusive democracy, and individual liberty. We can analyze this practical Quakerism in terms of processes for discerning truth. As noted above, early generations of Friends confirmed the teachings and stories of Scripture as they found themselves living them out, participating in them. So, for example, when George Fox affirmed, "This I knew experimentally," he was witnessing to personal experiences framed by his reading of the Bible. Thus, early Friends arrived at a coherent set of convictions as they found correspondence between the Bible and their own experience. That interaction of coherence and correspondence constituted the truth-content of their faith. In terms of practice, they evolved a set of lived testimonies and spiritual discernment processes that were consistent with biblical teaching, such as Jesus's advice on how to resolve conflicts in the community (Matthew 18). They were not unconcerned with practical outcomes, but they trusted that God would provide good outcomes if they were faithful to the appropriate processes of discernment and action. The interplay of appropriate processes with practical outcomes was their truth-mode.

In the Progressive Quaker renewal, then, we see a shift in emphasis toward practical outcomes at the expense of traditional processes of making decisions in unity (as seen in their choosing to vote). Individuals were free to follow their own lights, within a framework less oriented to the Bible, which had become hard to believe as a coherent set of propositional truths. They gravitated instead toward a set of Enlightenment principles, or "sentiments," which included democracy, universal human rights, peace, and justice. Voting thus made sense as democracy. And with the deregulation of belief, decisions made in unity would be hard to reach in any case. In effect, then, Progressive Friends had migrated toward the Enlightenment model of the civil contract, or constitution.[49] Their discernment process partook of free inquiry, debate, and political advocacy—modes Penn had described in the 1670s as he theorized the true constitution as residing among the people, in constant evolution. Hence, Progressives had departed from the more closed system of covenantal peoplehood, still cherished among conservative Hicksites, and into a Quaker subset of the wider American struggle toward a more perfect democratic society.

The use of the word "sentiments" in this milieu is noteworthy. The word typically suggests some combination or interaction of feeling and opinion. That energetic interplay of cultural affects and cognitive reflection during the heady days of the early to mid-nineteenth century is the driving force of change among liberal-progressive Friends—and their evangelical counterparts—in this period.

The Civil War and After

The Fugitive Slave Act of 1850 moved the nation toward a binary stalemate over slavery and related North-South issues.[50] The wave of optimistic cultural affects that had fueled the Progressive rebellion against Hicksite conservatism waned. Starting in the latter 1850s, most Progressive yearly meetings and associations fell apart. Most Progressives either returned to the Hicksite fold, joined other churches, or remained unaffiliated. But their impact on Hicksite Quakerism continued to grow.

The aforementioned shift of Progressive truth-mode toward practical outcomes and toward individual liberty of conscience augured for ends beginning to justify means. That tendency began to show before the outbreak of the Civil War, in Progressive and Hicksite responses to John Brown's violent action at Harper's Ferry, Virginia in October 1859. Fager has traced the growing Progressive Quaker sympathies with Brown. During the six weeks between his sentencing and his hanging in December 1859, it became morally tenable for more Friends to praise him as a martyr to the cause of abolition. With her usual adroitness, Mott parsed her Quaker regard for Brown:

> It is not John Brown the soldier that we praise; it is John Brown the moral hero; John Brown the noble confessor and patient martyr whom we honor, and whom we think it proper to honor in this day when men are carried away by the corrupt and proslavery clamor against him.[51]

In the binary stalemate just before the war, my enemy's enemy became my hero.

After the Civil War broke out in 1861, Hicksites were united in lamenting it. Certainly, it represented a major stumble in the march of progress. In 1861 correspondence, Lydia Foulke of Philadelphia Yearly Meeting found it "passing strange that in this enlightened age no other means can be resorted to but fierce and bloody war to settle differences."[52] Official Hicksite periodicals warned against political and military involvements, but a number of Northern Friends volunteered for service in the Union army. In Indiana, among all Quaker groups, one-fourth of draft-age Quaker males joined the Union army, compared to two-thirds of the same group in the overall state population.[53] There are no definitive statistics of Quaker participation in the war, but Hamm finds twenty-seven men from Race Street Meeting in Philadelphia and at least twenty from Wilmington Meeting in Delaware noted as having enlisted.[54] These counts may be low—it was not a development Friends were anxious to document. But they were not ready to discipline their enlistees either. Even after the War was over, few Quaker soldiers were disowned or even eldered for their military service. Friends chose instead to respect their liberty of conscience. As Fager summarizes:

> The Civil War was a watershed, a game-changing event in American Quakerdom. Not just the Progressives, but the Hicksites generally, reached an informal but real accommodation with ambiguity: the testimony against war as evil and unchristian remained. But a crucial qualification was added, first in fact, eventually as policy: adherence to this standard was shifted from a group-enforced norm to a matter of individual conscience.[55]

Moreover, a public antiwar witness was fraught with ambiguity, since most of the antiwar movement in the North was proslavery and racist in tenor. Even those who remained committed to peaceful resistance found the "war spirit" seductive. Some refrained from reading newspapers during the war. Some conservative Hicksites felt that if Friends had retained their unity and integrity better in preceding decades, their example and witness might have helped the nation avert war.[56] But traditional Quaker faith and practice had become an opaque or empty signifier, even to many Friends. It's hard to imagine how it would have posed a "bright and shining light" to such a polarized and alienated nation.

After the war was over, some northern Hicksites went south to aid and educate freed slaves. This was the most ambitious and uncontentious project Hicksites had initiated since the Great Separation, and it led to long-term focus and commitment to work for racial equality and justice.[57] Hicksites founded thirteen schools for freed slaves in the South. For example, Martha Schofield started a school in Aiken, South Carolina and remained there until her death in 1916.[58] As we shall see, the Schofield and Laing Schools were objects of continuing attention at Friends General Conferences in the next century.

Despite their involvement in education and abolition, Hicksites showed no interest in starting Friends meetings or promoting Quakerism among black people. William Tallack, an English Friend visiting among American Friends on the eve of the Civil War, observed that "although the American Friends are truly zealous for the liberty and improvement of the negroes, they do not generally feel it necessary to depart from the ordinary customs of white society in respect to non-intimacy with the coloured race."[59] In any case, the surge of interest in educating freed slaves flagged after 1869, when Friends were recruited by the Grant Administration's "Peace Policy" to work with Native American peoples. Hicksite and Orthodox Friends were given different geographical "superintendencies" in the Great Plains. Some Friends who moved west for this short-lived assignment for the government stayed in the region and contributed to the founding of Illinois Yearly Meeting.[60] Nevertheless, the ephemerality of progressive concerns and initiatives becomes increasingly apparent over time.

Thomas Hamm sees three key consequences of the Civil War for Hicksite faith and practice. First, despite the number of Friends who fought in the war, Hicksite concern for peace was strengthened. For example, Lucretia Mott and others joined the Universal Peace Union. At a women's peace rally in 1876, Mott said, "If we believe war is wrong, as everyone must, then we ought to believe that by proper efforts on our part it may be done away with."[61] (But with that more active approach, the peace testimony was becoming more a matter of public advocacy than personal resistance.) Second, and related to the first consequence, Friends abandoned their aversion to "creaturely activity" and "mingling" with other groups. Cooperation with the federal government on Indian work would have been unthinkable before the war. (On the other hand, it led Friends into regrettable efforts to "civilize" and assimilate tribes into American culture.) A third interrelated consequence was a relaxation of the discipline. Hicksites came to see corporate discipline as coercive, a "war upon conscience." Hamm concludes, "This is the final paradox: a significant step toward Hicksites becoming the 'liberal Friends' came from a series of compromises with war."[62]

The Emergence of Liberal Quakerism

The Quaker Israel no longer dwelt alone in melancholy among the peoples; a diaspora of Quaker conscience had been won at last. As Hamm summarizes, by the latter nineteenth century, Hicksite Friends had:

> Utterly eschewed any limits on the freedom of thought of their members; indeed, it had become fundamental to their conception of themselves as Quakers. . . . They defined themselves largely in opposition to the evangelicalism that dominated American Protestantism in the nineteenth century. By 1900, Hicksite Friends had transformed themselves from a peculiar sect into a branch of liberal Protestantism, still distinctive in theology and methods of worship, but no longer outwardly, or intellectually, separate from the larger world. . . . While often critical of the world around them, they no longer feared its influence. They were confident both that they could make it better and that it was moving closer to Quaker ideals. Perhaps more important, they were also confident that they could safely borrow ideas from it, even that most standard of evangelical

institutions, the Sunday school. The close of the nineteenth century would see the Hicksite yearly meetings form a national organization, Friends General Conference, which would become the central institution of liberal Quakerism in the twentieth century.[63]

As early as 1867, the reform-minded Hicksite periodical, *The Friend*, articulated a renewed Quaker mission in the world: "Instead of standing apart as a peculiar people ... go out into the world, and show our faith by our works." To the reformers, the old Quaker symbolics of plainness no longer communicated anything more than "conceit and imbecility."[64]

By the 1870s, the older, more conservative Hicksite leadership died off, and the remainders of the "hedge" were mowed down. Progressive Friends left their collapsing yearly meetings and helped swell the reformist ranks among Hicksites. Living on into 1880, Lucretia Mott survived to see her vision confirmed. New leaders were emerging, including Jonathan and Hannah Plummer of Illinois Yearly Meeting, Aaron Powell of New York Yearly Meeting, and Howard Jenkins of Philadelphia Yearly Meeting, all of whom were influential in the formation of Friends General Conference at the end of the century. The Plummers worked widely among Hicksite yearly meetings, making key connections that culminated in the formation of FGC. Jenkins was a journalist who merged *The Friend* with *The Friends Intelligencer* in 1885 to create the first sustained Hicksite periodical, which further consolidated the liberal vision among the yearly meetings. Quaker leadership was finding new forms.

Still, numbers continued to decline in Hicksite yearly meetings. Philadelphia Yearly Meeting Hicksite was three times larger than its Orthodox counterpart by the end of the century, but it equaled all the other Hicksite yearly meetings combined. Migration westward was one factor. Many didn't find or found a meeting in their new surroundings. Moving out of traditional Quaker milieus, some simply lost interest. Illinois Yearly Meeting was the first new Hicksite yearly meeting in forty years when it was founded in 1875. Some bemoaned a lack of ministry in meetings. Few new ministers were appearing. But by the 1890s, some suggested that ministry needed to come more from the body of the meeting, and less from the gallery of ministers and elders. By the 1880s, "marrying out" to non-Friends was no longer considered a hazard to Quaker quality-control. Some even suggested it was a way to spread Friends' principles.[65]

Hicksite schools often failed, but Friends felt free now to send their children to non-Quaker colleges such as Oberlin, Antioch, Brown, Yale, Dartmouth, and Harvard. These outstanding colleges in turn served as templates for the founding of Swarthmore College in 1869. Meanwhile, Friends were leaving private business and agriculture for white-collar professions such as law, medicine, teaching, and management.[66] They were steadily becoming more prosperous and finding more time to pursue literature and the arts, take part in lyceums, and so on. Scientific progress continued to be a focus of much interest. Mott preferred science over theology, because it was based upon "fact, demonstration, or self-evident truth."[67] Her words reflect the growing emphasis upon empirical, observable truth, which complemented the Hicksite concern for a faith with practical results. A few worried that scientific materialism would overwhelm Quaker spiritual sensibilities. But Friends drew upon wider sources to balance the material and spiritual. As Hugh Barbour and J. William Frost summarize, "Quaker liberalism began in the academy and was propagated by educators who wanted to train their pupils in a way that would preserve faith without repudiating science."[68]

A case in point is Darwinian evolution, which tied many churches in knots—including some Gurneyites—in the latter nineteenth century. By contrast, most Hicksites felt that it confirmed their belief in progress. In contrast to the "social Darwinists" who saw "survival of the fittest" as scientific validation for cutthroat competition and exploitation, Hicksites and other liberal Christians saw modern human progress as a spiritual extension of biological evolution, auguring a kinder and gentler future. We will hear a great deal of evolutionary ideology in the formative years of FGC Conferences, up to World War I. Parallel developments were underway among British Friends in the same period.[69]

The Formation of Hicksite Conferences

A concern grew to draw Hicksite Friends together from across the seven yearly meetings, to encourage and learn from one another. The

Jonathan Plummer. Courtesy of Friends Historical Library of Swarthmore College.   Hannah Plummer. Courtesy of Friends Historical Library of Swarthmore College.

first embodiment of this concern developed around Sunday schools, a key institution among Protestant churches which Gurneyites had already borrowed with great success in their rapid growth. Hicksites adopted the practice, rebaptized as Firstday schools. These spread among the yearly meetings in the 1860s, notwithstanding some traditionalist misgivings over yet another form of "creaturely activity."

Jonathan Plummer[70] was the son of a conservative Hicksite leader in Richmond, Indiana. He and his wife Hannah moved to Chicago in 1874, where he began a successful pharmacy business. He was involved in the founding of Illinois Yearly Meeting in 1875 and by 1877 he was founding groups for noncontroversial religious and social discussion. Plummer's irenic spirit and patient networking were keys to developing the conferences. In 1878, he commented, "I have great faith in the quiet, careful persistent labor of our Society, when its aggressive element is at work, modified and controlled by its co-operating conservatism."[71] With conservative leadership passing from the scene and Progressive Friends having outgrown their initial boisterousness, the time was ripe for a mediating figure like Plummer, a Midwesterner who could stand at some distance from the more entrenched positions of eastern Friends.

Plummer participated in a meeting of concerned Friends convened by Eli Lamb of Baltimore Yearly Meeting in 1867. They organized the first First-Day School Conference, held the following year at the Race Street Meetinghouse in Philadelphia. Pooling experience from the different yearly meetings proved useful. By 1890, there were 8,500 pupils, including some adults, in 150 Hicksite First-day Schools. Some 40 percent of participants were non-Friends, demonstrating significant outreach.

Plummer envisioned multiple conferences formed around various Quaker concerns. As Clerk of Illinois Yearly Meeting, he advanced in 1877 a "proposition being laid before the [Yearly] Meeting to invite consideration of the other Yearly Meetings upon the subject of holding a general conference once in five years or oftener, to cooperate in labor, and increase our influence upon the various questions involving our testimonies."[72]

The Plummers initiated conversations and correspondence the following year with Friends in other yearly meetings. The result was The Friends Union for Philanthropic Labor (FUPL), to give focus to the wide-ranging work of service and reform among the yearly meetings. There was resistance at first: some Friends feared the FUPL might serve as a vehicle for the centralization of power, even a standardization of doctrine and practice (the old bogeyman, Orthodoxy, was apparently still at large). To clarify the purpose, Plummer explained in 1879 that "we especially desire that the Conference may be ... prohibited ... from any consideration of doctrinal subjects, disciplinary provisions, or the internal affairs of any yearly meeting."[73] Hannah Plummer further qualified the initiative the same year: "I think the proposition clearly indicates that the conference need have nothing to do with Society in its local work. . . . [It would promote] Union of all our forces where it would be profitable, separation where it is proper and best."[74]

This loose, confederal constitutional logic slowly took hold. The first FUPL Conference was held in Waynesville, Ohio in 1882. It "brought together many Friends who had been active in the Underground Railroad and who were now working ardently for peace, temperance, women's rights, education for Negroes, social 'purity,' and other reforms." They were soon working on ten or more different fronts, and meeting in the same place with the First-Day School Conference, immediately following its sessions.[75]

The older, more established yearly meetings of the East were slow to endorse this Midwestern initiative, however. Determined, the Plummers and their collaborators brought FUPL east, meeting near Baltimore Yearly Meeting in session. Baltimore and New York Yearly Meetings soon joined the FUPL. As Fager narrates, "By November 1886, Plummer was ready for a direct assault on the citadel of reluctance: the Union gathered in Philadelphia itself, alongside the conference for First-Day Schools."76 Philadelphia Yearly Meeting finally joined in 1890, at the urging of its young Friends. Genesee held out longest, joining the FUPL and the First-Day School Conference in 1893.

Another joint gathering of the First-Day School Conference with the Friends Union for Philanthropic Labor was held in 1892 at the Goose Creek Meeting in Lincoln, Virginia with seven hundred Friends attending, many of them young Friends. A number of local Young Friends Associations had been reading and discussing Samuel Janney's four-volume Quaker history (published 1859-1868), written from a Hicksite perspective. Janney's history was often mentioned in the sessions at Goose Creek,77 perhaps suggesting a growing historical self-consciousness among Hicksite Friends. Swarthmore had already become the first Quaker college to begin collecting historical materials in 1871, eventually resulting in the Friends Historical Library. Evolutionary science and historico-critical study of the Bible had not only displaced static, traditional Christian doctrine but engendered a growing interest among Friends in their own history.

Along the way, new styles of communication were also appearing: rather than waiting upon prophetic utterances from recognized ministers, Friends presented papers on their concerns and their work, followed by discussion. The effects of wider reading and academic intellectual formation are evident.

Resulting from his wider progressive connections, Jonathan Plummer was part of the planning committee for the World's Parliament of Religions held in Chicago during the Columbian Exposition of 1893. He attempted a joint committee of Hicksite and Orthodox Friends to represent a united voice to the Parliament, but that quickly fell apart. Plummer led the Hicksite presentation with the opening words:

CHAPTER 1 Pilgrims of Progress

An occasion like this has been unknown heretofore in the religious history of the world. A new day is dawning. A day of clearer vision in which we can see that all human beings, wherever living, and holding whatever religious vision they may, are children of the same spiritual Father, however differently we may name him.[78]

Friends were pleased to see their views more widely accepted than before. Lavinia Yeatman concluded, "our sweet, small doctrine, "Mind the Light,' . . . is now an accepted belief, a central point in Protestant churches."[79] She may have overestimated Quaker influence, but the Parliament was a watershed for Hicksite engagement with the wider religious world and growing confidence in their relevance to changing times.

During the Parliament, Howard Jenkins in particular expressed the concern for more concerted liberal teaching among Friends. Another new organization resulted, the Friends Religious Conference. Unlike the first two conferences, this one was not composed of yearly meeting representatives but was simply a gathering of Friends concerned to define and broadcast the Quaker message for new times. The Chicago gathering further resolved that the three Conferences would find synergy by meeting at the same time. This was accomplished the next year, 1894, in Chappaqua, New York with more than a thousand Friends attending. At that gathering, Edward Magill, recently retired president of Swarthmore College, suggested that greater coordination was needed among Quaker schools and colleges (George School, the Hicksite boarding school near Philadelphia, had been founded just the preceding year). Hence, a fourth conference was born: The Friends Educational Conference.

The Young Friends Associations added a fifth element. Rising stars Jane Rushmore and Jesse Holmes were among the speakers at Chappaqua. The venerable Aaron Powell presided over the gathering, imparting an atmosphere of intergenerational solidarity. As Karl Mannheim notes in his sociology of generations, certain forerunners from a preceding generation or two often serve as key mentors to new generational cohorts of emerging leadership.[80] For example, Elias Hicks had purposefully cultivated alliances with younger generations. But of course, the new generation will have its own ideas and initiatives, emerging from new cultural affects

A group of Friends at the Chappaqua Conference, 1894. Friends General Conference Records, courtesy of Friends Historical Library of Swarthmore College.

and shared formative experiences. The story of the Friends General Conferences through the decades will be in part the story of successive generational cohorts, their intergenerational alliances, and their new affective and intellectual syntheses.

The next year, 1895, the Young Friends Associations, which were local groups devoted to reading and discussion, formed a Central Committee to foster greater coordination. Members of that key group included Jane Rushmore, then 31 years old, Jesse Holmes, also 31, and William Birdsall, 40. All three would be important voices in the future of Friends General Conference.

Conclusion

Hicksite Friends were still declining in numbers but perceived their influence growing. In an 1894 epistle, Indiana Yearly Meeting Friends witnessed:

> We feel glad in the thought that, while our members do not increase as we would wish, yet we feel consolation and encouragement by

the conviction that the light shed upon our hearts and minds is fast sending its beneficent beams into many hearts and minds not of our fold. Ideas held by Friends, long time almost alone, are many of them public property.[81]

It seemed as if the world were "coming our way" at last. Friends had indeed contributed significantly to several progressive causes in recent decades. But they had also been coming the world's way. And many of what they considered to be traditional Quaker convictions had been significantly reframed in modern, liberal terms along the way. The primary point of convergence was the wider progressive movement, burgeoning by the end of the nineteenth century, primarily among liberal Protestant churches, solidly middle-class in its sensibilities. We will devote attention to that wider phenomenon in the next chapter.

We have followed a remarkable trajectory—or rather, two trajectories—of American Friends over the nineteenth century. We have seen the breakdown of Quaker unity at the start of the century, and the recrudescence of the two Seeker outlooks that had been fused together in the early Quaker apocalyptic spirituality and revolutionary movement. We have only briefly described the Orthodox shift toward evangelical Protestantism. Gurneyite Friends looked at early Friends and saw precursors of John Wesley's Methodist outreach to the poor and unchurched in early industrial England a century later. By contrast, Hicksite Friends looked at the same early Friends and saw early universalists with progressive social values and activism. Both made legitimate claims upon the rootstock of their tradition. And both were wildly revisionist. They drew upon the tradition from their experience among the affects and ideas of a different age. Neither would have felt comfortable around the strange folk that first earned the epithet "Quaker" and gloried in their share in Christ's sufferings. But both were doing impressive things in the world.

The Gurneyite hybrid of Quakerism and Methodism had grown rapidly as it moved westward. The combined Orthodox and Gurneyite yearly meetings swelled from 55,700 in 1871 to nearly 98,000 in 1908, largely by linking with the wider Holiness revival movement of the Third Great Awakening. (Without resorting to those alliances, Philadelphia Yearly Meeting Orthodox shrank from 5,500 to 4,400 in the same period.)[82] By the end of the century, they were starting to mount world missions. Their 1887 Richmond Conference and resulting Richmond Declaration had begun to stabilize the evangelical Quaker hybridization into some normative definitions.

The Hicksite hybrid of Quakerism and Unitarianism was not growing in numbers but collaborating in many directions with an invisible church that included liberal Protestants but also began contemplating a wider world of faiths and philosophies, arts and sciences.

Meanwhile, the Wilburite and Conservative drop-outs from these Quaker reformulations maintained a more traditional faith and practice in small, mostly rural yearly meetings from North Carolina to California.

Hicksites and Gurneyites had traveled so far—and so far apart—by 1900 that they were less threatened by one another, barely aware of each other most of the time, and pleasantly surprised when they met like-minded individuals from across the chasm. When the Friends General Conference was formed in 1900, the term "Hicksite" was dropping out of use. They would henceforth be "Conference Friends."

CHAPTER 2

A Quaker Chautauqua
FGC's Formation and First Conferences, 1896–1904

To Jonathan W. Plummer belongs the great credit of having been literally the pioneer of this modern awakening in the Society of Friends.... These gatherings are the outcome of the early conception in the mind of our dear friend, formulated in propositions which at first were not welcomed by our yearly meetings, but which are now accepted practically by all.

— Aaron Powell, 1896 Swarthmore Conference[83]

By 1900, the population of the United States had reached seventy-six million. Out of that total, thrifty five to forty million were of the laboring classes. Wage earners in manufacturing were paid an average of $435 per year, domestics $240, and agricultural laborers $178 with room and board. Middle-class clerical workers in industry averaged $1,011. One-third of the population was either immigrant or had at least one immigrant parent. African Americans totaled ten million and Native Americans 237,000 thousand. There were approximately four thousand millionaires in the country.

The middle class had grown to twelve to sixteen million, approximately 20 percent of the total population. As historian Michael McGerr[84] summarizes, the middle classes were disgusted at the extravagances and social arrogance of the rich and appalled by the social conditions and degraded morals of the poor in this "gilded age." They were preparing to remake America in their own image through the Progressive movement. This phenomenon merits some attention at the start of this chapter, as it poses an important context for, and influence upon, the early development of Friends General Conference.

Progressives championed a phalanx of social causes, many of them grounded in the middle-class ideal of domesticity. Temperance was a central concern. But other vices—prostitution, gambling, tobacco, and narcotics—were also gathered under the general campaign for moral "purity." As Frances Willard, the driving force of the Women's Christian Temperance Union summarized, the goal was "to make the whole world Homelike." Another reformer praised "the restraining influence of the sober, level-headed middle classes—the true police of the world."[85]

The middle classes were growing in numbers and strength, but they also felt challenged by larger social and economic forces. Since the 1870s, corporations had initiated strategies of vertical and horizontal integration of production and distribution, creating huge trusts, corporate mergers, and monopolies. Small businesses, the economic foundation of middle-class life in previous generations, were being forced out. Young men were migrating to salaried white-collar jobs in corporate bureaucracies. Between 1880 and 1900 male clerical workers in the US tripled to 550,000. Big business and the upper classes whose interests it served became targets of progressive reform. But growing labor struggles by the turn of the century also made middle-class people uneasy. They felt caught between the hubris of the upper classes and the immorality of the working classes. Many supported labor unions as forces not only for economic justice but also for moral uplift. Some even espoused state socialism. Many progressives wanted stronger governmental control to counter the power of big business. The Civil War had reoriented democratic thought from community-based, republican virtue to a preoccupation with large, impersonal organizations. Progressives often viewed expanded governmental bureaucracy as the answer to controlling runaway corporate bureaucracy.

Despite its various concerns for a more just and equitable society, the progressive movement was largely acquiescent to racial segregation.[86] Progressives did little to oppose the flood of Jim Crow legislation in the South in the latter nineteenth century. They were sympathetic to the African American situation but viewed

CHAPTER 2 A Quaker Chautauqua

segregation as a way to limit racial violence—both the growing number of lynchings in the South and the urban race riots starting in the North, as the Great Migration of African Americans got underway. It would be easier to help black people, in both the North and the South, as long as the boundaries remained clear. A number of black leaders, most notably Booker T. Washington, encouraged white progressives in this strategy. And progressives had little actual experience with black people on a socially equal basis. Theodore Roosevelt, a progressive President, considered strict segregation the best solution to "the terrible problem offered by the presence of the negro on this continent."

Native Americans, whose population continued to decline even after hostilities had finally ended in the latter nineteenth century, were another concern for progressives. Friends and other religious groups had worked with the Grant Administration starting in 1869 to detribalize, "civilize," and assimilate Indians into European American culture.[87] Both the forced segregation of African Americans and the forced assimilation of Native Americans were terrible policies. But again, a concern for the sheer survival of these minorities against white hostility and governmental aggression pushed progressive attitudes in these directions.

The most unambiguous and successful equality crusade of the progressive movement was women's suffrage. Progressives united more easily on this issue, as middle-class women were the prime defenders of the domestic sphere in the first place and figured prominently in most progressive causes. Carrie Chapman Catt and the Quaker Alice Paul were among the standard bearers for this movement which continued to gain momentum in the new century.

The annual Chautauqua Assemblies, starting in 1874, might be called the cradle of the progressive movement. An evolution from Methodist camp meetings, these large summer encampments of liberalizing Protestants on the idyllic shores of Lake Chautauqua in western New York combined family recreation, informative lectures, and ecumenical fellowship—all made possible by the advent of the middle-class summer vacation. Tennis, hiking, picnics, and sailing were interspersed with concerts and lectures on religious questions, science, social issues, and public policy, even foreign language courses.

Women attended in larger numbers and were increasingly featured as speakers. One observer noted, "Man has a subdued look, no matter his pounds or whiskers, at Chautauqua."[88] Besides their ecumenical reach, the Assemblies grew more inclusive ethnically, but not racially.

Those who attended the summer assemblies returned to their home communities as reformers and activists. Local Chautauqua Associations were started in hundreds of towns across the country, harnessing middle-class ambitions for self-improvement and greater cultural enrichment. Swarthmore, Pennsylvania had a strong Chautauqua Association, with Swarthmore College professors Jesse Holmes and Paul Pearson as favorite speakers. The two also traveled and spoke extensively on the commercial Chautauqua Circuit during their summers, until the Chautauqua phenomenon faded in the latter 1920s.[89]

The philosopher, psychologist, and Boston Brahmin William James lectured at Chautauqua in the summer of 1896 and viewed its influence with mixed feelings. He called it "the middle-class paradise": "the realization—on a small, sample scale of course—of all the ideals for which our civilization has been striving: security, intelligence, humanity, and order.... You have the best fruits of what mankind has fought and bled and striven for under the name of civilization for centuries." But personally, he found "this unspeakable Chautauqua" intolerable. "Let me take my chances again in the big outside worldly wilderness with all its sins and sufferings."[90] Perhaps for an intellectual like James, the problem was less the middle-class than the middle-*brow* moorings of Chautauqua and the progressive movement it nurtured. A middle-class consensus with social and political force could not venture very far in any direction intellectually but needed to build agreement and resolve at a mid-level of insight, "the unlovely level of 10,000 good people," as James described it.[91]

Historian Andrew Rieser finds Chautauqua an important institution in shaping modern American liberalism, not only for the influence its own Assemblies, Associations, and Circuits, but also for the wider variety of offshoots it produced.[92] The Friends General Conferences, as we find them evolving in the same period, are surely part of Chautauqua's wider influence.

CHAPTER 2   A Quaker Chautauqua

Friends in the big tent on the Swarthmore campus, 1896. Friends General Conference Records, courtesy Friends Historical Library of Swarthmore College.

The 1896 Swarthmore Conference

The gathering of Hicksite Friends on the campus of Swarthmore College August 19-26, 1896 was the culmination of the formation and convergence of Conferences that had begun in 1867. These now included the First-Day School General Conference, the Friends' Union for Philanthropic Labor, the Friends' Religious Conference, and the Friends' Educational Conference. The Conferences still met as separate entities on different days but were open for all to attend. Thus, the overall event was still titled the "Friends General Conferences," but the arrangements were handled by an *ad hoc* Central Committee, presaging the advent of a consolidated organization. Proceedings of the Conferences were published separately at first, but then combined into one book later that same year. Some brief attention to the different Conference proceedings offers brief glimpses of their respective efforts at this juncture.

John William Graham. National Portrait Gallery, London, United Kingdom.

The First-Day School General Conference, the longest-standing group, met for its twentieth session the opening two days of the gathering. Their time was mainly taken up with reports from the seven Yearly Meeting Associations of the Conference: Genesee, Illinois, Indiana, Ohio, Baltimore, New York, and Philadelphia. The Conference's Executive Committee noted that its duties were now lighter than for many years, because the work was generally well organized. But the production and dissemination of the "Lesson Leaves" curriculum required much work by the Literature Committee. Two abiding needs stood out: first, teachers needed more preparation on the subjects embraced by the Lessons; second, adult classes needed to be started and expanded, to embrace the whole membership of

CHAPTER 2 A Quaker Chautauqua

the meeting. Adult classes would bring better cohesion to the adult membership. The yearly meetings were experiencing gradual shrinkage, not the runaway growth pains of the Gurneyite yearly meetings. These observations suggest a concern that viewpoints, interests, and attitudes were proliferating as numbers dwindled; some focusing and gathering of adult members was needed.

John William Graham, a leading liberal reformer from Manchester, England, had attended the Chappaqua Conference and was taken with what he saw developing among liberal Friends in America, parallel to developments in Britain. At the epochal Manchester Conference of British Friends in 1895, Graham had offered a glowing vision of the future for Friends: "The religious world has come round to the Indwelling Voice as its central conception, and so essential Quakerism holds the future in the hollow of its hand."[93] Graham brought the same sense of moment to the Swarthmore Conference. And for their part, Hicksite Friends, after decades of being shunned by British Friends in favor of the Orthodox branch, surely felt validated by Graham's presence and encouragement.

Hoping to foster transatlantic cross-fertilization among liberal Friends, Graham spoke about "Adult Schools in England," already fifty years old among British Friends, that served as an outreach to working men and women. Classes were taught by Friends of "good education and standing, but self-governing and cooperative, democratic in form."[94] Graham reported that in addition to the Bible, his own class studied tenets of Buddhism, "Mohammedanism," texts from John Woolman, and discussed current moral and social questions. In the Birmingham area, a number of nonconformist churches had started adult schools which brought out ten thousand on a given First-Day morning. Of that total, four thousand were attending Friends adult schools. Graham suggested that these schools had played a role in saving Quakerism in England. Otherwise, numbers would have slowly diminished and Friends might have resorted to a paid pastorate.

The Friends Union for Philanthropic Labor met for its ninth conference later in the week. Here too, all seven yearly meetings reported on their work on various fronts. In addition, there were reports by the superintendents of the various FUPL committees:

Purity; Demoralizing Publications; Tobacco and Other Narcotics; Temperance; Gambling, Lotteries and Kindred Vices; Capital Punishment; Prison Reform; Indian Affairs; Work for the Colored People; Peace and Arbitration. This list has much overlap with the moral concerns of the wider progressive movement, but augmented by traditional Quaker concerns about prison reform, capital punishment, Native Americans, African Americans, and peace. On the other hand, industrial relations were not yet part of the Quaker purview.

The report for the Work for the Colored People Committee was given by its superintendent, Anna Jackson, who deserves some introduction here. Born Anna Price Davis in Greenwich Village in 1848, she lived most of her life in New York City. Married to William Jackson, their home was a center for Friends, especially young Friends. She attended every Conference until 1920 and used her wider connections to bring a variety of speakers of interest to Friends. She was a charter member of New York's Political Study Club, whence a number of women emerged into prominence in public life. According to her obituary in *The Friends Intelligencer* (1/15/1921):

> Among Friends she is best known by her work for the colored people. She devoted much time and study to their welfare; and was acquainted with the leaders of this work. She [was] especially interested in the welfare of the Laing and Schofield Schools. She was a manager of the Colored Orphan Asylum, New York, being at the time of her death the oldest director of that institution.

She worked with Theodore Roosevelt during his term as New York's Police Commissioner, to introduce matrons to police stations. She also advocated for prison reform, police regulations, the care of children, and the suppression of immoral publications.

In her report, Jackson challenged Friends to increase their support for the Schofield and Laing Schools for black children in South Carolina. Contributions from the seven yearly meetings amounted to about $2,000 per year, but the needs were closer to $8,000 per year. She still met with objections to supporting them, hearing comments such as, "Colored people are not a well-behaved race." She countered that all classes of people need education, which prevents crime and enables moral and economic advance. She concluded, "Almost every interest of the Union [FUPL] is promoted in these schools. The causes of temperance, purity, mission work among women and children, peace, the prevention of crime, can be positively and immediately strengthened by the enlargement of the scope of these schools."[95] Friends generally supported Booker T. Washington's counsel that African Americans should focus on improvement through education, rather than challenge iron-clad segregation laws.

Besides Anna Jackson, other Superintendents giving reports included Jesse Holmes for the Temperance Committee, Aaron Powell for the Purity Committee, and Marianna Chapman for the Prison Reform Committee, all of whom we will continue to note. Later in the FUPL sessions, Swarthmore College professor John Russell Hayes read his poem, "The Grave of Lucretia Mott," after which the group rose and stood silently in her memory. The nursing mother of liberal Quakerism in America was still revered sixteen years after her death.

The Friends' Religious Conference met for the second time after its initial gathering at Chappaqua two years before. In his opening remarks, Chairman Aaron Powell stated the Conference's purpose: "There is still a mission for the Society, there is still reason why it should exist and why it should act as hitherto, as an interpreter of spiritual truth, fundamental spiritual truth, of which the world has never been in greater need than at the present time."

Among various papers presented, Jesse Holmes addressed "How Shall We Make Quakerism Reach the Masses?" Holmes had earned a PhD in 1890 from Johns Hopkins University in chemistry, while also studying philosophy. At that time a teacher at George School, he observed that the church has two missions: one to the masses, and one to its members. It starts out emphasizing the first and ends up preoccupied with the second. "Instead of seeking for sufferers, it sets up offices and waits for patients." The point is the advancement of humanity, not of Quakerism. In that work, "Our allies are all Christian people, within and without Christian churches." He concluded:

> The world calls for pioneers in a new movement against caste and for brotherly kindness. It needs leaders not necessarily of great powers, but of great love, willing and determined to dedicate their

Jesse Holmes. Courtesy of Friends Historical Library of Swarthmore College.

lives to leading others into paths of peace. Who in this great audience will here and now make this dedication?[96]

Concluding with this liberal-progressive "altar call," we hear an early Jesse Holmes. The sense of Friends as part of a trans-Christian progressive movement is clear here.

John William Graham spoke at this Conference as well, on "Three Needs of the Church." Some 2200 Friends packed and surrounded the large tent on the College grounds for this highpoint of the week. First, Graham emphasized "the need of consecration to aggressive work" on behalf of Friends. "It is not very convincing to the world for us to talk much of the Christ within, and not to look at all like Christ without, not to show any sign of his endless compassion." Friends refuse to separate out a clergy, but "then refuse to be a clergy ourselves."

> Quakerism is not like some great automaton, which maybe left to look after itself. We are every one of us needed to do our share of its service. . . . Sooner or later, unless we are willing thus to work for our Church, its membership will dwindle, its aggressive quality with lapse, and it will die, either by extinction or by the adoption of a pastoral system.

Second, and relatedly, Graham pressed the need for renewed ministry in the manner of Friends. He found hardly any young ministers at the Conference. This trend could prove disastrous, for "the old cannot speak the language of the young." But as a calling to be followed, "ministry earnestly discharged should cost us something, as everything worth doing does; it is just part of a devoted life." Finally, Graham found among American and English Friends alike "not enough living, modern knowledge of the Bible. . . . [O]ur whole religious life needs the enriching which comes from . . . the precious heritage of tradition."[97] With modern study and interpretation, the Bible becomes an agent against superstition. We will hear these concerns raised repeatedly by a variety of Friends. With the progressive focus on the new and the next, its shift from covenantal polity to constitutional politics, and its kaleidoscopic array of social concerns and reforms, the membership and internal cohesion of Friends were eroding.

At a session of the FUPL, Clement Biddle amplified Graham's last concern. He noted that Orthodox Christians criticize Friends for their lack of biblical knowledge. He urged Friends to study the Bible anew, with or without modern critical methods. Otherwise, Friends will sink

> to that low standard of human mind . . . which criticizes it, and wants to have nothing but what it can comprehend . . . searches through the Bible for the passages which it can criticize and find fault with, and searches through in the hope of finding something to confirm some preconceived ideas—ideas that, as we grow and advance in religious thought, change; and the time may come when ideas and thoughts now rejected may no longer be to us a mystery.[98]

Tent-camping Friends on the Swarthmore Campus, 1896. Friends General Conference Records, coutesy of Friends Historical Library of Swarthmore College.

Biddle thus challenged a liberal Quaker skepticism that had become more reflexive than genuinely questioning. We can hear traces of the early and traditional Quaker reading of Scripture that might be called participational or mystical. As we noted in the preceding chapter, that subtler sensibility had largely succumbed during the nineteenth century to rationalistic and moralistic diminutions of the Quaker spiritual formation.

At the end of the Religious Conference, Rufus Jones and Isaac Sharpless, professor of philosophy and president of the Orthodox Haverford College respectively, offered brief comments. Jones commended Friends for their efforts to speak to the conditions of a modern world. Sharpless was also complimentary, suggesting that if Friends were better acquainted with one another across their divisions, they would find more agreement than difference.

Surprisingly, Jonathan Plummer didn't attend the 1896 Conference—or any of the following ones. But Aaron Powell acknowledged his role in founding the Conferences and bringing them together (see the epigraph to this chapter).

Finally, The General Education Conference of Friends held its first sessions. Chairman Edward Magill, former president of Swarthmore College, explained how the idea for this new Conference had arisen two years before at Chappaqua. Friends recognized the need to unite around their interest in secular education as well as First-day schools, though he was quick to add that Friends should not differentiate between secular and religious aims. Papers were presented on Friends and public schools, athletics in public schools and colleges, the influence of higher education on the Society, professional training for Friends as teachers, and Friends schools in areas with few Friends.

In all, the Swarthmore Conference was a huge success. Almost all the sessions were plenary, held in a large tent on the campus grounds. Overall attendance ran as high as 3,200—approximately 15 percent of all Hicksites at the time. Some 1,442 Friends were lodged in college buildings, while 150 more camped in private tents pitched on the grounds. As many as nineteen hundred a day commuted by train. Clement Biddle, Treasurer for the Conference, announced that the ten-thousand-dollar cost of the gathering had been successfully raised by the time of the event. He added, "The very act of raising the money, of giving it, has done us good. The religion of our Society is too cheap, and sometimes I fear we value it at its cost." *The Friends Intelligencer* (9/5/1896) report summarized:

> Very encouraging to the Society of Friends were two features: the religious feeling and the participation of young people. The meetings were devotional, from first to last. The solemn pauses, the deep and living silences, combined with the spoken word and appealing supplication, made many of the sessions seasons of a remarkable experience. Young Friends, who had questioned perhaps whether the system of their Society was really impressive, and whether, in the tremendous pressure of other and far larger religious bodies, it could bear comparison, were convinced, we believe, that there is a vital and enduring force in Quakerism. The impression thus made will not soon pass away. The Conferences this year, the culmination in many ways of a decade's growth, will be long remembered amongst us.

The large Conference tent outside Richmond's Hicksite meetinghouse, 1898. Friends General Conference Records, courtesy of Friends Historical Library of Swarthmore College.

The 1898 Richmond Conference

The shift of the next Conference to Richmond, Indiana—nearly 600 miles west of Swarthmore College—honored the midwestern origins of the Conference movement. A special train from Philadelphia was chartered for Friends to travel together. But midwestern Hicksite Friends being far fewer, this event was inevitably smaller, drawing just over a thousand Friends. Some sessions were held in the large, Gurneyite Fifteenth Street Meetinghouse (where Friends had approved the evangelical Richmond Declaration eleven years before). The gathering was welcomed to Richmond by Dudley Foulke, formerly of New York Yearly Meeting, who called Richmond the "Quaker City of the West."[99] Citing past Quaker work for the abolition of slavery, equality of the sexes, and religious tolerance, he concluded, "The world and Friends are coming nearer together; the world is following that which Friends advocated long ago."

But in other respects, the world was not coming Friends' way. The Spanish-American War had begun a few months earlier. American aggression was triggered by the convergence of several factors: industrial expansion begun during the American Civil War, the closure of the American frontier, the hubris of new wealth, and a nationalistic Protestant mainstream eyeing new frontiers beyond

CHAPTER 2   A Quaker Chautauqua

North America. Vast new resources and untapped labor across the seas were there to be exploited, and millions of souls waited to be saved. Monopoly capital with growing global aspirations engendered a new, militaristic imperialism. Democrats and Republicans alike were ready to facilitate, even sanctify such aspirations. Albert Beveridge, the junior senator from Indiana, declared to the Senate:

> We will not renounce our part in the mission of the race, trustee, under God, of the civilization of the world.... He has made us ... the master organizers of the world to establish system where chaos reigns.... He has made us adept in government that we may administer government among savage and senile peoples.... And of all our race, He has marked the American people as his chosen Nation to finally lead in the regeneration of the world. This is the divine mission of America, and it holds for us all the profit, all the glory, all the happiness possible to man. We are trustees of the world's progress, guardians of its righteous peace. The judgment of the Master is upon us: "Ye have been faithful over a few things; I will make you ruler over many things."

Clearly, the divine law of "progress" could mean very different things to different people. Senator George F. Hoar responded to Beveridge with another quotation from the New Testament gospels: "The Devil taketh him up into an extremely high mountain and showeth him all the kingdoms of the world and the glory of them and saith unto him, 'All these things will be thine if thou wilt fall down and worship me.'"[100]

The Friends Union for Philanthropic Labor produced a "Memorial" to be sent to President William McKinley, expressing concern over the international arms race and its economic burden. A general atmosphere of militarism was turning minds from productive pursuits to the destructive and wasteful impulses of war. In particular, they said Europe was becoming an "armed camp." They urged the President to end the present war (Spain had recently sued for peace) and establish a just settlement. American territorial gains threatened to "lead the nation into adventurous and perilous paths." In addition, McKinley should establish a standing arbitration treaty with Great Britain, a bilateral commitment to peaceful resolution of differences, to set an example for other nations to follow. Finally, "We

Aaron Powell. Courtesy of Friends Historical Library of Swarthmore College.

have been alarmed at the efforts openly made... to make the United States a military power, binding the people to the yoke of compulsory military service."[101]

Addressing the advent of military training in schools, Susanna Gaskill queried how Friends should respond in "these days of rapidly expanding ideas, as to the place the United States holds in the world, and our mission to mankind." Alluding to Quaker participation in the Civil War, she admitted that Friends had "relinquished the more vigorous observance of our distinctive customs." Still, "Ought we not to advocate the peace principle, even in the midst of war?... Do we not believe that the progress of the world has been brought about by the arts of peace, and not by the art of war?" She urged Friends: "Feel deeply, and weigh the subject in its true bearing, and if there is any ethical earnestness in us, we shall stand as one man against this monstrous innovation."[102]

The Religious Conference, the last to meet, opened with the reading of a letter from Aaron Powell, who missed the Conference due to philanthropic travels in England. He reflected:

> In England and in America social conditions, in the last two and a half centuries, have undergone great changes in so many particulars, but in both countries as in the world at large, a practical religion is still a well-nigh universal need. While this need continues the mission of Quakerism will not have been accomplished. Of ritual, ceremony, and technical religious propagandism there is much; of applied Christianity, the doing of the will of the Master, far too little.[103]

Papers were read and discussed on "Religious Culture in the Home," "Are Friends Clear of Materialism?," "Our Smaller Meetings and Isolated Friends," and "Early and Modern Friends, Their Methods and Service."

Near the end of the Richmond Conference, a new voice, that of Henry Wilbur, was heard. He witnessed:

> The great help, intellectually and spiritually, which [this conference] has been to me. It is the first time in my life that I have attended such a Conference of Friends. For thirty years I wandered away from Friends' associations; but I was never so thankful as to-day that amid all these wanderings I held on to my birthright. There has been developed enough spiritual and intellectual power in this Conference, if it be wisely transferred to our several meetings, to create and produce the revival in our Society which we so much wish. But let us not forget that the high tide of this religious body is not stimulated or secured altogether in these large gatherings. It depends upon individual faithfulness, upon every one of us, who, under our peculiar system, is a priest unto God, that we go back to our individual meetings, and bear with hearty earnestness and faithfulness our service and our testimony. The world never needed us so badly as it does to-day.[104]

Born in 1851, Henry Wilbur[105] had grown up a Friend near Albany, New York. His parents were committed abolitionists who made their home a resting place for anti-slavery reformers and a refuge for runaway slaves. He was concerned for temperance and for equal suffrage from an early age. He went on to a career in journalism in New Jersey and New York City, retaining his membership despite his inactive status. He reflected in later years that he was glad to have been born in time to receive the moral stamina developed during the anti-slavery struggle and Civil War. Two years after Jesse Holmes's liberal "altar call," Henry Wilbur's moment of awakening at Richmond would lead to great service among Friends.

Nevertheless, Wilbur's testimony identified a continuing dilemma for the nascent Friends General Conference. How could the fervor produced by these large gatherings be transported back to local meetings? Could the affective intensity of the Conferences turn the melancholy of local meeting life into the spleen of renewed ministry and service? Or would it merely serve as a summer vacation from it?

The *Proceedings* of the Richmond Conference were published together from the start this time, as a publication of The Friends Intelligencer Association. *The Friends Intelligencer* had already published a number of the addresses in its issues. The coalescence into one body was now all but official. A Reorganization Committee was named and charged with making recommendations to the next Conference.

The 1900 Chautauqua Conference

During the Richmond Conference, an invitation was received from Methodist Bishop John Vincent, Superintendent of the Chautauqua Assembly, to meet at Chautauqua in 1900. The invitation was accepted. The 1900 Conference was a marriage made in progressive heaven, with 1,200 Friends gathered in "a place devoted to all the high interests of a broad spiritual and intellectual culture . . . a strange, but by no means unfriendly environment." The editor of the *Proceedings* added:

> In the spiritual and intellectual uplift both given and received by our people mingling with the people of Chautauqua . . . a higher standard of excellence was set for future gatherings, and . . . the Conference of 1900 inspired a brighter hope for the future growth

CHAPTER 2   A Quaker Chautauqua

William Birdsall. Courtesy of Friends Historical Library of Swarthmore College.

and usefulness of our Friendly body as one of the world's family of religious denominations.[106]

The word "mingling," used negatively by conservative Hicksites through most of the nineteenth century, had become a positive term by the twentieth. The Chautauqua experience confirmed to Friends their kinship with a wider array of progressive churches and groups. It also set a new tone of willingness to hear from "hireling" ministers and experts from universities and government bodies. Indeed, Chautauqua can be seen as the decisive moment of Quaker transition from sect to denomination, "one of the world's family." Nevertheless, in some respects we will hear abiding sectarian tendencies in perennial, anxious questions as to what it means to be a Quaker. Ben Pink Dandelion's paradoxical term, "liberal sect" (mentioned in the Introduction) is apt.

William Birdsall addressed "What Quakerism Stands for" in the opening session, probably intended in part to interpret Friends to others staying at Chautauqua. He observed that while modern sociology focuses on "man in the mass," "Quakerism maintains the importance of the individual." Jesus preached that the kingdom of God is within; likewise, Quakerism stresses that each individual has the light of Christ. "Inner light," therefore, sums up Quakerism:

> The individualism of the Quaker is not a selfish withdrawal from social service; on the contrary it requires of him his full share of such service.... Quakerism still stands for a noble individualism; it ... best represents and exemplifies that liberty of conscience which ... has been the goal of all progress in religion ... it stands for the brotherhood of men because it realizes the fatherhood of God.

The wider progressive movement was often critical of individualism as self-seeking. But since Hicksite and Progressive Friends had so strongly emphasized liberty of conscience, they viewed individualism more positively. A century before, the collective processes of group discernment had priority over individual opinions and leadings. By now, the individual had wrested that priority from the collective.

As noted in our introduction, "The brotherhood of man and the Fatherhood of God" was a popular formula among progressive Protestants of the day, a handy formula to square the circle of unity in diversity. A blurring of collective identities—sectarian, ethnic, gendered, class—into universal individualism helped the formula work. But various androcentric, Eurocentric, and Christocentric assumptions remained more or less intact for decades to come.

Birdsall observed that the individual faithfulness of early Friends had revived the

> Christian morality of meekness, piety, benevolence, purity, truthfulness, peacefulness, and passivity. Certain of these testimonies presently resulted in peculiarities. Plainness of dress became "the plain dress," and finally almost a uniform.... There could be no greater treason to its vital principle than to make it consist in particular external acts or practices, however important these may have been in the testimony bearing of a particular time.[107]

Birdsall's comment indicates some historical perspective and balancing, after decades of rebellion against the traditional forms,

CHAPTER 2   A Quaker Chautauqua

Howard Jenkins. Courtesy of Friends Historical Library of Swarthmore College.

which we heard one reforming Friend in 1867 call "conceit and imbecility." But by 1900 Quaker "peculiarities" had been largely planed off, leaving a sleek new profile that moved easily in wider circles.

It is also worth considering the term "Quakerism," which dates to the seventeenth century. Like the term "Quaker" itself, it was coined by opponents. It was used by Friends only in answer to criticism, not as a self-designation. In their own minds, they were "the people of God, known to the world by the name Quaker." But after a century of reform and remodeling, Friends viewed themselves from the outside as much as from the inside. They confidently breathed the fresh affects of a wider culture as much as the musty air of old meetinghouses. Thus, the term "Quakerism" expressed a double persona, private and public. W. E. B. DuBois observed at this time that only people of privileged race and class in America could enjoy such double status.[108] Friends were collectively no longer the strange "other" but "one of the world's family."

Conference Chairman Howard Jenkins, publisher of *The Friends Intelligencer*, addressed the same opening session with further historical perspective. He presented a brief, evolutionary review of Christian history, showing "priestcraft" giving way to the Reformation until finally Quakers came to proclaim that God is the teacher of his people himself. This outlook was finally finding acceptance: "It is no longer a dangerous heresy to declare convictions like those of Fox and Barclay. . . . It is not yet the millennial day, but a day of new proving, new sifting, new endeavor, and so we trust of new advancement."[109] Thus, the threshold of the twentieth century appeared like the high noon of progressive revelation and evolutionary development to liberal Friends and many others.

The Conference continued using the different pre-existing Conferences as program formats, with a Young Friends Association program added. All sessions continued to be plenary. Business meetings of the Central Committee and other committees and associations were interspersed with the plenary schedule.

John William Graham did not attend the Chautauqua Conference, but the brightest young star of the British liberal renewal, John Wilhelm Rowntree, had planned to come. He and Rufus Jones had become close friends in 1897 and were allies in Quaker renewal. But Rowntree's health was failing and he chose not to travel. (He died in Rufus Jones's arms in 1905, at age thirty-seven.) His paper was read to the Conference by Jesse Holmes. Rowntree affirmed evolutionary processes of development in both nature and culture. Evolutionary theory "reveals a universal law of continual progressive change" that applies to everything including religion. "Truth is one, and science, if true, cannot be in antagonism to what is true in religion."[110]

Isaac Roberts delivered a eulogy in memory of Aaron Powell, of Plainfield, New Jersey, an important figure in Hicksite renewal over the second half of the preceding century. Born in 1832, he had studied at Antioch College under Horace Mann. He became an antislavery lecturer in 1851 and editor of the *Anti-Slavery Standard*. Some of his lectures were broken up by violent mobs, and he was seriously injured in one such incident. After the Civil War, he was the organizer and first president of the National Purity Alliance as well as editor of *The Philanthropist*. He made nine trips to Europe to coordinate American and European reform movements. A recorded minister among Friends, he was beloved for his peaceful manner and mediating influence between reformist and traditional Hicksite Friends. He collapsed and died in 1899 while speaking at a meeting of ministers and elders at the Race Street meetinghouse in Philadelphia. *The Friends Intelligencer* obituary (5/20/1899) commented, "The loss to the Society of Friends is very serious. We are indeed ill able to spare him."

Two years after his Quaker rebirth at Richmond, Henry Wilbur gave a plenary address on "The Duty of Friends to Social Reform."

CHAPTER 2   A Quaker Chautauqua

Henry Wilbur. Courtesy of Friends Historical Library of Swarthmore College.

Again, evolution was a major theme: "In obedience to the law of evolution our race is growing more religiously social.... Under this impulse our theology has become more kindly, more inclusive.... In short, our conception of salvation has become more social." He concluded, "The Friend of the new time, true to the mark of his high calling, is the fulfiller of prophecy; the divinely appointed instrument by which the testimonies of the fathers regarding social purity and peace shall become vital and actual attainments in the lives of men."[111] We hear the variety of moral concerns under the banner of "purity" in these early conferences.

The struggle for women's suffrage was also coming to full strength among Friends. Marianna Chapman spoke on "Woman as Citizen." She noted that:

> Women are now defined as citizens, and, as such, are amenable to all law, can hold property, sue and be sued, enter into all professions and business relations, and fill a public office if elected or appointed;

but through some strange logic, or no logic at all, cannot except in four States of the Union, be electors.... It is only through the ballot that we attain to a government with the consent of the governed.

Martha Schofield. Courtesy of Friends Historical Library of Swarthmore College.

Just as we heard Anna Jackson argue in 1896 for the wider social benefits of negro education, Chapman predicted that women's suffrage "will decrease the percentage of the criminal element . . . increase that of sobriety and of the church, and decrease the proportion of the saloon element, the gambling element, and the fighting element." It would also add to national life the strongest peace force in society: "Women are fundamentally peaceful." She urged Friends to work for suffrage: "It is most fitting that a society which first made woman an equal in the church should stand for her as an equal in the State. One of its first armor-bearers was Lucretia Mott. Have we not grown to her stature?"[112]

Then Martha Schofield, still working with sharecroppers and educating black children in South Carolina, intersected gender and race with "The Womanhood of the Negro Race":

> Inherited tendency can only be brought under subjection by the broader growth and development of a true womanhood. As yet, the mothers of men know not their own powers.... Will not our race reap as we have sown, unless we put the sickle in, divide the tares from the wheat, and go forth sowing the seed, and planting that which will develop, strengthen, broaden and uplift the womanhood, wifehood, motherhood of the negro woman, and thus solve the "better-half" of the negro problem?[113]

Like many in the wider progressive movement, Friends saw women's rights as pivotal to social transformation on many fronts.

CHAPTER 2   A Quaker Chautauqua

Suffrage would break down the social paradigm of "separate spheres" that had left men free to indulge their vices away from home. Again, the middle-class domestic vision of a "home-like" society was central to the progressive cause.

(Note: Nearly fifty lynchings took place in Aiken County and its wider area in South Carolina during the decades Martha Schofield maintained her school there. The fact that those in her school and wider network were spared such atrocities may suggest at least some beneficial aspects of white paternalism [or in this case, maternalism] under those daunting historical circumstances. [114])

This feminist agenda came into further expression with Edward Janney's address on "Personal Purity and Its Influence upon Character." He began with the gospel story of the woman caught in adultery, asking why the man was not also held accountable. He went on to examine the double standard of morality in modern life. He found an attitude, ancient and modern, in which woman was an inferior "whose chief duty is to minister to the pleasures of man." This, he claimed, led to a "deterioration of character" for both women and men, with women and children suffering most. Prurient stage-plays, both popular and serious, are commercially successful but detrimental to society. "Purity is the cornerstone of the home; the home is the unit of the State; destroy purity and the nation will soon disintegrate."[115]

We heard Henry Wilbur pair "social purity" with "peace," another area of rising Quaker activity. Howard Jenkins spoke on "The Outlook for Peace." The Spanish-American War was past, but trouble continued to brew in Europe, as the recently united Germany came into its own as an industrial and military power with expanding imperial ambitions. Jenkins articulated the "escalator of progress" ideology so popular at the time. "We are taught that these processes [of growth and change], however slow, have a continuous and consistent direction, and their direction is upward. No evolution goes from higher to lower, from refined to crude, from the perfected to the elementary. This being true, we cannot doubt that we shall ultimately emerge from darkness into light." He spoke at length on the historic Quaker "peace position," urging Friends not to be discouraged by new threats of war. Friends were told that world peace is an impractical ideal. But "toward the ideal we look; toward it we endeavor. And thus there comes the forward and the upward Process of Growth."[116]

The traditional Quaker peace testimony had been a loving but stubborn refusal of war. By 1900 it had become more a "position" and an "ideal." Ethical idealism was a hallmark of liberal Christianity in this period. But inter-imperialist war loomed, threatening a materialist blow against idealism, a resurgence of the "crude" against the "refined."

Jenkins made reference to the Hague Conference of 1899 as a promising development. Friends and peace societies around Europe and America had hoped the Conference would create an international court for compulsory, binding arbitration of disputes. Most of the countries, including the US, Britain, Russia, and France favored it. But the provision was vetoed by a small coalition led by Germany. Still, a Permanent Court of Arbitration was created, to be enacted on a voluntary basis, and international laws regarding war and war crimes were established.

One expression of this rising tide of Quaker peace activism was the American Friends' Peace Conference held in Philadelphia in December 1901, bringing together Friends from all the branches.[117] The epistle of invitation to yearly meetings declared this to be a critical time for "Christian civilization," requiring an active, urgent movement for peace. Friends were "in a position to-day to speak with greater intelligence and wisdom, and therefore with greater power, than ever before in history." Drawing upon the cumulative lessons of Quaker history and world history, Friends owed it to themselves and the world "to restate in a united and new way the pressing question of peace and ... the rescue of mankind from the awful iniquities and crushing burdens of modern militarism."[118]

Rufus Jones spoke at that conference in evolutionary terms. He said the spirit of fighting is strong in children, but they slowly wean themselves from it, and civilization is on a similar path of development. Old ways still have a strong hold upon us, but "the warmer currents of the Gulf Stream are slowly flooding the world."[119] British Friend Anna Braithwaite Thomas called Friends to an "aggressive spirit" of peacemaking. "We must let them see that we are actually getting things done in Christ's way."[120] Several speakers found hope in the 1899 Hague Conference, noting that its provisions followed the general lines of William Penn's *Essay towards the Present and Future Peace of Europe* (1693).

The Friends Intelligencer (9/8/1900) reflected upon the Chautauqua Conference, finding a steady development over the past decade: "a more mature and more definite understanding and sense of purpose were disclosed" at Chautauqua. More non-Friends were present, due to the ecumenical location. "What is the effect of these conferences upon us? We cannot believe it is slight, or that it quickly passes away."

The Organization of Friends General Conference

The renewals that had so transformed both Orthodox and Hicksite Friends over the preceding century reached their constitutional moments at the turn of the century. The 1887 Richmond Conference of Orthodox-Gurneyite Friends had produced some basic evangelical definitions of Quaker faith and practice. They affirmed most of what had developed over the past half-century. They passed over the question of pastoral leadership but drew a line against recent innovations such as the introduction of outward sacraments. The Gurneyite Ohio Yearly Meeting dropped out, but the remaining yearly meetings joined together in 1902 as a new body, the Five Years Meeting. They approved a uniform discipline, establishing a small degree of authority in the new body over its constituent yearly meetings. This federal constitutional tilt toward centralized authority confirmed the misgivings Hicksite reformers had harbored against the Orthodox all along.

Meanwhile, the Chautauqua Conference of 1900 resolved to consolidate the pre-existing entities: "The several organizations and interests represented at the Conference [shall] be united in one organization, to be known as 'Friends' General Conference'. . . . Its affairs [shall] be under the management of a committee, to be known as the Central Committee, composed of one hundred members."[121] The First-Day School Conference, Education Conference, and Union for Philanthropic Labor would each appoint thirty members, with balanced representation from the seven yearly meetings. (The percentages of yearly meeting representation were proportional to membership, with Philadelphia given 47 percent, New York and Baltimore 18 percent each, Indiana 7 percent, Illinois 5 percent, Genesee 3 percent, and Ohio 2 percent.) Ten more members would be appointed by the Executive Committee of the Friends Associations. Edward Janney was named as Chairman of the new body.[122] Deborah Haines[123] notes that while the Religious Conference was left out of this equation, it attained better representation of its interests in 1902 with the formation of a Committee for the Advancement of Friends' Principles (described later in this chapter).

The slow development of the Conferences had by now assured Friends that this would not become a centralizing and disciplinary organization. Thus, a looser, confederal constitutional sensibility united the seven constituent yearly meetings.

Friends General Conference and the Five Years Meeting might be seen as Quakerly correlates to the consolidation and standardization that had been underway in the corporate world since the 1870s. Their federal and confederal constitutions articulated organizationally the developments and discernment of the preceding seventy years. As such, the two bodies reflected the different sides of the dialectical tension built into the US Constitution. Would they further their respective centralizing/federal and decentralizing/confederal tendencies? Or would balancing forces come into play?

In the meantime, a rebalancing of the business-government equation was soon underway in national politics. Wealthy businessmen in Chicago had literally danced together the night of President McKinley's election in November 1896. They could look forward to a government that would see things their way. But within a year after McKinley's 1900 re-election, an anarchist immigrant assassinated him. "The party was over," Cornelius Vanderbilt IV later remarked.[124] Theodore Roosevelt, a New York progressive who had been nominated as Vice-President to balance the Republican ticket, was suddenly thrust into the White House. The Roosevelt family was certainly wealthy, but it was the old wealth of New York, with a certain sense of *noblesse oblige*. The progressive movement suddenly had decisive political representation. FGC came into focus at a privileged moment.

CHAPTER 2   A Quaker Chautauqua

Edward Janney. Courtesy of Friends Historical Library of Swarthmore College.

The 1902 Asbury Park Conference

Friends migrated to another Methodist-founded center for their next Conference. Asbury Park on the Jersey shore was founded in 1871 by the wealthy philanthropist and developer James Bradley, inspired by the Methodist camp-meeting resort of Ocean Grove, New Jersey. The Central Committee accepted Bradley's invitation to use the resort's facilities.

Edward Janney, who would Chair the Conferences for two decades, opened the Conference, noting that attendance was already nearly two thousand. Janney was a homeopathic physician and a recorded minister in Baltimore Yearly Meeting. After Aaron Powell's death in 1899, he took over as President of the American Purity Association and was involved in a variety of reform causes. His steady leadership of the Central Committee was a factor in FGC's continuing progress. At his death, he would be remembered for "his boundless energy and enthusiasm, his initiative, his devotion, his unfailing optimism, his cheerfulness" (FI 12/20/1930).

The Conference received an impassioned address by Anna Cooper on "The Ethics of the Negro Question." Opening with the Proverb (29:18), "Where there is no vision, the people perish," she bemoaned the ethical blindness of America's opulence. "Things without thoughts are mere vulgarities. . . . A nation cannot long survive the shattering of its own ideals." She foregrounded the issue of race: "It is no fault of the Negro that he stands in the United States of America today as the passive and silent rebuke to the nation's Christianity, the great gulf between its professions and its practices."

Cooper hearkened to the great moral cause of abolition Friends and others had pressed half a century ago. "Today all this is changed. White and black meet as strangers with cold distrust or avowed hostility." She enumerated the current plagues of lynching, economic injustice, and unequal education. "It is no popular task today to voice the black man's woe. It is far easier and safer to say that the wrong is all in him. The American conscience would like to rest from the ghost of the black man. . . . If at such times we cannot sing 'America' it is not because of any treason lurking in our hearts. Our harps are hung on the willows—and in the Babylon of our sorrow—we needs must sit down and weep" (see Psalm 139). Cooper prophesied, "God is not dead. Neither does He sleep. As a nation sows so shall it reap. Men do not gather grapes from thorns nor figs from thistles. To sow the wind is to reap the whirlwind."[125] Cooper's prophetic address was more a lament than a call to action, perhaps because the wider progressive movement had made peace with segregation. But clearly, not all progressives were content with this separate peace.

Cooper's address was followed by a short presentation by Matthew Anderson, pastor of the Berean Presbyterian Church of Philadelphia, and one of the first non-Quakers invited to speak at an FGC Conference. He offered some statistics on Negro migration from the South to Philadelphia. In 1890 the black population of the city was 40,370. By 1900 it had reached 64,020, an average yearly increase of 2,385. But Philadelphia offered few opportunities for their moral, religious, and economic advancement. Atlanta, with a black population of only forty thousand, had many more public schools, manual training schools, and colleges open to negroes. Northern philanthropy supported negro education in the South. But in Philadelphia, the little Berean school for manual training was struggling for survival in the basement of his church. Anderson's brief report offered a useful supplement to W. E. B. DuBois's landmark sociological study, *The Philadelphia Negro*, published in 1899.

Mariana Chapman continued to press the "Equal Rights of Women," focusing the lack of men in teaching positions. As long as women could be paid less, they would be hired more:

> It all comes back to equality of opportunity and equality of rights... since women are in the economic world and have come there to stay, it is just that they should have their opinions counted concerning the law makers and the officials who govern their world of labor and life.

With their 200 years of experience with women's leadership and share in decision-making, Friends were needed at the forefront of work for suffrage. "It is a political question only so far as it is a question of right and wrong, of fair dealing, of morality, of the God-given right of self-government and opportunity for service."[126] Her address received a long, affirmative response from Carrie Chapman Catt (no apparent relation), president of the National American Woman Suffrage Association.

Shifting focus toward internal concerns, a panel of nine Friends addressed "The Greatest Need of the Society of Friends." Janney urged speakers not to focus on criticisms of the past but on hopes for future. A blend of traditionalist and activist voices shared common hopes for deeper worship and more Friends willing to serve in roles of leadership, including ministry and First-Day school teaching. One bemoaned the influence of education and intellectual culture, leading to unprofitable vocal ministry: "A rambling, disconnected discourse, without point or logical conclusion, tends to discourage rather than encourage an entrance into our Society." Another urged renewed simplicity. Resorting to the practices of other religions in order to attract new members would not succeed. Another pressed the need to rethink and repurpose the select meetings of ministers and elders—perhaps just eliminate the ministers. Henry Wilbur was the last panelist to speak, with sustained passion: "Have we not become sufficiently saturated with the spirit which ought to go out to minister and to teach and to inspire, that we shall take to our homes the uplift and the inspiration and the consciousness which we have had here?" God is "pleading with us to labor in the vineyard for the uplifting of men as the only way of advancing the Glory of God."[127] The offerings of the panelists indicate a continuing concern for the internal health of meetings, in order to sustain FGC's expanding social vistas.

John William Graham returned to speak on "War and Evolution," lauding evolution as a "marvelous upward career." He noted the past century of relative peace. (Indeed, the British regime of colonial conquest and capitalist expansion had combined stable prosperity with enough naval and military dominance to keep rebellious forces at bay.) Viewed in evolutionary terms, war had played a role in the establishing of modern nation-states, but it was now becoming obsolete. The world was advancing from militancy toward sympathy. Graham's outlook was surprisingly rosy, considering that Europe continued to arm and the United States had begun to flex its muscle.

Graham also spoke on "Isaac Penington, a Quaker Mystic," concluding that Friends "are the purest type in England and America of the church mystical and philanthropical, and our call is to abide in our calling."[128] "Mysticism" was a word seldom heard in Hicksite usage thus far. But it was becoming a catchword among liberal Christians in Europe and America as they attempted to relocate a spiritual center that could hold amid the disruptive forces of modernity. Rufus Jones became the major popularizer of mysticism among liberal Friends and other progressive Christians in America.[129]

The Friends Intelligencer printed a number of the addresses given at the Conference. In its summary report (9/20/1902), it observed that these biennial meetings had become "a very important feature in the life of our Society." Growing experience helped the organizers run them more smoothly and efficiently. "No one will doubt that our religious body, as the result of those general meetings in the past twelve years, has become more unified and single-minded."

The next issue (9/27/1902) reported the Central Committee's sense that "a more general work should be carried on, and that it should be more systematic, more energetic, and more continuous." An ad hoc committee was formed, with Jesse Holmes as its secretary, to develop the idea further. This was the kind of work paid clergy undertook in other churches. The notion that Friends "are not a proselyting body" had retarded such initiatives. But Friends "have a duty to be instrumental for good." The Committee for the Advancement of Friends' Principles was formed later that year, with Henry Wilbur as its Chair.

The 1904 Toronto Conference

FGC's first visit to the Jersey shore at Asbury Park was a foretaste of things to come. But like ancient Israel wandering in the wilderness with a portable ark and tent of meeting, the Conferences continued to itinerate in these early years. The next Conference in Toronto honored the Canadian element of Genesee Yearly Meeting. The initiative for renewed Quaker outreach, described in the preceding paragraph, took flight in these sessions as well. John William Graham visited again, clearly aiming to keep the British and American liberal renewals in conversation. He spoke on "The Friend and His Message" at an opening session aimed to engage interested non-Friends from the area. He described Quaker beginnings as a fresh awareness of the light in every one. The resulting Society of Friends might be called "the Community of the Holy Spirit."

Continuing to live into its newly integrated structure, FGC renamed its conferences "committees." The Philanthropic Committee sustained focus on racial justice as Anna Jackson addressed "The Race Problem in the United States":

> With race riots in the North, as well as in the South, with terrible crimes committed by negroes, followed by barbarous lynchings in both South and North, many people are appalled. They see no light. They tremble in the present, and look with dread to the future. Many, even of the old-time friends of the Negro feel discouraged, and fill the air with denunciations of the evil-minded black, and suggestions

as to his segregation or enforced emigration. Other friends of the Negro, with Booker Washington at their head, urge further education as the remedy, and again the cry comes, 'Education has spoiled the Negro.'

Jackson suggested that Friends might best focus on raising money to create settlement houses in urban areas of the North, run by colored people themselves. Meanwhile, Friends could work for uplift in their own communities: "A man free from prejudice will tend to remove prejudice from the minds of those around him. . . . I ask you to mold public opinion to the side of justice." She suggested Friends raise their own consciousness in three ways: *First*, judge "the colored race" by its history and opportunities, remembering that it has emerged from slavery only in the last forty years; *second*, keep in mind that personal progress for the black American comes at a greater cost than for the white; and *third*, teach that our government is founded on inalienable rights "for the Afro-American along with everyone else."[130]

Building upon a Quaker tradition of interracial advocacy, Friends such as Anna Jackson and Anna Cooper were far ahead of the European American mainstream, ahead even of the mainstream of the progressive movement. But their perspective was still informed by limited interracial contact in contexts of relative equality. Inevitably, it retained a certain paternalism.

Purity also received sustained attention in these early Conferences, in this instance through a series of short presentations on purity in the home, school, press, and church. Purity was posed as a positive way of addressing a variety of social ills. The home was again framed as "the very heart of human society—upon the home as a foundation-stone rests our social order, and . . . all social uplift." In joining with the purity campaign, Friends could unite with a broader ecumenical movement "going in advance and blazing the way to a higher and broader and nobler civilization." In the session's concluding presentation, Henry Wilbur asserted that the purity campaign would never succeed until it could:

> Establish it as a rule that the father of a family should be as tender and decent and delicate as the mother; that the two sexes should

be brought up with equal delicacy and equal decency . . . the two sexes will rise or fall together; and the point is to keep them clean, rising together . . . teach boys and girls that every organ of the body is divine, made for divine ends and purposes, to be used for divine ends and purposes. If you can once imbue them with that thought, the whole purity question is settled.[131]

In these continuing addresses on purity, we can hear how these Friends integrated feminism, pacifism, social justice, and moral concerns.

Jesse Holmes introduced the peace session, noting that wars are usually justified on some moral principle, the end justifying the means. But even the most celebrated American wars, the Revolution and the Civil War, produced many disastrous ends alongside the stated ends of independence and emancipation. Moreover, peace as the absence of war is not peace. The United States was resounding with the din of industrial war and trade wars. Schools glorified the soldier, clergy prayed for victory, criminals were treated with the idea of revenge. As long as these trends predominated, it was neither a peaceful nor Christian nation. We thus hear a more integrative Quaker understanding of peace converging with integrative definitions of purity. These trends advanced as Friends drew increasingly upon the social sciences, sometimes explicitly referenced in Conference addresses.

At this Conference, the First-Day School Committee presented a new graded curriculum for use among the seven yearly meetings, featuring updated approaches to teaching the Bible. To call attention to this achievement, the Committee invited Rufus Jones to make his first full-fledged FGC presentation on "Teaching the Bible." Jones was starting to have an impact beyond the Quaker world with the publication that year of *Social Law in the Spiritual World*. He spoke at an evening session that probably attracted a wider local audience. He began by remarking that "Friends are never quite happy unless they are engaged in some reform." He then stressed the Bible's historic role in reform:

> No other book in human history has so profoundly influenced the race as has the Bible. It has been an incalculable factor toward

progress in all lands that are civilized. It is probably not too much to claim, if we say that the Bible has done more than any other single thing to promote Anglo-Saxon supremacy in the world and to produce the virile moral power of these dominant peoples.[132]

A century later, these words do not sound like an endorsement of the Bible to our ears. If anything, they approximate many liberal complaints about the Bible and Christianity today: racial dominance, androcentrism ("virility"), and all the mixed feelings words like "progress" and "civilization" evoke for us today. But we must bear in mind that these speakers were European Americans who had come of age during the Victorian era. They were still absorbing the implications of the new world they heralded.

Jones expressed concern that the Bible was losing its cultural and moral influence as it was no longer taught in public schools or in the home. Moreover, Sunday Schools were often dogmatic in their approach. Bible stories could still be powerful influences on the morals and faith of young people. Jones hoped that if Friends learned to teach the Bible as *stories* rather than doctrines, public schools might adopt their example and include the Bible in their curricula.

Appraising the Toronto Conference, *The Friends Intelligencer* (8/27/1904) noted that "concerned young men and women were present in larger proportion than ever before. . . . One of the most distinctively Friendly sessions we had was that under the care of the Young Friends Associations." In addition, the Committee for the Advancement of Friends' Principles was energetically "nurturing the spiritual lives of Friends and Friends meetings, through correspondence, visitation, and the holding of small gatherings for scattered and isolated Friends."[133] But the work demanded more focus and energy. "They therefore recommended that a suitable Friend be employed as a permanent secretary, with headquarters in Philadelphia." This person must be "a man or woman of discernment, for the work will be far more than clerical." More fundraising would be needed to support this new position. Subsequent to this report, Henry Wilbur, still in his early fifties and the emerging public voice of FGC, was appointed to the position. He began work early the next year with prodigious energy. As Chuck Fager observes,

CHAPTER 2   A Quaker Chautauqua

Wilbur became the first Hicksite "hireling."[134] Given the delicacy of this innovation, the Advancement Committee was left with the responsibility to raise Wilbur's salary. We will continue to follow his meteoric Quaker career.

NOTE: This book's Appendix, "A Quaker Moral Compass," offers reflections on the integration of peace, racial justice, moral purity, and other concerns we see developing over the course of these Conferences.

CHAPTER 3

The New Normal
FGC Conferences 1906–1914

We are a busy people [engaged in arduous occupations, in the work of the world, sometimes losing sight of the higher interests of life]. And so we have been getting together every two years among other things to catch fresh inspiration from the look into each other's faces, to learn from each other what can be done, what is being done, in the various fields of right and elevated effort, and to renew our zeal to build afresh the fires of inspiration.

— William Birdsall at the 1906 Conference[135]

The 1906 Mountain Lake Park Conference

Ecumenical affinities continued with the next Conference, held at Mountain Lake Park, the Methodist-founded Chautauqua Assembly site in Maryland. Some 2,500 Friends attended. In the opening session, William Birdsall, who had become President of Swarthmore College, praised the Chautauqua movement: "The chief glory of the work of these assemblies is that they have joined religion to other interests of man ... connected the work of intellectual development, of intellectual culture, of human refinement, with ... the promotion of religious truth and of religious living."[136] He found these qualities convergent with the longstanding traditions of Friends. (Once again, "the world is coming our way.") Birdsall also reflected cogently on the emerging pattern of the Conferences (see the epigraph above). It is a telling description: Friends experience affective refreshment as they "look into each other's faces," while receiving intellectual uplift as they "learn from each other what is to be done," and are then affectively recharged "to renew our zeal" for reform.

CHAPTER 3   The New Normal

Friends at the Mountain Lake Park Lodge, 1906. Friends General Conference Records, Friends Historical Library of Swarthmore College.

Joseph Walton, principal of George School, offered the keynote address. A recorded minister in Philadelphia Yearly Meeting, Walton had led the school through a period of major expansion. He spoke on "Quakerism: A Normal Religion." He first clarified his intention: it was not to show a certain doctrine or "ism" to be normative, unfolding a truth beyond all others. Quakerism is about experience. Something stirred among early Friends "that was and is normal in religious life."

Walton observed that civilization and education enlarge human desires and ambitions. These ambitions breed social inequality and war. By contrast, Quaker worship emancipates one from such drives, while also motivating a new kind of engagement with the world:

> It reorganizes the man and puts him in his proper place in the world, in society, in the home and in the church. He has found himself, and as a result peace abides with him.... This kind of life is normal; it is the kind of life that we yearn for in our calmer and wiser moments. Here is something normative and something partaking of immortality. Finding one's place in the world, and in the hearts of others, a

Joseph Walton. Courtesy of the George School Archives.

place no other personality can fill, is a practical method of deepening one's roots in immortal life. It is the struggle for identification with the Father.

If, then, there is in man a personality whose die was cast in the image of God, and if the things of this world are necessary when put in their true place to aid the unfolding of . . . that personality which has no duplicate, then Quakerism is normative and calls all men to come and find that in themselves of God's own planting.[137]

Walton echoes the personalist philosophy that had strongly affected Rufus Jones during his year of study at Harvard in 1900 and the resulting manifesto, *Social Law in the Spiritual World* (mentioned in the preceding chapter). Like Jones, Walton recognized key points of convergence between traditional Quakerism and this new stream of philosophy. They found in personalism a *lingua franca* that could aid in the wider spread of Quakerism.[138] Once again, Friends recognized themes in their own tradition that were becoming popular, perhaps eventually normative, in the wider culture.

Among the recorded responses to Walton, Lavinia Hoopes of Philadelphia Yearly Meeting heartily agreed. But "I have just thought of a few of our little peculiarities that have been taken on by our Society, and which seem to me entirely abnormal." She singled out the strange tone of voice still used by some in vocal ministry, calling it "an old superstition":

> It is our business to drop them [these "mistaken ways"] and reform our ministers. . . . We desire a normal life, expressing itself in a simple, normal way, that when a stranger comes to our meeting . . . they need not have to ask why this cadence, why this peculiar modulation, why this sometimes rapt manner.[139]

Hoopes's comments underscore a key dilemma for Quaker renewal. Pushing Quakerism into the mainstream also pushed the mainstream into Quakerism. Along the way its peculiar ideas and affects were swapped for more popular ones. The results were often but not always beneficial.

Continuing concern for the rapid decline in biblical literacy motivated William Jackson of New York (husband of Anna) to speak on "Ignorance of the Bible a Loss to Society." He affirmed that the preceding century of scientific discovery and evolutionary theory had assailed old theories with new evidence. These advances now informed the modern study of the Bible:

> We learn from the same Bible the evolution of the purer religion that recognized the universal brotherhood of men in the universal Fatherhood of God, and we marvel that in the nineteenth century human slavery was defended by ministers of Christian Churches, and that taking human life by the State, and declaring war by the nation, still find excuses in quotations from Mosaic legislation.
>
> He who goes to the Bible to find his spiritual life there will be disappointed, but he who reads it with a discerning spirit will not fail to find in the records of the lives of a multitude of seekers after the

truth, struggling to emerge from spiritual darkness, an instructive lesson and an inspiring stimulus that can be found in no other book nor be taught in any better way.[140]

Typical of this early period, we find a confident moral teleology in Jackson's evolutionary reading of the Bible and human history. But the historical study of the Bible required more effort than the average Friend had time or inclination to devote to it. Moreover, the coming storms of the twentieth century soon battered this easy confidence.

Emergent trends among FGC Friends were voiced in a session organized by the Young Friends Associations, titled "A Young Man's Religion." The panel of young Quaker speakers (indeed, all male), suggested, among other things, that:

> The young man to-day wants a simple, a plain religion. He is loth to believe that the great essential truths and relations of his God have been different from those of any people in any age.... If this be Quakerism, let us have more of it.
>
> The religion of a young man is positive and an affirmative religion; there is not in it a single negation. Yet there must be in it a reasonable and satisfactory explanation for mistakes and failures. There must be room in it for a sense of sin, and there must be some way out of sin, a way that is open to every man.[141]

With the new Quaker outreach led by Henry Wilbur, this fresh input was of vital interest. FGC had begun holding weekend conferences, an innovation borrowed from British Friends. Marie Jenkins reported that six successful weekends had been held in various locations since the last Conference, on various topics reflecting FGC concerns. One Friend felt they were "too sensational, too much in the nature of proselyting." Henry Wilbur responded that "on that mere word proselyting altogether too much nervousness is exhibited.... I believe that the Society of Friends ought to proselyte."[142]

Other presentations at the Conference included Charles Burleigh Galbreath on capital punishment: "The death penalty does not reform, does not deter, does not protect, does not accomplish a single legitimate end of punishment. It has been tried; it has failed."[143] Russell Smith, of the University of Pennsylvania addressed ethical investment. He observed that many who would never steal or bribe will own shares in and take dividends from corporations that steal, and bribe and are corrupt. The whole is composed of its parts. The ordinary American Christian of to-day has not advanced to the point where he sees all his investments are his, morally as well as financially. He sees that the dividends are his, but he asks few moral questions about how they are achieved.[144]

This was a first appearance of broader socio-economic questions at FGC Conferences. It would not be the last.

The Friends' Intelligencer (9/8/1906) counted 2,500 attending one of the Conference's meetings for worship, with seventy-five elders and ministers crowded onto the platform. Ministers and elders still occupied a place of honor, but that place and its honor were increasingly questioned within FGC's egalitarian ethos.

The 1908 Winona Lake Conference

FGC continued to itinerate, making another stop in the Midwest, at a lake resort in northern Indiana and the home of one of the largest Chautauqua Associations in the country. Again, a special train from Philadelphia was arranged and carried 160 Friends to the Conference. Six hundred attended the opening session. Henry Wilbur continued to gain momentum. His plenary address, "Speaking to Twentieth Century Conditions," clearly aimed toward Quaker outreach. He cited the great material and intellectual progress of the last century. Even religion had been "rationalized and softened, the bitterness of the old time having been diluted with the milk of human kindness." But the world still suffered major blights of materialism and lust for power.

> Any word that we speak to-day must be directed to the twentieth century heart of hope. Turning our backs upon the conquered material world, we face the moral wilderness as yet almost untouched by the pioneers of spiritual progress.... The delights of that superlative moral conquest may be the experience of our present progressive civilization, if we as men and women are supremely true to the heavenly vision set before us, and to the high ideals which are at the center of our better nature.[145]

Wilbur was an enthusiastic promoter of the faith he had rediscovered in middle age, if not a major thinker. His rhetoric exudes the moral idealism of the prewar period. The material world was now "conquered" and the "moral conquest" was at hand. His enthusiasm was infectious, however. He aired his proposal for "Friendly Propaganda," to produce six newspaper columns worth of text every six weeks and send the printed product out to one hundred newspapers. These "in the main should deal with questions related to our testimonies, such as Peace, Temperance, and other movements for human betterment, treated in the Friendly spirit and from the Friendly standpoint."[146]

It was also reported that forty Quaker representatives attended the International Congress of Religious Liberals, held in Boston the preceding year. (Henry Wilbur had been a founder and the first president of the National Congress of Religious Liberals.) The representatives reported, "[W]e believe that no harm was done either to our members personally, or to the Society generally, by Friends thus meeting and mingling with the adherents of other religious organizations."[147]

Native American concerns received a first major airing at this Conference, with significant differences of interpretation. Joseph Janney enumerated main points of Theodore Roosevelt's "Square Deal" for Indians: Indian rights were finally to be recognized and enforced by the federal government; tribal lands were to be broken up and allotted to Indians individually; laws against the sale of liquor to Indians would be strictly enforced, and so on. Janney enthused that these steps would work "toward the disappearance of the Indians as a separate nation or people and their ultimate absorption into the great mass of our population." Meanwhile, government and denominational schools for Indians were increasing: soon there would be few Indian children still out of school. Friends "by their quiet influence and intelligent comprehension of the real needs of the Indian, contributed in no small degree to the accomplishment of this result."[148] Evidently, Friends had still not gained perspective on their complicity in what today we would call cultural genocide.[149]

Responding to Janney, Marianna Burgess spoke less glowingly, based upon her thirty years among Native Americans. She reported, "The deplorable condition of those Indians in that new state of Oklahoma is something to make one almost sick. There is much to be done and much for Friends to investigate regarding this Indian matter. The government has simply played with the Indian question during the last three to four years. Much as we can commend the actions of President Roosevelt, this country has made many and grievous mistakes on this Indian question."[150]

Anna Jackson reported on race relations and negro education in a paper read for her by Elizabeth Stover. "We are now in the shadow of a terrible crime," she wrote. Federal troops had been mustered to quell a race riot in a northern city. Lynchings were growing more frequent in the South and occurring even in the North. Consciences were gradually benumbed to it all. Quakers, traditional friends to the Negro, were succumbing to prevailing prejudices. The grandchildren of Friends who had risked their lives and fortunes for the oppressed slave were heard "talking flippantly or maliciously of 'the worthlessness of the nigger.'" She concluded, "If we call ourselves Friends, we should prove ourselves friends to those who need friends." The first step must be the "education of the white people in the principles of toleration and justice." Secondly, Friends needed to support their own Schofield and Laing Schools in South Carolina. Jackson concluded with a query: "What can I do to bring justice and peace to this country? How can I aid my Afro-American brother?"[151]

Aside from a few incidentals, *The Friends' Intelligencer* made little comment on this Conference in the wilds of the Hoosier state.

The 1910 Ocean Grove Conference

Friends were drawn back to the Jersey shore and to their Methodist cousins at this camp-meeting mecca. They were welcomed by E. A. Ballard of the Ocean Grove Association, who made affirmative comparisons between George Fox and John Wesley. Edward Janney, Chairman of the Conference, did not return the compliment, but in classic Quaker self-reference allowed that Ballard would make "a pretty good Friend himself." He explained that Friends had gathered again this year to be "learners in the spirit of Christ: and to listen to those who have spent many years studying the subjects they will present."[152] Indeed, this Conference evinced a growing tendency to draw upon non-Quaker expertise regarding the great questions of the time.

Friends gathered at the Ocean Grove Conference, 1910. Friends General Conference Records, Friends Historical Library of Swarthmore College.

But the proceedings began within the Quaker fold, with Jesse Holmes, now Professor of Biblical Literature at Swarthmore College, speaking on "The Sense of a Larger Fellowship." Friends had emerged from a long period of being "peculiar": "It's not plain why to be a peculiar people is a source of pride; but in our case it has often resulted in making us seem exclusive. We have come to be an isolated people." While other churches formed unions of all kinds, Friends found themselves standing around the edges. When the "Federation of Christian Churches" (perhaps he meant the Federal Council of Churches) met two years ago in Philadelphia, "We were told in a very public fashion that, while we were very good people, we were not Christians." Such Christians apparently felt that "the method of saying Lord, Lord is essential, and that character and conduct are no sufficient test."

Holmes concluded, "We're looking the wrong way for fellowship." Creedal churches are mistakenly gathered: "No religion depending essentially on an order of events has a secure foundation." Faith is something more intimate: "It is not necessary to define God to know God. I cannot define my nearest friend—but he influences deeply my every thought and act. I watch my conduct through his eyes." So where should Friends look for a wider fellowship? Some missionaries to India were "teaching the life and character of Jesus, presenting him as a teacher not as a God, ignoring all dogma, and accepting the native Buddhas as messengers divinely sent." A missionary had told Holmes, "The East has something to teach to Western Christianity." He finished by reiterating the "practical righteousness" theme: creeds, traditions, churches, and meetings are of value "only as they help us do God's will, make us more loving, and show us how to serve."[153] Holmes, becoming more iconoclastic, was also becoming a favorite, perennial speaker at the Conferences.

After Holmes, the main addresses of this Conference came from further afield. The second session heard the socialist Scott Nearing, professor of economics at both the University of Pennsylvania and Swarthmore College, speak on "Social Religion." Nearing found the invitation to speak about economics and society at a religious conference "one of the most hopeful signs of a most hopeful age." Condescendingly, he added, "I rejoice to think of the change in your viewpoint and activities which must inevitably follow from a fuller realization of the facts of the society in which you live."

Jesus had made social welfare part of religion. Nearing cited several examples from the gospels. He also reframed "purity" in more sociological terms: "America reeks with prostitution to-day. Girls are let down, pushed and dragged down, into an inferno that beggars description; and society and the church draws back the hem of its garment and passes by on the other side, forgetting that it was Jesus who said, Neither do I condemn thee." Like the Hebrew prophet Amos, Nearing inveighed against the pomp and glory of mainstream Christianity, financed by those whose wealth rests upon "sweating dens in the slums." He summarized, "You cannot found a social religion on the proceeds of social injustice." Lest Friends might take too much comfort in their plain meetinghouses, he added, "Because you profit by [the poor's] existence, you are responsible for their continuance."

Nearing concluded with an impassioned call:

> Your religion must be a social religion. You must teach the truth... about brotherhood, and co-operation in industry, about social religion.... It is the duty and the opportunity to tell the boys and girls of the future generation that progress must be made, that progress is being made, and that you are helping to shape the future, with its uncounted possibilities.[154]

The recorded responses that followed quickly dissipated Nearing's impact in several vague directions.

Arthur McGiffert, professor of church history at Union Theological Seminary in New York, brought further revelations from beyond the Quaker ken with "The Present Trend of Religious Thought." He began by noting that religious *feeling* was encouraging in all quarters, but religious *thought* varied greatly. Evolutionism had brought religion down from the skies to the earth, leading people to look for change from within rather than from without. The new psychology of religion had resulted from this shift of attention:

> Religion is a natural growth of the human spirit, and is to be accounted for not by a supernatural impartation of truth, or of inspiration from above, but is to be accounted for by the natural growth of the human heart.... Now revelation is conceived... as the gradual awakening of the human mind to truth which it discovers for itself in the process of development.

Thus, according to the present trend, religion is a natural product of the human mind. McGiffert mentioned the pragmatist philosopher William James, whose *Varieties of Religious Experience* had been published just six years earlier. He also mentioned Martin Ritschl, the leading German exponent of natural theology. He concluded that religion is not a gift from above or from the past, but we make it ourselves and we apply it to our world. We test our faith in God by our common experience. This is pragmatism: we are led to God out of our need, and in our own experience we prove God, or we don't have God at all.[155]

McGiffert's talk must have shaken some foundations, even among progressivist Friends. This was a thoroughly naturalistic theology, cut loose from any transcendent source of revelation, entirely immanent and unified in its processes.

CHAPTER 3 The New Normal

Henry Wilbur came along the next day to reassure Friends that the world still revolved around their Religious Society. "The Society of Friends and the Present Trend of Religious Thought" began in Quaker-centric fashion by citing the second century church father Clement of Alexandria as "the first Quaker." Clement had written of "the divinity in our humanity" and "the innate character of the moral perceptions, the divinely planted impulses to righteousness in the human heart." Wilbur went so far as to say that "The present trend of religious thought is a by-product of Quakerism." He topped that by suggesting that it would take the combined efforts of every religious thinker that ever lived to match the insights of George Fox and Elias Hicks. Statements such as these threatened to take Friends from peculiarity straight to solipsism. The intellectual quality of FGC's early decades was more aspirational than realized. Speakers like Wilbur and Holmes were in over their heads.

Wilbur summarized the Quaker task at hand: "It is the business of the Society of Friends to discover the final way of yoking the splendid individualism which has characterized our faith to the required collectivism of modern civilization and of modern thought." Wilbur was not the only FGC speaker of this era to define Quakerism as individualism. After a century of insistence upon "liberty of conscience," Quaker processes of collective discernment were in eclipse, not only in practice but even in theory.

Wilbur was on surer ground when he suggested that Friends should offer the world the quiet of their worship: "The quiet which waits and considers, which softens and sweetens, is vital to our present-day world." This quiet could counter the "spiritual nervousness" of modern times. He called Friends to abandon their aloofness and "mingle" with the world, to communicate "the heart of divine sympathy" to the poor and the weary. "This is our new trend of thought. As a body we need to revive the original missionary spirit of the founders."[156]

Later in the Conference, Edward Clarkson Wilson of Baltimore Yearly Meeting spoke on "Conditions That Make for War," with a more sobering view of the European situation than earlier speakers had offered. Extremist rhetoric in both England and Germany was driving even moderate minds to drastic conclusions. Perhaps

Wilson felt the need to counter the wishful optimism that often predominated in these early Conferences. He observed, "A pessimist is someone who lives with an optimist."[157]

The *Friends Intelligencer* (7/30/1910) reflected:

> Those of us whose privilege it was to be at the Conference, and to listen through the week to addresses and messages, and thereby felt inspired to do great things, and to say the great thoughts, when we return to our several homes and meetings will doubtless feel great discouragement when that Conference time of enthusiasm wanes, and we realize that our talents are weak and the aspirations of that time are not being fulfilled.

To counter that melancholy relapse, the article suggested that each Friend can "watch his every thought at every waking moment of his life that there be no place in his consciousness for aught but thoughts of love, of charity, of purity, of constant kindliness." Another Friend, evidently inspired by Scott Nearing's address, suggested in the next issue (8/6/1910) that Friends continue studying industrial relations.

At a September 1911 Central Committee meeting, Bird Baldwin expressed the hope that the next Conference would emphasize "historic and present Quaker principles." Baldwin's comment exemplifies a continuing concern in some sectors of FGC leadership that the internal coherence and cohesion of liberal Friends were eroding as the scope of social, economic, and global concerns continued to expand. We will continue to hear such expressions occasionally. But there was no stopping the trend toward issue-driven programming.

Henry Wilbur and the Committee for the Advancement of Friends Principles

Wilbur's energetic commitment to Quaker outreach continued. In 1910, he wrote 2,246 personal letters, received 551 visitors, and attended 49 First-Day meetings and 14 meetings at other times. He also addressed 70 meetings at times other than First-Days, two weekend conferences and three yearly meetings. In addition, he published "The Life and Labors of Elias Hicks" and a sixteen-page booklet, "Friendly Fundamentals." He and the Advancement

Committee busily organized weekend conferences, reading circles, and summer schools. But as Roger Hansen summarizes, outreach beyond the Quaker world proved more challenging. Wilbur hoped to engage with industrial workers, but that work never took shape. He interacted eagerly with African Americans but with little outcome. He had more ready connections with the International Congress of Religious Liberals. One Friend described him as "the central personality and the moral leader" among religious liberals in America.[158]

Wilbur's work for the Advancement Committee had become so central to the identity of FGC that his title was changed to General Secretary in 1911.

The 1912 Chautauqua Conference

The election year of 1912 marked a tidal wave of progressive expectations. Theodore Roosevelt, after losing his bid for the Republican Party's nomination to William Taft, founded the Progressive Party, which split Republican sympathies. Woodrow Wilson, a strong progressive without Roosevelt's zest for military adventure, received the Democratic Party's nomination on the forty-sixth ballot. The progressive movement was about to find its most coherent and effective political representation. Wilson warned, "If you are not a progressive, you better watch out."[159]

These developments strongly affected FGC's return to Chautauqua for the last Conference before the outbreak of World War I. It proved to be the high watermark of FGC's initial phase. Friends were again greeted by Chautauqua's leader, John Vincent, who affirmed Friends as Christians and a legitimate branch of the Christian Church (perhaps in reference to the ecumenical rebuff Jesse Holmes mentioned during in the preceding Conference). He noted the importance of tolerance and generosity in studying the origins of the church's different branches. He added that "Methodism" means "followers after the way," a way similar to that of Friends.

Again, Edward Janney did not return the compliment. He rather ungraciously suggested that while Friends were a much smaller body than the Methodist Church, they were like the small amount of leaven in the lump. But he praised Chautauqua for "exerting such a marvelous influence." Janney reflected that much had happened since their last meeting at Chautauqua twelve years before, when they came together officially into one body. Under a single FGC, "We are united and its work has spread out far wider than it could possibly have done before." In addition, "We have grown more liberal in our thought . . . not only among our own members but extending to other religious workers and religious associations." Janney finished with a remark signaling a shift in Conference style: "We have in the past studied much; but now the time has come to do constructive work."[160] This Conference added one-hour round tables on various subjects, held for five of the mornings. The format of these smaller groups is not described in the surviving publications, but it appears that they were smaller and perhaps more interactive than the plenary sessions. This innovation marks an important shift in Conference style that would develop slowly over decades to come.

The opening session featured a sweeping, programmatic keynote from Jesse Holmes, "The Modern Message of Quakerism." He continued his pivot away from the wider Church, suggesting that for centuries Christendom had assumed that truth comes from some earlier, more authoritative source, usually the Bible. That orientation had produced endless hypocrisies, pretenses, and cowardice: "Men are afraid to give the hot truth straight from their hearts."

By contrast, the foundational message of the Society of Friends was to "trust your best self. Play your own part and speak your own message under your own name. Show its correspondence indeed to the truth of other days or other lands . . . but put yourself back of your gospel." (Note that "inner light" could now be reduced to "your best self.") He continued, "Truth to be of any value . . . must so enter into life and conduct as to make some difference, and that difference is the constant test." Thus, Holmes balanced between the traditional correspondence theory of truth (tradition or theory must correspond to, be confirmed by, experience/experiment) and the more recent *pragmatic* theory (propositions are true if they lead to desirable results) advanced by William James and others. Holmes summarized:

> The tragedy of Christendom lies in the fact that it has striven to live in the ruined tombs, rather than to build more noble temples from their masonry. It has set its face backward instead of forward. It

has asserted that "the truth" consisted of unverifiable assertions of historical fact—fact untestable, unusable and often improbable. Our generation is experiencing one of the great periods of change. Every denomination is feeling it.

Revelations of the divine are not transcendental informations about heaven and hell, or the end of the world, or even the future that is in store for us; on the contrary they show themselves in electric lights, and sanitation, and taxation, and tariffs, and above all in every unselfish endeavor by which human misery is alleviated and mankind moves to higher levels.

This was a natural theology, rationalist, non-transcendent, and highly leveraged upon belief in progress and progressive revelation, without grounding in the mystical element being advanced by Rufus Jones at this time. Holmes concluded with a call to merge religious duty with democratic citizenship. "The great religious duty of our time then is the duty of the citizen of the democracy. The making over of our barbarous industrial materialism into a real democracy is just the task of the Lord's Prayer—to make the kingdom come on earth."[161]

As the title of his paper hints, Holmes was shifting toward a more definitely *modernist* stream. The wider progressive movement and most progressive Friends stopped short of radical attack upon traditional Christian thought. Progressives found modernism too anomic and rebellious to aid in the middle-class political consensus just about to succeed. Holmes may have offended listeners at some points, but they liked his fiery affects. He continued to be a favorite FGC Conference speaker.

John William Graham crossed the Atlantic again, to address the Conference with "What Is Worth While and Why." After a brief meditation on the Prologue of John's Gospel, he observed:

The world we live in is full of strife, with victory and defeat. . . . We are called to take service under [God] against his enemies and ours, to subdue the earth, to tame wild nature, to guard against famine and disease. Growth, progress, evolution, is the law of our life, and of the Divine Life in us that grows from less to more, or shrivels up.

Since George Fox's time the Society has never had such a chance as it has now. On both sides of the sea nations need a mystical church, and we are the only permanent, steady and sane mystical church they have. We have plenty of tasks to keep our faculties tense. ... A mystical church cannot be maintained without mystics.... We want more ministry and good ministry... earnest inwardness. If we are ready vehicles of the Divine we shall have a message given us.

Like Holmes, Graham was charged with the promises of progress. From the perspective of a century later, we can recognize environmental disasters developing in the way science and capitalism were "taming wild nature and subduing the earth." And with war impending ever closer in Europe, this rhetoric sounds rather desperate.

Still, British Friends had managed their theological differences more successfully than had their American cousins over the past century. This allowed them to advance impressive social experiments under the patronage of their wealthiest families:

> Our Friends the Rowntrees and Cadburys in England have opened up a new industrial era by showing the way to the better treatment of employees. I can count four or five Quaker model villages or districts. The same Friends now own half a dozen important newspapers, and have saved the press of London from falling into wrong hands. We are an order to be reckoned with already. We once did much to put down slavery. We have still to do much to put down war. We once helped to purify prisons. We must now purify slums. There is nothing in all America so well worth your youthful loyalty as the Society of Friends.[162]

The Rowntree experiments in York and the Cadbury experiments in Birmingham served as models for progressive industrial relations in Britain. Moreover, the Rowntrees and Cadburys had leveraged their chocolate fortunes in 1903 to start Woodbrooke, a Quaker study center on one of the Cadbury estates in the suburbs of Birmingham. And rather than scorning their Protestant neighbors as Holmes did, they had created a consortium of denominationally based adult schools in the Selly Oak neighborhood around Woodbrooke, raising the religious lives, cultural competence, and vocational skills of the local working classes.

Still hoping to "put down war" even as it loomed, a session on peace led off with Arabella Carter's reflections on Quaker engagement with the wider peace movement. She reflected that the joint peace conference of Friends in 1901 (briefly described in the preceding chapter) had proven to be a watershed. The sense of association among the different branches produced "something beautiful, something lasting." Another joint conference had been held in New York in 1910, showing that "The time has come when we as Friends must not only stand for peace as in the past, but move forward for it."

The chair of the session countered that "One of the bitter complaints of our time is the multiplicity of organizations. It seems as though we are organized almost to death." But the next speaker, Charles McDowell answered that in this "day of opportunity" Friends should either organize or "join some peace society outside of our own membership." As the oldest and finest peace society, Friends could help newer ones such as the American Peace Society, publisher of *The Advocate of Peace* with a wide readership. "The world is now entering, probably, the greatest change in human history, the ending of war between civilized nations; and it is something to be a part, a little part, of that great movement." (Unfortunately, "civilized nations" had other ideas.)

Leander Williams hoped that another joint peace conference of Friends could be organized in time to make a statement to the next Hague Conference, scheduled for 1915 (but pre-empted by the outbreak of war). He continued:

> This country is suffering seriously and embarrassed by the enormous amount of money it has to pay for war. When the war ceases the expense does not. We are now paying $120 million to pay the pensions of those that served in the Civil War. We are paying pensions to those who have served in the Cuban-Spanish War, and that is continued as long as the men who are receiving those pensions live. We are paying enormous sums to keep up the army itself; to provide and carry warships all over the world and to that we must look. Provided there were no pensions to pay, no military organizations to keep up, this country would be the most prosperous, probably, in the whole world.

This is early sighting of what would eventually be known as the permanent war economy. And the US was by no means prepared for war in Europe.

Graham added further economic dimension to the peace discussion. He pointed to the enormous increase in international trade and credit and the rise of the United States on the world stage in the past forty years. War between England and Germany would stop hundreds of millions in trade per year between the two:

> The whole of this world is bound together now not by specie payments, but by one spider's-web of international credit. Credit exchange has taken the place of cash payments as in early days cash payment took the place of barter. In these days property is intangible and cannot be reached. We cannot destroy the enemy's property without destroying our own.

With prosperity so interlinked, "It will pay every nation in the world for every other nation in the world to become rich."[163] Christ's teaching of human unity was at last being realized by the world economy.

This Conference saw FGC confronting issues of class conflict and industrial relations. William Jackson's address on "Industrial Conditions" was a substantive response to Scott Nearing's challenge to Friends two years before. He began by noting the traditional adage, "It is no disgrace to be poor." But it is a disgrace, he insisted, the greatest blot on civilization. "And the shame is not to the one who suffers, but to us who let such conditions continue."

> Industrial conditions have reached such an acute state that it is imperative, for the preservation of our nation, that they be promptly adjusted. There is a discontent among the poor such as the world has probably not known since the days of the French Revolution. Perhaps the fact that Industrial conditions is the central feature of the present presidential campaign indicates its importance.

Jackson noted that the new Progressive Party had presented a platform largely devoted to issues of justice and economics. It was "the first time in history that a non-socialist party recognized the class struggle, recognized the great economic revolution, and recognized the fact that the tool users of the nation are not the tool owners, but must become such if we are to remain a free nation." Woodrow Wilson's speech accepting the Democratic National Convention nomination had also dealt with industrial questions and pledged reforms.

CHAPTER 3 The New Normal

Jackson presented some of the issues and statistics:

> Thousands of men and women work long hours, at a driving rate of speed, and receive pay that will provide only for the poorest lodgings, and food that scarcely sustains life.... The average wage for a farm hand in New York State is $1.65 a day, without board.... Industrial conditions are better to-day than ever before in the world's history ... and yet there is more need for a change of these conditions now, than at any previous time.... For everywhere there is now the belief that a man is a man—and he shall not live like a dog—to be fed by a master, and to come and go at the bidding of another.... There is a demand that those who have more than they need shall share with those who have not enough.... Call this what you will, it is the feeling that is stirring throughout the world.

Thus, Jackson attached no particular analysis or political solution to this phenomenon but pointed to the social conditions and affective currents underlying the variety of political positions.

He reviewed three major movements in industry and politics—trade unions, the Industrial Workers of the World, and socialism—concluding that none of them would produce the needed reforms. Wealthy philanthropists were pouring millions into education. "As education caused the present unrest, so will more education work for its adjustment." The churches had a role to play in bridging class differences. "But as long as we think of those who labor as of another class ... and have not love—the workingman will have none of us or of our so-called religion."[164] Just as Friends endorsed Booker T. Washington's solution to racial inequality, Friends trusted that education, in concert with religious outreach, would also heal the nation's class divisions.

The 1912 Conference manifested the apogee in FGC's prewar optimism, even hubris. The evolutionary ideology voiced by Holmes and Graham is as grand as any we have heard. Apparently, the speakers met with enthusiastic approval. Meeting during the Conference, the Central Committee considered "taking formal measures to suppress applause." Still, the growing concern over poverty, industrial conditions, and class conflict indicated that progress might not come so easily and inevitably. Edward Janney's introductory remark that FGC was shifting from educating Friends on the issues to preparing them for action was not strongly borne out by the published proceedings. Perhaps the round tables, which were not recorded, focused more on action.

The 1914 Saratoga Springs Conference

The Central Committee received invitations from Columbia University, Cambridge, Massachusetts, Washington, DC, and Saratoga Springs, New York as sites for their next Conference. Saratoga Springs won out. A chartered excursion boat took 473 Friends up the Hudson River to this upstate summer resort town. Round tables were featured again at this Conference, but this time they met only three mornings instead of five. Except for members of the Central Committee and other standing committees, Friends were free during the afternoons for excursions and recreation. The Chautauqua format of edifying lectures interspersed with recreation, socializing, and family time was well established by now. One long-time Conference attender reflected that "light festivities were no longer taboo."[165] *The Friends Intelligencer* (9/12/1914) reported that registrations totaled about seven hundred, much the same as two years ago at Chautauqua, but with more participation by young Friends. Informal attenders probably swelled these numbers somewhat, but participation appears to have sagged in inverse proportion to the rising rhetorical tone we heard at Chautauqua.

President Woodrow Wilson and a Democratic Congress had begun reforming economic life, with the graduated income tax law, the Clayton Anti-Trust Act, and the creation of the Federal Trade Commission and the Federal Reserve. But he cast a blind eye to racial segregation, resisted women's suffrage, and was ineffective in advancing the conservation measures begun by Roosevelt. And as the Saratoga Springs Conference opened September 2, war had broken out in Europe in late July, taking some oxygen out of the room.

The opening session of the Conference revealed Friends in disarray. Henry Wilbur presented a paper, "The Spirit That Should Guide Us," making some mentions of the war, but often drifting into vague platitudes. The ensuing discussion by leading Friends was recorded.

CHAPTER 3   The New Normal

One Friend suggested the Conference produce a minute stating the Quaker position regarding war. Alice Robinson responded with the traditional Quaker testimony: "It seems to me that we have always taken the ground that no war is justifiable. I stand on that ground to-day. I never felt the Revolutionary War was justifiable; and I never felt that any war, according to a strict sense of right and justice, was justified. If we are followers of the Prince of Peace nothing would justify war on any ground." Wilbur responded that quite a few Friends had served the Union in the Civil War. And there began the waffling. William Jackson remarked that Friends oppose wars of aggression, but wars of defense are different: "For the preservation of the people of your own nation, of your own family.... Let us keep this in consideration ... we are all in favor of mediation, in favor of removing the causes of war."

Rachel Knight added that she would rather the Conference make a statement favoring a constructive policy for peace than take a stand against the present war. "It is a great problem to the Friends of England to know what the stand of their young men shall be at this time." (One third of eligible male Friends in Britain enlisted over the weeks and months to come.) Wilbur responded to Jackson, observing that the Kaiser, the Czar, and the King of England all claimed they were fighting a defensive war, and perhaps actually believed it. Jesse Holmes blew more smoke into the room: "Life is not by any means simple, so that a set of formulas can be laid down that will fit every situation that arises." He added that the Society of Friends stands for brotherly kindness, arbitration, but that of course depends upon a Christian spirit, clearly absent in this situation:

> This does not mean that we approve of war, even if we go into it.... I would fight for my life in a minute; because I don't think it is desirable to allow people to go around killing other folks; it is a very general development of every civilization that going around killing other people should not be lawful.... Each individual has got to face each situation as it arises.... I am myself a believer in the principle of peace, and that these principles will ultimately prevail.[166]

Decades of confidence that the escalator of progress was taking the world past war, that Friends could appeal to reason and goodwill everywhere—the growth of a pacifist ideology—had eroded the prophetic resistance to war that constituted the traditional peace testimony and had helped make Friends "a peculiar people," the reputation for oddity these Friends were so anxious to shed. It was finally resolved that the Conference would produce a minute of sympathy for British and Australian Friends, who were facing this crisis most acutely.

But Friends in the United States were only beginning to register the crisis. Many papers were probably prepared before the war broke out. Jesse Holmes reaffirmed progress in "Experimental Religion as a Motive Force." He began by positing God's presence in the human conscience as the driving force of human history. From there, he reached some startling conclusions:

> If god is a power that strives for human betterment, then he is not the god of the animal kingdom in the similar sense that he cares for, or strives for the interests of animals, except incidentally when their interests coincide with ours. We regard the extermination of savage beasts—of cobras and rattlesnakes, of lions and tigers as a carrying out of the divine plan. We enslave the horse and dog, we devote oxen and sheep to our needs as food, we wage relentless war on parasites and microbes and do not question that it is all in accord with "the Kingdom of God." Of course this is also the Bible teaching: "Let them have dominion over fish and fowl and cattle and all the earth, and everything that creepeth upon the earth." The power which from earliest time has driven man to progress and in dominion, acts from within and not from without. It rouses man to the challenge of an insolent and menacing world. . . . For [some] content is victory. But not so with the strong! For them the voice of God has been a trumpet call to uncontent, to unsatisfaction. It led man from the cave, to the house, to the palace. It drove him from the wild seeds of swamp and prairie, to the grain field, the orchard, the garden. Under its spur he took the roadside weed and made the rose of Sharon and the lily of the valley.[167]

Holmes's faith in progress sounds truly desperate here. A century later, we easily recognize the environmental disaster inherent in such a vision, not very different from the competing imperialisms that had led to the war.

CHAPTER 3 The New Normal

Carrie Chapman Catt visited Friends again, to speak on "Woman Suffrage." She began by noting that talking to Friends about equal rights was like carrying coals to New Castle. But she added that Friends were not as strong in their advocacy as they had been a century before:

> There is no question but that woman's suffrage is coming; because the plea for it is the fundamental plea for democracy. It is the same argument which brought the vote for men. There is no question but that thrones, emperors and nobilities are doomed; there is no question but the people of the world will rule and govern themselves; there is no question but that there will be a federation of the world; but when. When you are ready, you and other Americans, are ready to stand true, first of all, to your own principles.
>
> Women must be taught to want this thing, why? Because tradition binds their hands and enslaves them to old customs, exactly as the millions of men in Europe today, blinded by their traditions, or enslaved by their old customs, are marching under the orders of Czar or Kaiser to their death, because they do not dare to claim an independence from that tradition.
>
> O arise men and women, you who have led the way in equality of rights for men and women in the long ago, rise once more, and lead another great, strong, energetic, emphatic movement onward. As one who has not been a member of the Society of Friends, I have regretted to see the Society seem to drift apart, to lose its national characteristic, to lose its national farsightedness. With all that you have, in your ideals; like one, great powerful body, strive, I ask you, for this old ideal of yours.[168]

Catt recognized that the march progress, still sounding inexorable, had been dealt a major setback by the war. Even the suffrage movement in America continued to struggle. Her middle-class idealism reckoned with the moral inertia of tradition and custom, but it did not countenance the material resistance of capitalist economics and hungry masses.

David Snedden, Commissioner of Education for the State of Massachusetts was another expert from beyond the Quaker fold, speaking on "The Relation of Education to Morals." He noted that as society becomes more "civilized," the complexity of human relations increases, and so does the need for systematic moral education. But with little direct moral teaching in schools, society will encounter growing problems. He concluded, "We shall never go back to teaching … by dogma, by precept.... We shall appeal more and more to the understanding. If we do not live up to these requirements, modern society is going to find that in its emphasis on democracy and its emphasis upon freedom of thinking, it has created Frankensteins that may, sooner or later, work the destruction of society."[169]

During the Conference, the Central Committee produced and the Conference approved a letter "To the President of the United States and Lovers of Peace Everywhere" (published in FI 9/26/1914). The letter explained that Friends:

> have no desire to condemn those who see their present duty in the ways of conflict, offering themselves in sacrifice for their ideals of patriotism. We appreciate and sympathize with their devotion. Yet never was more plainly demonstrated the futility of the system which now drives millions of industrious and kindly men to slaughter and disaster, without their choice and without their understanding. A balance of mutual hatreds and jealousies, backed by armies and navies, has failed utterly as a basis for world organization.

The letter went on to identify the causes of war in group hatreds according to creed, class, and race; desire for territorial gains; the ambition of rulers or peoples for power. It advocated formation of a world parliament of nations, a world court, and world police to maintain peace. It concluded, "this moment when civilization totters, offers us the greatest opportunity in history. The ending of war, instead of being an Utopian dream is within the reach of democratic statesmanship." As a neutral power, the United States was in a position to influence nations at the end of the war.

After one of the evening sessions, Henry Wilbur, sixty-three years old, collapsed and died of a bronchial hemorrhage. The following afternoon, a memorial meeting was held. Thirty messages of grief and gratitude were spoken. Wilbur was extolled as a Friend who believed in "consecrated common sense." At a later session of the Conference, George Miller remarked "A leader has fallen. We have some leaders left. We need a great many more. It is our duty to develop them; and I feel that the great work that Henry Wilbur had on his mind, that is, the school at Swarthmore, is our great opportunity."[170] Indeed, new leadership was urgently needed to confront a new world situation. Other FGC leaders had recently died prematurely: William Birdsall in 1909 at the age of fifty-four; Joseph Walton in 1912 at fifty-seven. As Miller suggested, a broader base of leadership was needed. The next month, *The Friends' Intelligencer* (10/17/1914) reported significant progress toward "the school at Swarthmore," which was expected to open early the next year. We will hear more of it in the next chapter.

Conclusion

Henry Wilbur's death, along with the outbreak of World War I, adds emphatic punctuation to this first period of FGC's history. The emergence from sectarian seclusion and peculiarity was more or less complete. Perhaps some degree of over-correction was inevitable. At the outbreak of the war, even leading Friends in the FGC orbit appeared caught off-guard and unsure of their moral center. During the course of the war, more prophetic voices and initiative would arise, largely from sources outside FGC.

In her biography of Rufus Jones, Elizabeth Gray Vining reflects:

> It is difficult for generations that have come to maturity since 1914 to realize fully the impact of horror and betrayal which the war made upon people's minds. A few here and there, it is true, had seen it coming, and realized that, as Rufus Jones wrote, "Beneath all overt acts and decisions the immense subconscious forces, charged with emotion, have been slowly pushing toward this event." To most people, however, the world had entered upon a period of inevitable progress and war had been relegated to a dark age of barbarism now happily past. The only enemies to be slain were poverty and ignorance. . . . The disillusion that resulted when the German divisions rolled over Belgium and the treaty of friendship was tossed aside as a "scrap of paper," was swift and bitter. Not only the goodness of God became a matter for agonizing question but the very possibility of His existence in a world such as this had demonstrated itself to be. Theories of the upward march of humanity were seen as false and flimsy in the lurid light of man's capacity for evil.[171]

The Marxist cultural theorist Fredric Jameson remarks that, without a deep appreciation of the role of failure and contradiction, the resistance of the social substance, the historical process easily becomes "a banal and uplifting saga of inevitable progress."[172]

Even Rufus Jones, having made multiple trips to Germany and Britain over the preceding two decades, still experienced the outbreak of war as a "terrific jolt."[173] But the powerful collective affects of hatred and envy overwhelmed all rational strategies to avert the war. Jones's work to advance mysticism in American life was, among other things, an attempt to reach those affective registers that rational religion cannot tap. William James's *Varieties of Religious Experience* (1902) had helped to reintroduce mysticism, and Baron von Hugel's *Mystical Element in Religion* (1904) had shown that it could be healthy, creative, and progressive. But as Gary Dorrien, historian of American religious liberalism, suggests, Rufus Jones became the true "apostle of mysticism" among liberal Protestants in America.[174]

Dorrien summarizes the position of American liberal theology: "All claims to truth, in theology as in other disciplines, must be made on the basis of reason and experience, not by appeal to an external authority." In the early nineteenth century, there were few religious liberals. By the 1880s, they had grown to become a movement, led by pastors but linked with the rising progressivism in American politics and religion. By the early twentieth century they were a force that redefined mainstream American Protestantism. Progressive liberals believed that God is immanent in the evolutionary processes of nature and modern cultural development. However, "Their sweeping optimism and success set them up for a hard fall, and they were slow to recognize that their appeal to the 'best of modern knowledge' often turned academic and cultural fashions into new external authorities."[175]

Thus, we can recognize the Quaker story we have been narrating in these first three chapters as part of a larger liberal Protestant transformation. Hicksites had not transcended their Protestant foil as much as they believed but were being carried along by many of the same affective currents and intellectual trends. Even Rufus Jones's mystical emphasis was part of a larger movement.

CHAPTER 3   The New Normal

Friends claimed that early Quakers had articulated some of these commitments well in advance of modern liberalism. But in doing so, they also reframed early Quaker witness in modern, progressivist terms more than they realized. Still, their concerns for peace, racial justice, and women's rights—part of that deep Quaker legacy—drove FGC Friends ahead of the mainstream liberal consensus. It is there we will find them quickly emerging from the crushing disillusionment of World War I.

CHAPTER 4

Progress Revised
FGC Conferences 1916–1928

Since four years ago, the Society of Friends in America has had a rebirth. Since the days of George Fox and William Penn, there has never been a time when we were so gripped by a feeling of responsibility for the world . . . we have joined with Friends in England in a work that has circumscribed the globe. . . . It is to be regretted that it took the entrance of the United States into war to stir us truly into action.

— Vincent Nicholson at the 1920 Conference (FI 8/14/1920)

As war of unprecedented scale raged on in Europe, President Wilson maintained American neutrality. This and his reforms earned him a second term with the 1916 election. He was the first Democratic President to be reelected since Andrew Jackson in 1832.

British Friends experienced the crisis of the war acutely from its outbreak in August 1914. Brian Phillips[176] has described the "hubris and folly" of British Friends in the late Victorian and Edwardian periods leading up to the war, very similar to the inflated confidence we heard from the FGC Conferences of the same period. The displacement of evangelical doctrine by liberal optimism starting with the Manchester Conference in 1895 inspired a strong sense of destiny among British Friends. The rise of peace societies in Britain and Europe, the praise of Quakers by leaders of other denominations, and the exchange of peace delegations with German clergy buoyed expectations among British Friends, as evidenced by John William Graham's FGC addresses in the preceding two chapters.

With Friends entering the mainstream and the mainstream entering Friends, the outbreak of war swept a third of eligible British

Quaker males into enlistment with the British forces. Still, many others chose alternative service with the Friends Ambulance Unit or other channels. The English evangelical Friend Henry Hodgkin was the leading figure in founding the Fellowship of Reconciliation before the end of 1914. The creation of an ecumenical rallying point for pacifists in Britain, even to the point of engaging in counter-recruitment, was highly unpopular. The FOR was attacked by mobs in London and investigated by Scotland Yard. The next year, Hodgkin came to the United States to found an American chapter of the FOR, with the help of Rufus Jones and others. We will hear again of this pioneering British Friend near the end of this chapter.

Some young Friends in Britain had been suspicious of the older Quaker generation's optimism even before the war. More than 140 of them became draft resisters during the war and were subjected to harsh treatment, including solitary confinement and hard labor. One of them, Corder Catchpool, concluded that the peace testimony still contained more of the cross than progressive Friends had wished to believe. Writing in his prison cell in 1919, Catchpool looked back on the drift of Friends leading up to the war:

> The cause of Peace has suffered from old men, good old men, bless them, sitting talking around tables—good men, but old. Congresses, Conferences, even Leagues of Nations, may help. But the past has revealed their utter inadequacy, in the hour of trial. Enough of Peace on paper. It shrivels up and fades away as smoke in the fiery furnace.[177]

This shift from progressive optimism to prophetic resistance thrust young Friends like Catchpool into leadership among Friends during the inter-war period. While the American experience of the war was less acute, we will find a new generation of prophetic leadership rising among American Friends during and after the war.

The "new school in Swarthmore" mentioned in the preceding chapter was named the John Woolman School and opened January 1915 in a three-story stone house near the campus. Eleven students studied the Bible, Quakerism, psychology, social work, economic issues, and race relations. Henry Wilbur's dream found fruition. Following the example of Woodbrooke in England, studies were

Barnard Walton. Courtesy of the Walton family.

offered in three ten-week terms per year. Leading lights such as Rufus Jones and Jesse Holmes gave lectures. Extension courses were added in 1916. Elbert Russell became director in 1917, taking a break from his doctoral program in biblical studies at Johns Hopkins University. Recognizing that the Woolman School itself would necessarily remain small, Russell increased his energies in extension teaching around the wider region. He found eagerness among younger Friends to find common ground between the Hicksite and Orthodox streams.[178]

J. Barnard Walton, son of Joseph Walton, replaced Henry Wilbur as General Secretary in 1915, a position he would hold for the next thirty-five years. Besides advancement work, Walton was also much involved in the work of organizing Conferences.

The 1916 Cape May Conference

Since 1911 the Central Committee had been exploring a permanent location for future Conferences. They had first looked at Asbury Park. The Jersey shore offered a family-friendly setting close to Philadelphia, Baltimore, and New York Friends. This time they chose Cape May, New Jersey. A Conference flyer showed families on the beach, urging Friends to "Take the Children to the Conference," and promising special classes and activities for them. Regarding programs, one Central Committee member complained, "We need more inspiration and less information!" "Quakerism today" and "the inner spiritual meaning of life" were suggested themes. With war having shaken the easy confidence of Friends, such suggestions found traction.

There were already 1,200 Friends present at the opening session, a resurgence in participation. Chairman Edward Janney reflected that the war was just underway two years ago when they met at Saratoga; it was hard to believe that it still continued. This was a time for Friends to:

> Stand firmly on the Christian principle of peace and opposition to warfare and all preparations therefor. Jesus bids us to do this at whatever cost. Let us stand firmly and squarely upon that principle—receive the persecution, ridicule, blame, and censure from others that may come to us, and be willing to stand all that for the great cause, peace among men.

Janney's call sounds far different from the doubt and disarray we heard among leading Friends during the opening session two years earlier. No doubt, reports from British Friends contributed to this more prophetic tone. His three uses of the verb "stand" echo the language of spiritual warfare in Ephesians 6. Quaker faith was starting to sound less "normal."

The opening address, "The Development of the Religious Life," was given by George Walton, part of the emerging generation of

George Walton. Courtesy of George School Archives.

leadership. He was in his second year of a thirty-six-year tenure as Principal of George School. He too called Friends to a tougher witness:

> The golden days of this Society are ahead. The heroic age of Quakerism is ahead. We have a little something in the kind of life . . . that would be useful to the whole world. . . . We are too feeble, not in numbers alone, but in intelligence, and above all in the power of the spirit.[179]

Elbert Russell gave four biblical lectures on the Christian message in the synoptic Gospels, the Gospel of John, the letters of Paul, and Hebrews. He also voiced concern for the Woolman School's precarious finances and expressed disappointment that Swarthmore College had not taken it under its auspices. (In these years, some Friends worried that the College had lost much of its Quaker identity and sense of purpose.)

The Conference heard reports of Friends' continuing work on prison reform, capital punishment, purity, women's rights, "work among colored people," Indian affairs, child welfare, and "proper publications and amusements."

The war absorbed considerable interest and time. William Hull, professor of history and economics at Swarthmore College, spoke on "The Quaker Solution to the War Problem." George Nasmyth of the World's Peace Foundation addressed "International Reconstruction after the War," suggesting that democracy would not survive without a world system of justice and law. William Penn and others had envisioned this solution for centuries but had remained isolated voices crying in the wilderness until now. He predicted that the peace movement would become the greatest constructive movement in modern history. This Conference did not feature an address by Jesse Holmes, who was intensely occupied with chairing a joint emergency peace committee of Hicksite and Orthodox Philadelphia Friends.

This was the last Conference to produce a bound volume reprinting proceedings from issues of *The Friends Intelligencer*. Henceforth, they appeared only in issues of the *Intelligencer*. Specific issues will be cited from here onward.

The War and the Progressive Movement

Woodrow Wilson recognized that war threatened his progressive domestic programs. Speaking privately, he commented, "Every reform we have won will be lost if we go into this war." Jane Addams, progressive and pacifist, believed the war would "set back progress for a generation." But other progressives viewed the war as tonic to the movement. The educator John Dewey found it "full of social possibilities," to rein in individualism and assert "the supremacy of public need over private possessions."[180] Certainly, the war confirmed the progressivist conviction that bigger government was needed to tame big business. After the United States entered the war in April 1917, federal bureaucracy expanded enormously. By 1918, there were almost three thousand new agencies engaged in the mobilization, such as the War Industries Board, the Food and Fuel Administrations, the Shipping Board, and so on. The federal income tax was boosted, with the highest bracket at 63 percent and an excess profits tax on corporations was added.

Once in the war, Wilson also promoted the cause with a national Speakers Bureau of seventy five thousand "Four-Minute Men" to give brief, compelling arguments for the war effort across the nation. The president of the national Chautauqua Association headed the Bureau. Wilson brooked no opposition. Following the passage of the Selective Service Act, he added the Espionage Act in 1917 and the Sedition Act in 1918 to suppress anti-war activists. Left-wing labor organizers and socialists were also swept into the dragnet. One critic described Wilson as a man of high ideals and no principles.

Meanwhile, the Quaker Alice Paul and the National Women's Party began picketing the White House for women's suffrage in January 1917. Wilson finally endorsed the cause in September 1918 as good for the war effort. It was also good for the purity campaign. With women's votes on the horizon, the Eighteenth Amendment was passed by Congress in 1918 and the Volstead Act put Prohibition into law (over Wilson's veto) in 1919. The Nineteenth Amendment confirming women's suffrage was ratified the following year.

The Formation of the American Friends Service Committee

After the war, Rufus Jones reflected:

> When the Great War burst upon the world in the summer of 1914 Friends in America were not spiritually prepared to give an adequate interpretation of the ground and basis of their faith, nor were they clearly united upon a plan of action suited to and correspondent with their ideals of life.[181]

At the outbreak of the war, British Friends went to work to produce a volunteer ambulance unit, provide relief for refugees and other victims, and assist aliens and families coming into Britain. A newly formed Friends' Service Committee also worked with conscientious objectors of all kinds facing prosecution for their faith.

On the American side, a Friends National Peace Conference was held in 1915 at Winona Lake, Indiana. It created a Continuation Committee to formulate Quaker responses to the war. Meanwhile, as mentioned earlier, Holmes was busy in 1916 chairing a joint emergency peace committee representing the Hicksite and Orthodox Philadelphia Yearly Meetings. Finally, as soon as war was declared by the United States, an Emergency Unit was created at Haverford College to begin training Friends and other pacifists for service overseas. These three different initiatives converged in the formation of the American Friends Service Committee (AFSC) by the end of April 1917, the same month that the US entered the war. Rufus Jones was its chairman and Vincent Nicholson, a young Friend from Indiana, its first executive secretary. Relief and reconstruction work in France and Russia were the first initiatives, expanding quickly with wider work around Europe. In France, AFSC volunteers joined with the British FSC volunteers already well established in the work. This work proceeded as the three Historic Peace Churches—Friends, Mennonites, and Brethren—continued to negotiate with the federal government for a conscientious objection provision to military conscription.

But there was also widespread defection from the peace testimony among American Friends, and many draft-age male Friends enlisted or entered the draft. Overall statistics are hard to obtain. But by September 1917, the Advancement Committee was already concerned that "not only is there a questioning of the peace principles in a more searching way than during any previous war, but the whole issue is at stake whether the Society of Friends stands for anything vital and distinctive enough to justify its existence."[182]

The 1918 Meetings at George School

Cape May had invited FGC in 1916 to return in two years, but many questioned whether FGC should hold a Conference during the war. At a Central Committee meeting in March 1918, some felt their money should go toward AFSC's reconstruction work in France. Besides, with many younger Friends in the military, their participation would be limited. Perhaps one or more small gatherings would be more useful. Meanwhile, plans were already forming for a world gathering of Friends in London sometime after the war. The Central Committee concluded that some kind of meeting in 1918 would help "clarify our vision" for that event. A small gathering at George School near Philadelphia began September 12 on the theme of "Quaker Fundamentals."

On behalf of the planning committee, Jesse Holmes noted that for the first time they would meet without prepared papers. During a devotional period, George Walton affirmed that "the group mind multiplies the power of the individual mind, and together we may reach a revelation of truth wider and dearer than any of us could reach alone."

FGC was producing a series of study lessons on "Social Order," written by Jesse Holmes. (This too followed the example of London Yearly Meeting.) Holmes observed:

> After the war must come the most radical changes in the social order.... But what is the new social order to be? To drift from a war which has largely destroyed the old order (as it has done in Europe, and is fast doing here), into a peace which will involve other enormous changes, and to neglect to prepare for the coming situation, would be to allow our world to fall back into chaos.

Reconstruction after the American Civil War did little to prepare the nation for a post-emancipation social order, "So the negro was kept in shameful conditions . . . a major setback to civilization in this country." Holmes recommended the British Labour Party's Four Fundamentals as a guide: a guaranteed minimum provision for every family's health; democratic control of industry; a revolution in national finance; and surplus wealth redirected toward the common good (FI 9/21/1918). In a later session, Holmes added that a standard of living should be set and no one allowed to rise higher until all had reached it. Though by no means an environmentalist, he also advocated that the government control all natural resources used to create wealth (FI 10/5).

Friends were aware that a poorly settled peace would only sow the seeds of future wars. William Hull, professor of history and economics at Swarthmore College, commented that William Penn's old peace plan had been newly articulated in Wilson's proposal for a League of Nations, "which, if adopted, may prevent a future even more terrible war" (FI 9/28). Meanwhile, Thomas Jenkins reminded Friends, "While we sit here comfortably, I hope we may not forget that some hundreds of Friends are in prison in solitary confinement or hard labor. They are fighting our battle." (Indeed, American draft resisters received treatment as abusive as what British resisters suffered.)

In a session applying Quaker fundamentals to the life of Friends meetings, Elbert Russell commented that Friends were "still under the shadow of Quietism. We seem to be more afraid of the consequences of doing than of not doing. The world may suffer from the things we don't do. We need to regain the work of the spoken word." The general tenor of this meeting suggests that Friends were clearer about the world's problems than their own.

In the final session, Elizabeth Powell Bond put race relations back into the conversation:

> If we have increased light, is it not laid on us that our light should be felt by others who have not had our opportunities? The colored race is not loved by many, is wronged by many. They are to-day the most friendless of all races, and more in need of our help than any other class. Shall we be satisfied if our yearly meetings do not stand as fast friends of this friendless people? (FI 10/5)

With the motif of friendship, Bond's query implies a more mutual relationship between white Friends and African Americans, which would grow only slowly over future decades.

Though limited in vision, this small gathering reveals Friends starting to rethink themselves and their world during the greatest crisis the western world had yet known.

The 1920 Cape May Conference

Notwithstanding attractive invitations from Chautauqua and Asbury Park, the Central Committee found energizing unity to return to

1920 invitational postcard. Friends General Conference Records, Friends Historical Library of Swarthmore College.

In the Convention Hall at Cape May, 1920. Friends General Conference Records, Friends Historical Library of Swarthmore College.

Cape May, with the theme of "Living Our Faith." Four years before, they had met in a large tent. Cape May had promised a better venue next time and now there was a new Municipal Auditorium built on a pier extending out over the water.

Between eight hundred and one thousand attended sessions at any given time. A few Orthodox Friends were starting to participate. Jane Addams was the big draw of the Conference. *The Friends Intelligencer* called her an "incarnation of womanhood ... a woman who has suffered because she loved. ... That is Jane Addams!" (FI 8/7/1920—a first Conference Supplement). The Conference was held July 7-14, earlier than usual, owing to the All-Friends Conference to be held the next month in London.

With the war over, the affects of renewal outstripped advance planning. "There were many little happenings during the week—happenings which had little bearing on the direct business of the Conference, and yet which showed the spirit of the gathering even more clearly than did the lectures to which it listened." Besides the scheduled round tables on race, prisons, and joint work by Hicksite and Orthodox Friends, other ones generated spontaneously about post-war reconstruction and the new Women's International League for Peace and Freedom. A gathering of young Friends from the different yearly meetings also materialized, strengthening its own generational ethos.

The Central Committee proposed three resolutions for Conference approval. One on Prohibition rejoiced in the Eighteenth Amendment and the passage of the Volstead Act to enforce it. This was a tenuous victory and the resolution urged Friends to support Congressional candidates who would oppose any weakening of the new law. Friends concerned for purity were emboldened to formulate a further resolution regarding tobacco, which "burns up $1.5 billion per year, ruins health, enslaves, demoralizes." It urged more education about tobacco's dangers. Finally, the Conference approved a resolution urging Friends to press Congress toward a League of Nations "dedicated to the Golden Rule among nations and true union of the people of the world to abolish war and bring equality of rights and opportunities to all nations and peoples."

Jesse Holmes, just returned from Europe, reported on his tour as American Commissioner for Friends' Relief Work there. The center in France had just finished its work. British and American Friends were feeding forty thousand children per day in Austria and six hundred children per day in Berlin. New Friends meetings had been started in Vienna, Berlin, and Frankfurt, attracting many whose first impression of Friends was their relief work. Friends working in Poland were fighting a typhus outbreak. With winter coming, many thousands across Europe and Russia faced starvation and disease.

In anticipation of the All-Friends gathering the next month in London, this Conference featured three papers on "Our Faith." Edward Janney, chairing his last Conference, balanced FGC's emphasis on rational inquiry and pragmatic action with Rufus Jones's mystical grounding. "The mysticism of our faith is a mysticism which impels to action. It is mysticism conjoined with common sense. It takes cognizance not only of the state of one's own soul, but that of our fellow men. It is a *do* religion" (FI 8/14). Gladys Brooke epitomized, "We believe in the individual.... Faith in man, and as a corollary to that, faith in God: that, to me, is the quintessence of religion." Thus, faith in the individual with God not too far behind.

The third speaker, Edward Palmer, affirmed, "We welcome all seekers after truth." (This is an early appearance of the term "seeker" at Conferences.) He also noted that even among members, liberal Quakerism is open to wide variations in interpretation. To illustrate the range of interpretations, Palmer offered a just-war statement of his own. He suggested that it took "a shamefully long time" for the US to enter the recent war:

> The peals of the great gong sounded across the ocean, and American manhood and womanhood set forth.... To make war implies hope of conquest ... or ... a thirst for revenge.... None of those motives which prompt men to war actuated us.... With a heavy heart we drew the sword.... It is inconceivable that any Friend chose his course except with conviction that therein lay his greatest service to mankind.... The world progresses only by the kind of devotion which does not consider the price [FI 8/14].

As we noted in Chapter 1 regarding the American Civil War, some Friends who heralded progress most boldly were willing to sacrifice peace—and human lives—upon its altar.

CHAPTER 4   Progress Revised

Russell Smith, Quaker and professor of economic geography at Columbia University, spoke more challengingly on "Our Faith and the Causes of War," affirming that

> Friends' principles and testimonies are good for what ails the world, including its present tendency to war.... We Friends are, of course, opposed to war, but do we not believe in, stand for, and help along things that tend to bring on wars? ... [T]he trouble is that we have not a sufficient spirit of self-effacement to endure a real brotherhood of men; we want special privileges instead, and we get them.

This assembly of white, middle-class Friends enjoying a week on the beach at Cape May found themselves caught perilously between the Scylla of Edward Palmer's just-war philosophy and the Charybdis of Russell Smith's challenge to a more sacrificial and integrative pacifism.

Smith also commented on the compromised future of the League of Nations: "The British seizure of Mesopotamia [for oil interests] was perhaps the greatest blow that the idea of a real League of Nations ever had," adding wryly, "if we may except American insistence upon the Monroe Doctrine" (FI 8/14).

Vincent Nicholson, mentioned earlier as AFSC's founding executive secretary, spoke on "Living Our Faith in Special Service." He opened by remarking on the American Quaker "rebirth" over the past four years (see the epigraph to this chapter). He offered an ambitious vision for the work ahead:

> We have harked back to the ideals of William Penn in the last three years; we have had the chance to carry to a wider field the true ideals of his Holy Experiment, and so to lay the foundation for a life in which the kind of thing we have witnessed in the last three years can never again happen [FI 8/14].

With AFSC's spontaneous creation and inspiring accomplishments, the high ideals of FGC's rhetoric had finally found traction. Ironically, however, we will find much of the initiative and leadership coming from Friends such as Nicholson from outside FGC's ambit.

Jane Addams had spent time in the previous year with the AFSC in Germany. She lauded Friends: "The Quaker is redeeming the name of 'American' in many parts of Europe. Personally I have more faith in

Jane Addams Collection, Swarthmore College Peace Collection.

you than any other group of people in America, because of the work you are doing, and because you are being judged by the work you are doing" (FI 8/14). The text of her speech, titled "Americanization," was to be continued in the next supplement of *The Friends Intelligencer* but inexplicably did not appear. A December 1919 manuscript by the same title[183] reveals what she probably went on to say at the Conference. She reflected that at the end of the nineteenth century, "nationalism" in Europe and America was pulling together all kinds of ethnic subgroups. In a similar vein, she described her Chicago neighborhood of the past 30 years as an "immigration colony." Her Hull House settlement had helped a wide variety of immigrants find themselves in American society.

But now in postwar Europe she saw "nationalism" pushing subgroups away. She saw the same trend in America, as wartime suspicion of Germans and other European immigrants carried over into a sustained nativist intolerance. This was a discouraging trend. But she further reflected that as she had traveled in Europe and Britain, she noticed that large swaths of those societies were still basically feudal. Capitalism was only slowly integrating them into its regime. She reasoned that similarly, socialist internationalism would probably advance slowly and unevenly (a century later we can say, very slowly and unevenly).

A session under the care of the Young Friends Movement featured three speakers responding to the query, "Friends—Why?" Most notably, this was a first speaking appearance of Rachel Davis DuBois, aged twenty-seven with a new doctorate from Columbia University. She urged Friends to continue on the vanguard: "We must go all the way; must take 'Thou shalt not kill' in all its phases or there is no reason for Friends. . . . If we do not say and act these things ahead of our time, as did John Woolman, Elizabeth Fry, and others, we have no excuse for existing as an organization" (FI 8/14). We will hear more from this pioneering spirit, particularly on issues of race. In the meantime, an earlier champion of African American progress was passing from the scene. This was the last Conference for Anna Jackson, who had attended every one of them. She died the following December. Her obituary in the *Friends Intelligencer* (1/15/1921) concluded, "She worked untiringly for what she believed to be right—without hope of reward or praise but that the world years hence might be a better place."

There were many rallying calls at this Conference. Elbert Russell pointed toward the next frontier, "The frontier of our own souls— there is a frontier indeed." (Russell had resigned as director of the Woolman School earlier that year and undertook a long, distinguished teaching career at Duke University.) Jesse Holmes called Friends, especially young Friends to "take your faith into politics, take it into society, take it even into your church" (FI 8/7). *The Friends Intelligencer* quoted one Friend's remark that "everyone seemed bubbling over with ideals, as we exchanged them with those we had never met before almost as freely with life-long friends" (FI 8/14). Enthusiasm may have been buoyed in part by the 1919 publication of FGC's first collection of 39 hymns and songs, which began to be used at Conferences. The affects of the moment were infectious. The 1920s were ready to roar.

The Decline of the Progressive Movement

After the Armistice of November 1918, Wilson was consumed with trying to advance the ill-fated League of Nations. He abandoned the progressive programs he had promoted so successfully up to that point. Overstretched, he suffered a stroke and his political capital collapsed. Meanwhile, most Americans were ready for prosperity and a lot more fun than the progressive movement had been willing to countenance. New consumer technologies such as "movies," radio, and the phonograph generated an expanding aesthetic space that tended to displace progressive ethical concerns. Meanwhile, northward migration opened up new opportunities for African Americans, who introduced blues, jazz, and new popular dance forms for white consumption.

Except in rural areas, which largely continued in dire poverty, Americans had more money to spend on the pursuit of pleasure. Average manufacturing wages increased from $435 a year in 1900 to $568 by 1915. The annual vacation had become standard for salaried workers. Historian Michael McGerr[184] identifies these technological and economic changes as keys to the progressive movement's decline. New realms of personal consumption stimulated larger affective currents in the culture, less aligned with family and local community. Even liberal Friends, who spurned the sheer pursuit of pleasure, can be seen projecting their social ideals more widely in the world while becoming less moored to the life of their meetings.

Meanwhile, with big business and wealth somewhat more regulated, the American electorate swung back toward a series of Republican Presidents—Warren Harding, Calvin Coolidge, and

Herbert Hoover—who extolled the virtues of American individualism. A "red scare" touched off by the Russian revolution and a spate of anarchist bombings in America led to the suppression of socialists and more left-leaning labor activists. Even moderates including Jane Addams were smeared as "parlor Bolsheviks" (note the earlier reference in *The Friends Intelligencer* to Addams as "a woman who has suffered because she loved"). Concomitant with these reactionary trends, racism resurged in both the North and the South. Confederate monuments were erected all over the South and the Ku Klux Klan spread in numbers and wider social influence even into the North.

Progressives, Puritans, and Pacifists

The decline of Progressive politics in America offers parallels with the decline of Puritanism in seventeenth-century England. The English Civil War provided Puritan victors with the political moment to enforce stricter moral codes upon the nation during the Commonwealth period of the 1640s and 50s. Theaters were closed and Christmas observances were suppressed, for example. But the Puritans were unable to produce a viable settlement of government and religion. When the Commonwealth collapsed at the end of 1659, the nation celebrated and soon clamored for the return of monarchy and a state-church establishment. In the following years, theaters reopened and London merchants successfully petitioned Parliament to lift the ban on Christmas. Puritanism was thoroughly repudiated. England embarked upon a distinctly anti-utopian domestic policy and an imperial foreign policy.

The young men and women who became early Friends were in many respects hyper-Puritans intensely concerned with personal morality and for social reform.[185] As Quakers, they waged moral crusades that made Puritans look lax by comparison. But their renunciation of the violent option generated very different politics. The Quaker Lamb's War was a nonviolent cultural revolution from below, diametrically opposite to the violent Civil War and the repressive politics of the Puritan regime.[186] Early Friends engaged in vigorously countercultural politics through their resistance to the established church, their willingness to suffer persecution, and their commitment to plainness of speech, dress, and lifestyle. All this was testimony, the communication of a divine life they had found together.

We also find similarity and difference between FGC Friends and the wider progressive movement in this period. Friends strongly shared the wider progressive movement's purity agenda and even took leading roles in forming ecumenical purity crusades. They were less quick to engage with the larger questions of wealth, poverty, and industrial relations, but some figures such as Jesse Holmes eventually adopted fully socialist politics. Owing to their vanguard work for abolition and with freed slaves in the preceding century, Friends were more attuned to the oppression of African Americans, though not ready yet to challenge segregation during the heyday of Jim Crow legislation.

We found Friends confused in their initial response to the war in 1914, and many in both Britain and America joined the military. But by 1916, the traditional peace testimony was reaffirmed, at least as peace *advocacy*, if not as definite *resistance* to military participation. The advent of the AFSC in 1917 helped channel the stronger pacifist impulses into opportunities for Quaker-organized alternative service in relief and reconstruction.

While the wider progressive movement fell apart during the 1920s, Wilson's rhetoric of "a war to end all wars" helped inspire a broad-based peace movement in America during the 1920s and 30s. Progressive Protestant clergy like Harry Emerson Fosdick had supported the war in the early stages but regretted it by 1919. Fosdick's change of heart may have been inspired in part by his friendship with Rufus Jones.[187] Like Friends, Fosdick recognized that the Treaty of Versailles had undone Wilson's Fourteen Points for a lasting peace. By 1923 he concluded that "War is the most colossal and ruinous social sin that afflicts mankind today . . . it is utterly and irremediably unchristian."[188] He attacked war the rest of his life. By the 1930s, many mainline Protestant leaders shared his views.

The Fellowship of Reconciliation became the central rallying point for mainstream pacifists. Campus organizations and the YMCA and YWCA were also important incubators of pacifism among the

CHAPTER 4 Progress Revised

Postcard announcement for the 1922 Conference. Friends General Conference Records, Friends Historical Library of Swarthmore College.

younger generation. "Peace evangelists" such as Sherwood Eddy and Kirby Page preached, lectured, and published books and articles critical of war and the economic structures that perpetuated it.[189] Reinhold Niebuhr and A. J. Muste were other Protestant leaders allied through FOR. An ordained Presbyterian minister, Muste aligned with Friends during the war.

Thus, progressive impulses found new focus in the peace movement. And Friends, with their historic peace testimony and the pioneering work of the American Friends Service Committee, emerged on the vanguard.

The 1922 Richmond Conference

The Central Committee initially accepted Cape May's invitation to return in 1922. But a rise in hotel rates changed their minds and they opted for another venture westward to Indiana. A postcard announcement of the conference featured a pen-and-ink depiction of retro-Friends traveling westward.

Perhaps the All-Friends Conference in London shortly after the 1920 Cape May Conference had inspired this decision to "mingle" with those of "the other Branch." The Five Years Meeting of Gurneyite Friends was scheduled to take place in Richmond shortly afterward.

Again, a train was chartered to take Friends from Philadelphia to Richmond. But the Conference register listed only about four hundred Friends. Only fifty from Indiana formally registered. Sessions were held at the large First Friends (Fifteenth Street) meetinghouse and the Grace Methodist Church on the next block (FI 9/23/1922).

During the opening session the new Conference chairman Arthur Jackson spoke of the increasing spirit of unity among Friends. He also expressed a concern for "a more uniform Discipline for use by all the Yearly Meetings of our Branch." After some "earnest" discussion, the Central Committee meeting during the Conference resolved to ask the Executive Committee to explore further the proposal "to produce one book of Discipline which may be adopted generally." Was it something in Richmond's Gurneyite air? Ironically, more than a century before, an Orthodox initiative from Philadelphia for a uniform discipline had become a flash point of Hicksite protest. The Five Years Meeting had adopted its uniform discipline at its founding sessions in Richmond twenty years before. Perhaps twenty years of integration into the Friends General Conference had convinced liberal Friends of the idea's merits. We will follow this development.

The Central Committee also approved an initiative from the Young Friends Movement, requesting that the Central Committee be expanded from one hundred members to 125, with the additional members nominated by the YFM. In addition, some young at-large members would be added to the Executive Committee. The decision marks the advent of a new generational cohort of leadership among liberal Friends and indicates the old guard's readiness to welcome it.

The Conference featured three talks on industrial relations, much emphasis upon social service, and many spontaneous group meetings. The struggle to grasp Quaker identity and purpose continued with two addresses and two sets of round tables "to help us define Quakerism in its relation to God and man." John William Graham came to America one last time and taught at Swarthmore College for the 1922-23 year. He attended this Conference in order to lead a round table on his new book, *The Faith of a Quaker*. Perhaps no other religious group was (and is) so absorbed in self-examination, as liberal Friends struggled to balance between an expansive cosmopolitan outlook and an abiding sectarian sensibility. Meanwhile, much Indiana watermelon was consumed.

Haridas Mazumdar, a young Indian from Bombay and adherent of the Gandhian movement, found his way to Richmond and spoke during an evening meeting for worship:

> Before the war, the average men had politicians do the politics. Now we are trying to think for ourselves. It is a very hopeful sign. It is directly due to this war that a new experiment in revolution, a bloodless revolution, is being tried out, under the leadership of Mahatma Gandhi. People are trying more and more to get in touch with one another. They show we do not want war any more. Let us not so much repent of the past as struggle for a better future. Call God what we will, He is today moving the hearts of people all over the world, and it is by this that we have hope for a better world in the near future. But we cannot hope for this unless each individual shall answer the call for himself. To fulfill one's duty is more important than to get one's rights [FI 9/30].

Here is an early notice of the new activism that would later revolutionize peace and justice movements in the United States. But at the time, most Friends and the growing mainline peace movement were sure that the horrors of the recent war would open the popular conscience to rational persuasion for peace. Of course, Gandhian nonviolence actually had much in common with the early Quaker Lamb's War. But that was poorly understood among modern Friends, who viewed early Quakers vaguely as founders of their beloved liberal sect.

Frank Aydelotte, Swarthmore College's new president, spoke on "Quakerism and Democracy." A newcomer to Friends, he saw modern Quakerism "showing a new and broader spirit—a sense of obligation to human needs. It has broadened so that it transcends the narrow limits of sectarianism." Aydelotte found "a fundamental similarity between Quakerism in the religious sphere and Democracy in the political sphere. In both there is a revolt against the setting apart of one man to lead" (FI 10/7). But in both spheres, a broad base of character and training is required. The College was working to challenge students to higher standards. Indeed, in the years to come, Aydelotte

Frank Aydelotte. Courtesy of Friends Historical Library of Swarthmore College.

succeeded both in making Swarthmore an outstanding academic institution and in renewing its Quaker identity and purpose.[190]

One of the *Friends' Intelligencer* supplements (10/7/1922) reported a candid conversation: "Why do we go to so many Conferences? All the time conferring, talking, discussing, and debating; nothing but problems and questions, addresses, talks, and round-tables: What does it all amount to?" The other Friend answered, "Hard to say. I go to get ideas; and then it is so pleasant to meet old friends and make new ones."

The 1924 Ocean City Conference

The Conference happily returned to the Jersey shore, a little north of Cape May. Ocean City had been purchased forty-five years earlier by Methodists hoping to make it a second Ocean Grove. It had many features in common with Cape May, including a boardwalk. About 900 registered, but estimates ran as high was 1,200 in attendance, a strong rebound from the Richmond Conference.

CHAPTER 4 Progress Revised

Poster for the 1924 Conference at Ocean City. Friends General Conference Records, Friends Historical Library of Swarthmore College.

At Richmond, the Central Committee had decided to make the tricentennial of George Fox's birth a focus of the next Conference. Indeed, a "George Fox Pageant" dramatized ten scenes from Fox's *Journal*. Photos in *The Intelligencer* Supplement (all in one issue that summer) show a cast of Friends dressed in campy early Quaker costume. This was as close as Friends were willing to come to examining their deeper roots. Arthur Jackson's opening address maintained focus on the present-future: "This Conference has been designed to stimulate avenues of thought which will move us to action." Education and young Friends figured prominently on the program. Frank Aydelotte was again a featured speaker.

Progressive economist Raymond Robbins gave five addresses on "Spiritual Values in Modern Civilization." He posed spirituality as a balancing force between the contesting powers of capital and labor and an antidote to the peril of Bolshevism. He bemoaned the fate of the League of Nations, now "at the mercy of nine men sitting in Geneva, one an American and eight representatives of secret diplomacy, imperialism, and wrong." He noted that slavery and alcohol were tolerated until enough people no longer tolerated them. The challenge of the day was to foster the public will to outlaw war.

Friends were anxious to offer leadership to the new mainstream peace campaign. A Conference class for "peace speakers" stressed the need to build public opinion for peace just as the Anti-Saloon League had built public opinion for Prohibition. But it was important to point to solutions to war, not just the problems.

Racial concerns resurged at this Conference, perhaps in response to the new wave of lynchings and the growing political influence of the Ku Klux Klan. John Hope, president of Morehouse College in Atlanta, challenged Friends: "The test of American Christianity is your treatment of the negro. Be square with the negro, and all your burdens will be easier. Are you willing to pay the price of Christian treatment of your negro brother at the door?" Anna Jackson Branson spoke of "The Negro's Gift to America," a significant shift from the rhetoric of victimhood. She was probably influenced by the publication that year of W. E. B. DuBois's *The Gift of Black Folk: The Negroes in the Making of America*. She commented that northward migration had made "the whole negro question" no longer a regional one but a national one—most of all, a human one. Noting that a third of workers in steel and iron industries were now black, she concluded:

> The negro is not a liability, he is an asset . . . [and] has made a contribution to the religious life of America. . . . We must have the same enforcement of law for white man and black, until the negro no longer gets ten years for an offense which the white man expiates

with three.... Get acquainted with the negroes; read their books, sing their songs; get acquainted with at least one phase of their contribution to our civilization; know what they have done and are doing.

While Branson's language implies continued social distance, clearly African Americans were becoming more real and more interesting to northern, European American Friends. The affective registers of personal acquaintance and singing black music were helping to shift the ground of thought and conversation. FGC published a supplementary collection of hymns and later that year, but no spirituals appeared until a 1940 supplement. Even if the progress of Quaker racial awareness was slow, the stubborn endurance of concern in FGC circles, against the tide in the wider culture, is impressive.

Meeting during the Conference, the Central Committee heard a progress report on the uniform discipline. The working committee shared mimeographed copies of their work thus far. They expected to complete a draft within a year. There was also conversation whether FGC should take *The Friends Intelligencer* under its aegis. There was hesitation; some were concerned that the periodical not become an official organ of the Society but remain a forum for individual viewpoints. The question lapsed but was revisited periodically in years to come.

Finally, FGC undertook further reorganization. In order to foster greater integration with constituent yearly meetings, yearly meeting clerks and the clerks of yearly meeting representative bodies were added to the Central Committee. A basic constitution was drafted. These are significant initiatives for consolidation. Unfortunately, minutes do not reveal the concerns that gave rise to them.

The 1926 Ocean City Conference

September 1925 Central Committee minutes indicate considerable discussion about the future of the Conferences, even whether it was useful to continue them. Any future gatherings should "meet a deeper mental and spiritual need and endeavor to raise the level of our vision and strengthen the purpose of our lives, with the consequent result of a better and more enlarged Christianity." Some Committee members continued to voice concern for greater internal coherence at the grassroots, to balance the expanding social vision. But Conference programs continued to favor the latter.

Finally, they decided to meet again in 1926 at Ocean City, on the theme of "Quaker Solutions to Social Problems." The Committee instructed the Planning Committee "that the Friendly point of view be emphasized, and that we secure speakers from the ranks of our own Society where possible." In other words, rely less on outside experts. The Committee also affirmed that "much profit is derived from the Round Tables, and those on Education at the Conference last year resulted in more interest in the work of our schools." Smaller-scale processes were slowly gaining ground in programming. Finally, the Committee decided to discontinue holding a large First-Day School meeting at future Conferences. Two or three smaller gatherings at other times might prove more useful.

This second Conference at Ocean City, held July 6-13, proved very different from earlier ones. Over 1,100 officially registered. Total attendance exceeded 1,200. In their desire for greater integration with the yearly meetings, the Central Committee requested monthly meetings to send delegates to attend and report back to their meetings. Five hundred such delegates representing monthly and quarterly meetings helped boost overall registrations. And a new Junior Conference for children under age fifteen drew ninety. Planners also tried a new format, with different sections (more or less round tables) meeting simultaneously, each a sort of small conference or summer school class in itself.

Arabella Carter, editor of *The Intelligencer*'s Conference Supplement, commented, "speaking as a Conference attender throughout a period of well over thirty years, I can safely say that this one of 1926 seemed far and away most worthwhile" (FI 8/14/1926). A non-Quaker observer was surprised to see the breadth of subjects treated at a "religious" gathering. "Sad, indeed, that the idea of service to fellow men being real religion has permeated so slowly." In another innovative move, *The Intelligencer* devoted less space in its Conference Supplements to plenary addresses, but printed them as lead articles in subsequent issues.

CHAPTER 4   Progress Revised

Chairman Arthur Jackson opened the sessions with the usual affirmation that "our religious life is bound by no creed or dogma. We do believe in the Fatherhood of God and the Brotherhood of Man." But he continued on a more challenging note:

> We are too selfish—want too much for ourselves, and are prone to accord the great principles little thought. Our younger members are interested and much better informed and prepared for life's duties than were we at their age. We hope in discussing at this Conference "Quaker Solutions to Present-day Problems" new light will be cast and new vigor given [FI 8/14].

Clearly, leading Friends were concerned that the cultural distractions and material comforts of the postwar era were taking a toll on the lives of Friends and their meetings.

Two sessions of the Conference focused on industrial relations and drew significant non-Quaker attendance. One speaker was Sidney Hillman, President of the Amalgamated Clothing Workers of America, who spoke on "Union Cooperation." He advocated more democratic processes in industrial life. Strikes are a weapon of the jungle, he said; legal processes would be much more constructive.

Caroline Norment, who had succeeded Elbert Russell as director of the Woolman School, reported that sixteen had registered for the summer term, from all over the nation, including some African Americans. Support for the school had also increased. In particular, Mary Lippincott of the Quaker publishing family had donated a large house and ten thousand dollars in endowment. Perhaps inspired by the round tables on education two years earlier, this Conference featured reunions of Swarthmore College, George School, and Woolman School alums.

The Conference registered concern over the declining international situation. Hans Gramm, who had worked for the AFSC in Germany, noted reaction against democracy in both Europe and America. The potential for another war was growing. Old-fashioned diplomacy would not avert the danger. More general goodwill and service were needed. The service of American and British Friends had inspired the formation of a new yearly meeting of German Friends.

John Nevin Sayre, secretary of the American Fellowship of Reconciliation, and Arthur Morgan, president of Antioch College, both spoke on the dangers of military training on campuses. Some sixty thousand students had been forced to take Reserve Officers' Training Corp (ROTC) for two years, fixing their minds on war as a natural, patriotic duty. Morgan quoted from the ROTC manual: "Pacifists are persons having impractical ideas or fisionary schemes as to the maintenance of peace. . . . They refuse to recognize force as the ultimate power, and decline to accept human nature as God ordained it." Following the war policy of Woodrow Wilson, the manual affirmed that "during the course of a great war every government, whatever its previous form, should become a despotism" (FI 8/14). Frederick Libby, secretary of the National Council for the Prevention of War, saw America moving toward war.

In a similar vein, Jesse Holmes spoke on "The Fruits of Imperialism." State imperialism "is in fact the imperialism of wealth, using the powers of government for its own ends." Similarly, wealthy men also try to make colleges their own through lavish grants. But he assured listeners that "our college at Swarthmore is one of the very small number in this country where freedom and independence are encouraged. Our Quaker tradition of free thought and speech is honorably maintained." He concluded, "American democracy is on trial. Can we maintain a government whose primary purpose is the life, liberty, and happiness of all its people? . . . Is property made for men, or men for property?" (FI 8/21). Holmes joined the Socialist Party in the 1930s and twice ran for public office in Pennsylvania.

Swarthmore president Frank Aydelotte continued the somber assessments. It was ironic that Wilson's war "to make the world safe for democracy" had been followed by the decay of democracy in Europe and America. But "[Wilson] has not betrayed us, we have betrayed ourselves." It was vital to "keep alive the Quaker spirit of protest" (FI 7/31).

The Section on Race Relations was led by Rachel Davis DuBois, now a high-school teacher in Woodbury, New Jersey, and Robert Kerlin of the West Chester Normal School. In contrast to most round tables/sections, this one was less presentation-oriented. Half of each period was devoted to group discussion. Kerlin spoke of the

CHAPTER 4   Progress Revised

Rachel Davis DuBois Papers, Friends Historical Library of Swarthmore College.

"Negro Renaissance" in progress in Harlem and elsewhere, mentioning Charles Johnson, Carter Woodson, Walter White, Countee Cullen, and Laura Wheeler. The Section featured a group exercise on "superior and inferior races." Davis DuBois reported, "We came to the conclusion that such a list depends on the ideals and experiences of those who make the list. One reason why there was only one Negro on the list was because of our lack of contact with leaders of that race." The group also looked at Japanese American and Native American issues. They concluded, "Although there may be many racial differences, we are all one in the spirit" (FI 8/21).

Rachel Davis DuBois is a key figure in the evolving group processes at FGC Conferences in this period. We first noted her appearance as a young Friend speaking at the 1920 Conference. She had grown up a Friend on her family's farm in New Jersey and became active in the peace movement in 1920. In 1924, two key events redirected her life. While traveling in the South, she met George Washington Carver and felt embarrassed by her ignorance on racial questions. She then read an article by W. E. B. DuBois arguing that war arises from racial problems. Thus, began a life-long concern to improve race relations and to nurture a greater appreciation of different cultural strains in American society.

While teaching high school in Woodbury, New Jersey, DuBois developed a curriculum of assembly-programs highlighting the contributions of particular ethnic and racial groups. Perhaps influenced by the KKK's growth in that state, some parents objected to her interracial emphasis. The controversy eventually led her in 1929 to return to New York, where she furthered her work in the public schools and other settings. One of her mottos was, "It's the not-me in thee that makes thee precious to me." Years later, the anthropologist Margaret Mead would call DuBois "the mother of intercultural education." We will hear more of her contributions to FGC Conferences and other work.

More early references to Gandhi appear in "Our Undeveloped Resources" by Wilbur Thomas, AFSC's executive secretary. He affirmed the limitless resource of God working through people. The AFSC adventure had revealed undeveloped resources in the Society of Friends, for example. On a larger scale, this power could accomplish great things: "Multiply the undeveloped power of Russia by a Gandhi and one begins to comprehend the possibilities of developing power." He concluded, "It is not foolish, therefore, to dream of a warless world. . . . If God's other name is love, why not tap that great reservoir of love and work for a warless world?" (FI 8/7). This former Friends pastor and Earlham College professor integrated the divine with the human drama in ways that could appeal across the American Quaker spectrum.

The 1926 Conference stands out less in terms of content than in format and reportage. Speakers clearly described a darkening prospect for the world, but their pessimism was counterbalanced by the creative genius, expanding work, and prophetic witness of the AFSC and by bright new leaders such as Rachel Davis DuBois.

Meeting at Ocean City, the Central Committee noted so far, Baltimore, Illinois, and Philadelphia Yearly Meetings had approved the reorganization plan. Meanwhile, the committee drafting the uniform discipline, with major input from the Philadelphia Yearly Meeting Discipline Committee, had circulated a completed draft among various groups. At a later session, the Central Committee and the Conference business session approved the 140-page text. "It presents a clear conception of Friendly faith, principles and business procedure in modern language, so that not only those accustomed to Friends' expressions, but any interested stranger can understand. The Conference passes this proposed Discipline on to its constituent Yearly Meetings, with the hope that they will adopt it as way opens." The drafting process had taken just four years.

In 1999, Chuck Fager rediscovered FGC's long-forgotten Uniform Discipline in the Friends Historical Library at Swarthmore College. He attributes the speed and success of the drafting process to the influence of two influential members of the drafting committee, Jesse Holmes and Jane Rushmore. (The latter had become the first clerk of the combined men's and women's business meetings of Philadelphia Yearly Meeting in 1924.) Amazingly, in just another four years, the Uniform Discipline had been adopted by all seven constituent yearly meetings, with only New York making substantive changes. Fager notes some salient points: there is no provision for select meetings of ministers and elders or the recording of ministers. The subordination of monthly meetings to yearly meetings is almost entirely expunged, a final triumph of congregational order. Emphasis shifts from a "gathered people" to the individual and his or her "Inner Light." "Plainness" becomes "simplicity," and "social mingling" is positively encouraged, along with work for social reform and racial equality. In effect, the agenda set forth by Progressive Friends in the mid-nineteenth century (see Chapter 1) had been fully embraced.[191] The Uniform Discipline codified changes that were once acts of rebellion against traditional faith and practice.

Finally, the Conference approved an epistle "To Our Friends and Workers Abroad," describing the theme and various presentations they had heard. It affirmed that young Friends had played a vital part in round table discussions, singing at night, pageants, and spontaneously organized devotional meetings on the beach. And the new Junior Conference was a triumph.

The 1928 Cape May Conference

Ocean City and Cape May seem to have been in competition for this large gathering of peaceful folk with disposable income. At a September 1927 meeting, the Central Committee seemed clear to return to Ocean City, but they ended up at Cape May, where they would return for many Conferences to come. Conferences were now settling into a regular early July time-frame. The postcard announcement stated the Conference theme, "The Place of Religion in Life," and promised "good fellowship" with "good speakers" and "peppy discussions of the big navy, industry, race, Quakerism." (Planning Committee minutes from the preceding November note that Reinhold Niebuhr, the fiery Union Seminary professor active

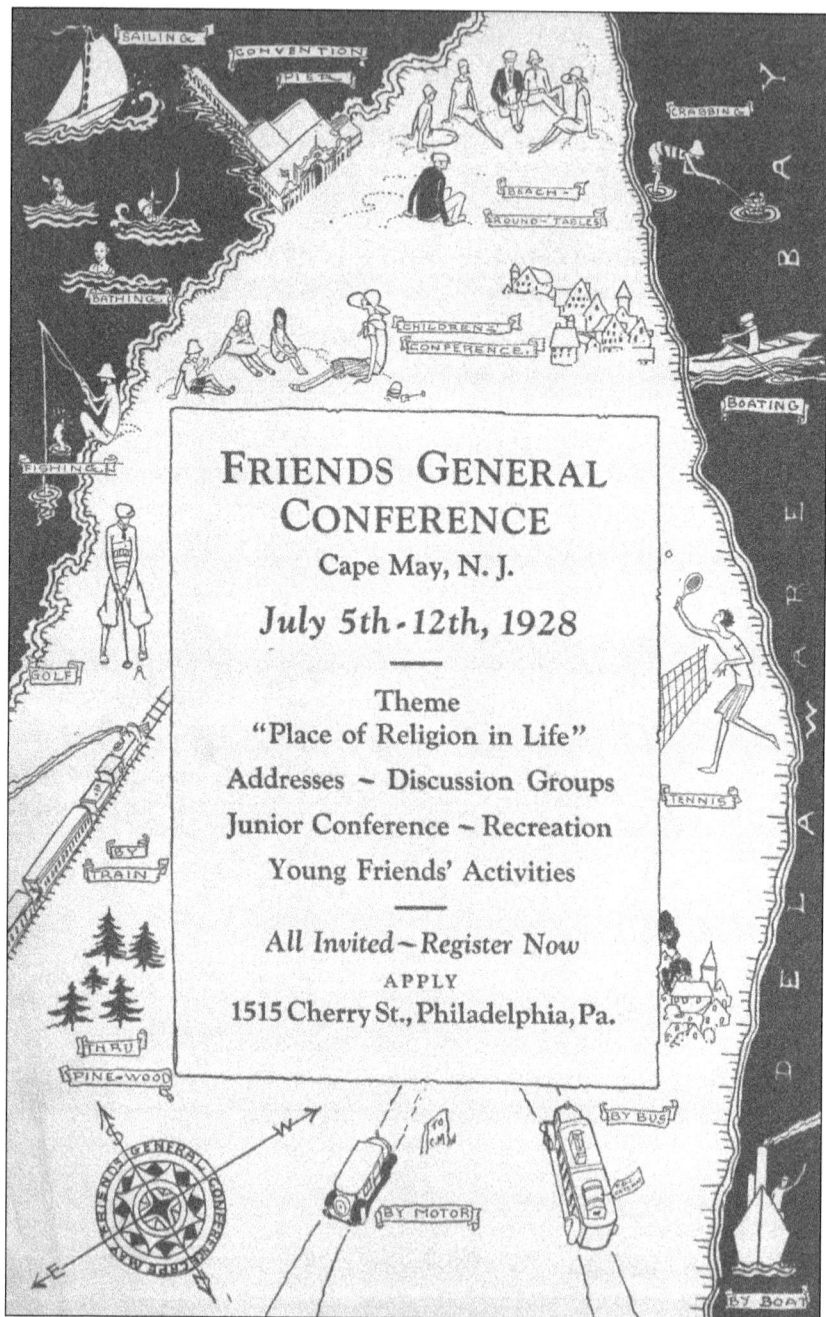

Poster for the 1928 Conference. Friends General Conference Records, Friends Historical Library of Swarthmore College.

CHAPTER 4   Progress Revised

with the Fellowship of Reconciliation, had declined their invitation to speak.[192])

The new Conference format was continued, this time with seven "sections" (round tables): Quakerism, Education, Religious Education, Peace, Race Relations, Industry, and a new High School Group. These met simultaneously at 11:15 am. Devotional meetings were held earlier at 9:00; plenary addresses at 10:00 am and 8:00 pm. Registered attendance was not quite as high as two years ago, but there were more one-day attenders. Young Friends were growing in participation; this was the first Conference for nearly half of them. Better amplification improved the plenary sessions. The Junior Conference continued its success. *Intelligencer* Supplement editor Anna Curtis commented that Conferences were becoming truly inter-generational, "more and more family affairs" (FI 7/28/1928).

Interest in rapprochement with Orthodox Friends continued to grow slowly, spurred by younger Friends. New York Yearly Meeting Friends had started an ad hoc "Joint Yearly Meeting" with Orthodox Friends. They challenged others to follow suit.

Popular push-back against Prohibition led to a plenary address by Martha Bensley Bruere, "Does Prohibition Work?" Yes and no, she concluded. The Eighteenth Amendment was a distinctly American product. Many immigrants were not part of the fifty-year process that had led up to it. The new freedom and citizenship of women was a factor for change. They were less willing to suffer with drunken husbands, but also felt more free to drink. Upper-class women were drinking more, lower-class women less. She summarized: "However, Prohibition is here. It is not a question of morals any longer," but a social and economic one. Notwithstanding much law-breaking, Prohibition was making a difference (FI 8/4).

The Race Relations Section was led by Rachel Davis DuBois and Crystal Bird. Bird, an African American working that year with the Interracial Section of the AFSC, had been hired to speak on "the problems, the needs, and culture of the colored race" at colleges, schools, churches, and public forums. DuBois described this Section as:

> A creative discussion group, not a company listening to a lecture course ... constant sharing of experiences, and a group-testing of convictions and prejudices, so that each might develop further, and

the problem as a whole be nearer a solution—the problem of race being the most fundamental, fascinating, and urgent.

In the first session, participants shared their "personal experiences with Negroes," which they found were limited almost exclusively to those of the laboring classes. Crystal Bird reviewed each day's discussion as "one who knows the Negro point of view from reality and not from sympathy alone."

DuBois reflected that the negro of *Uncle Tom's Cabin* was passing away. "All this brings a conflict of interests and desires; the races are drawing apart, with a cleavage, in some places, from the cradle to the grave." She observed that earlier generations had worked philanthropically *for* the negro; the time had come to work with the negro: "In this there must be new sacrifice, and new sufferings—a new Abolition movement to free us from our prejudices" (FI 8/4). (After an intensive year of travel and speaking for the AFSC, Bird moved on to other work, concluding that European Americans did not see African Americans as quite human.[193])

Edward Janney led the Peace Section, reviewing important new books from the wider peace movement, including titles from Sherwood Eddy and Harry Emerson Fosdick. Ray Newton reported on recent AFSC-sponsored peace conferences and ten peace caravans traveling around the countryside.

Jesse Holmes continued to fulminate against mainstream Christianity and to advocate socially engaged religion: "We must give up our desire to be rich if we truly wish for the kingdom of God, and with it must go an industrial system which puts the many under the domination of the few." He concluded mordantly, "What has religion to do with all this? Keep religion out of politics—keep religion out of business! Yes—keep religion out of life! Keep it for death-beds, for fear, for disaster" (FI 8/11).

Conference attenders enjoyed Holmes' rhetorical flourishes. But one wonders how much his skeptical impulses may have helped erode FGC's religious grounding over the decades of his influence. Would a PhD in chemistry have been hired to teach religion and biblical literature under Frank Aydelotte, who did much to raise Swarthmore's academic level and Quaker identity? In 1924, Holmes published a series of articles in the *Friends Intelligencer* on

CHAPTER 4   Progress Revised

Jesse Holmes. Courtesy of Friends Historical Library of Swarthmore College.

"Christian Theology," which he described as the noxious product of "the great Christian church machine," with "its finished codes and its supermen who hand out the predigested truth to the world of lesser men" (8/23/1924). By contrast, he described Friends as living a way of life aimed at the general good, dependent upon "an experience of a super-self which will enable us to continuously live in accord with that way of life. The expansion of these experiences into a theological system we leave to individuals." Friends were uniquely positioned "to offer to a scientific age what might be called a scientific theology on which to base a genuinely Christian way of life" (11/15/1924). Holmes expanded on this scientific theology later in the decade, as we will note in our next chapter.[194]

After Holmes's death in 1942, Brand Blanshard, wrote an appreciation for his friend and Swarthmore teaching colleague (*Friends Intelligencer* 6/6/1942). He described Holmes as a utopian:

> following always a gleam that came from another and juster world ... it was because he saw so vividly what might be that he was so impatient of what is. And on the other side there was a dash of Don Quixote in him. He was ready to champion anyone who could prove that he was the underdog, and he loved to set his lance against the irresponsible great of the earth.
>
> Jesse Holmes was an iconoclast in religion as he was in social matters, and for the same generous reasons. He was at war with all that was at enmity with joy.... He was quick to wrath, but like other men who think more of their causes than of themselves, he was slow to take offense.... He was a gay, brave, lovable, intensely human being.

The Growth of Liberal Book Culture

Edward Janney's mention of recent books from the mainstream peace movement is an early example of the growing role of liberal book culture at FGC Conferences. We will find a book display mentioned for the first time at the next Conference. Matthew Hedstrom[195] shows books to be crucial to the growth and success of liberal religion in this period, as they had been for evangelical expansion during the preceding century. Publishers Macmillan (publisher for Rufus Jones) and Harper's (publisher for several Quaker authors) started religion departments in the latter 1920s, and the Religious Book Club was founded in 1927 to stimulate sales. There was money to be made in promoting religious books to "a growing, socially-anxious American middle class seeking to better itself in the decades after World War I."[196]

CHAPTER 4 Progress Revised

Rufus Jones was a pioneer in producing popular books to spread new religious ideas. Near the beginning of Chapter 2, we heard William James's snide comments about the middlebrow culture he found at Chautauqua. Jones wrote *Social Law in the Spiritual World* (1904, mentioned earlier) to popularize for a mainstream readership some key ideas from James's *Varieties of Religious Experience*, published just two years before. Jones formulated a "mysticism for the masses." As he wrote in *Spiritual Energies* (1922), experiential religion was not just for saints, apostles and spiritual athletes, but for common everyday people, living busy lives. His "affirmative" mysticism was not aimed at mountaintop experiences but took experience as the starting point for action in the world. "The truth test is to be sought, not in the feeling-state, but in the motor effects." This was a pragmatic mysticism, oriented to social utility and middlebrow accessibility. Though Jones never broke through to full mainstream success, he strongly influenced Harry Emerson Fosdick and Howard Thurman, who did.

Books were important commodities for "middle-class Americans anxiously engaged with the emerging mass culture, hoping to solidify their tenuous social status with cultural markers acquired by reading the 'right' books."[197] As a liberal sect, Friends enacted a particular version of this wider phenomenon. The biennial FGC Conferences were an important mechanism for connecting Friends with the latest books and emerging ideas. The nurture of a religious and social consensus in a relaxing, family-friendly shore environment was key to the genius of the Friends General Conference. Settling into a regular return to Cape May strengthened the affects of FGC's formula, enacted with a nearly liturgical rhythm.

CHAPTER 5

An Expansive Depression
FGC Conferences 1930–1936

Across the world our messages have gone
Across the world to welcome the new dawn
When brotherhood and kindliness and love
Shall rank all worldly wisdoms far above
Each year has seen them flow in fuller stream
Such is our conference vision, such our dream
Born of those small beginnings far away
Down to this year of grace at bright Cape May

— from the Conference Pageant, 1930[198]

American society passed through enormous changes on all fronts during the war and over the course of the 1920s. The preceding chapter mentioned how the new technologies of radio, the phonograph, cinema, and the automobile expanded affective spaces in the culture, distracting many Americans from progressive causes. Moreover, for the first time, the majority of Americans were urban by 1920. Another six million farmers left the land over the next decade. The beginning of decline in rural and small-town America also boded the gradual decline of the Gurneyite pastoral Quakerism that had grown so rapidly there.

The total US population of 63 million in 1890 nearly doubled to 123 million by 1930. At least a third of the increase was due to immigration. Ten percent of Americans were foreign-born and another 20 percent had at least one foreign-born parent. Nearly a third of Chicago's residents in 1930 were foreign-born. Many new Americans were Catholic or Jewish, displacing somewhat the Protestant ethos of American society. The Great Migration of African Americans to

CHAPTER 5 An Expansive Depression

the North reached half a million during the war and a million more during the 1920s. But 80 percent of African Americans still lived in the South in 1930. These rapid racial, ethnic, and religious changes triggered reactionary, nativist politics; the Ku Klux Klan reached its acme of influence in many communities and some state governments during the 1920s.

The wealth gap was widening again. Much new wealth was amassed through market speculation, an option available only to those with capital to invest. The income of industrial workers also rose by 25 percent during the 1920s. But income in rural communities actually fell. The Great Depression of the 1930s was not much worse for rural America than the farm crisis of the 1920s.

The stock market crash of October 1929 was a massive market correction, to be sure. By mid-November $26 billion, about a third of the value of stocks in September, had evaporated. But the crash did not itself create the Great Depression. The newly elected President Herbert Hoover viewed it as a necessary break from an unhealthy economic cycle. Britain, still reeling from the war and losing its imperial command of global capitalism, abandoned the gold standard in 1930, and a wave of protectionist trade policies ensued around the world. Hoover objected to the Smoot-Hawley protectionist trade legislation voted by Congress that year. But he declined to veto the act. His veto would probably have been overridden anyway. Protectionist trade policies furthered the rabid nationalism already sweeping Europe (mentioned by Jane Addams in the preceding chapter). But more immediately, trade barriers exacerbated the international liquidity crisis, already a problem owing to the punitive economic measures taken against Germany in the Treaty of Versailles. The international banking system began to collapse, the final and decisive cause of the Great Depression. In the closing weeks of 1930, six hundred American banks failed, with many more to follow the next year.

It is curious that Herbert Hoover, the first Quaker elected President of the United States, received almost no mention at the FGC Conferences of 1928, 1930, or 1932. Perhaps his Gurneyite background led Conference Friends to ignore him.[199] He was considered a humanitarian hero and a transcendent candidate by many, and was elected by a landslide in 1928. In many ways, Hoover's rise to power marks the high-point of mainstream progressive aspirations among American Friends. His failure to grapple successfully with the early stages of the Depression may also suggest the limits of a Quaker religious sensibility amid the hurly-burly of mainstream politics.[200]

The Rapid Expansion of the American Friends Service Committee, New Independent Meetings

The AFSC began an ambitious expansion of programs as relief and reconstruction work in Europe wound down. Chairman Rufus Jones brought a number of midwestern Friends into the work. Indiana Friends pastor Murray Kenworthy headed the relief work in Russia until he caught typhus. Homer and Edna Morris, on leave from teaching at Earlham College, replaced Kenworthy. The work in Russia continued until 1927. Wilbur Thomas, another Friends pastor, took over for Vincent Nicholson as executive secretary of the AFSC in 1922 and quickly expanded AFSC's work to the domestic front, with work with unemployed coal miners in Appalachia in 1922.

Jones pressed the question whether the AFSC should lay itself down or reorganize for long-term service:

> It is extremely important that we should make no mistake about our future course. We should not go on unless we are sure that we have a vital mission to perform nor unless we can speak and act for the corporate membership of the Society of Friends. I do not want to see us go out and hunt for tasks to keep our machinery going.[201]

By 1924, the Board found clarity to continue and expand the work. Peace caravans of young Friends and other young pacifists began crisscrossing the country on speaking tours by the mid-twenties. Besides the main office in Philadelphia, the AFSC founded regional offices in Boston, Pasadena, and Richmond, Indiana in 1927 and 1928 at the same time as an Interracial Section was added. Jones drew Clarence Pickett, another Midwestern Friends pastor and Earlham professor, to head the Home Service Section in 1925.

Wilbur Thomas had wrangled with Herbert Hoover over the allocation of American relief resources in Europe and Russia during and

CHAPTER 5   An Expansive Depression

after the war. Thomas continued his antagonistic attitude toward Hoover after the latter began serving in the Harding and Coolidge administrations. When Hoover was elected President in 1928, Rufus Jones, a personal friend of Hoover and a mediator among different streams and parties of Friends, would no longer tolerate Thomas's antagonism. Thomas tendered his resignation in early 1929 and was succeeded by Clarence Pickett, who served as AFSC's executive secretary for the next twenty-one years.

Meanwhile, the British and American Friends Service Committees were founding Friends centers around Europe, building on the recent fame of this small, obscure religious group's humanitarian programs. The centers introduced interested seekers in Vienna, Berlin, Moscow, Paris, and Warsaw to Quaker practices and principles of peace.

The 1920s also saw a growing phenomenon of independent Friends meetings in campus towns and cities. These newly founded meetings, such as those in Cambridge, Massachusetts and Washington, DC generally fit the FGC mold but refused to join a yearly meeting and thereby conform to the old divisions among Friends. The new meetings had been inspired by the example of the AFSC's work more than by existing Quaker meetings.[202] Henry Cadbury, New Testament professor at Harvard, a founder of the Cambridge Meeting, and AFSC's new chairman after Jones's retirement in 1928, wrote letters in 1929 to FGC's Central Committee, the Five Years Meeting, and Philadelphia Yearly Meeting Orthodox. He asked these bodies to collaborate in welcoming the new independent meetings, and to encourage Friends living far from any established meeting to start more such meetings. He urged that each body go as far as their discipline and custom would permit in recognizing these meetings. The next year FGC's Central Committee appointed an ad hoc committee to explore the matter. We will hear more about these developments.

With Gurneyite successes starting to ebb, and FGC yearly meetings still declining in numbers, the AFSC became the driving force of American Quakerism, expanding into the Great Depression with visionary social idealism and consecrated leadership. As Gregory Barnes summarizes, by the latter 1930s the AFSC was "in the lead and pulling slightly away."[203]

141

Poster for the 1930 Conference. Friends General Conference Records, Friends Historical Library of Swarthmore College.

CHAPTER 5   An Expansive Depression

The 1930 Cape May Conference

FGC's Central Committee was now receiving invitations from cities such as Washington DC and Los Angeles as well as from resort towns. They debated whether Conferences might better be held in urban areas where more people would be attracted to hear the Quaker message. But the quieter environment of a family-friendly resort was by now the established mode. The Committee opted again for Cape May with the theme, "Quakerism as a Dynamic Religion for the Present Age." Hotel rates ranged from $15 to $56 per person for the week, with the large, fashionable Congress Hall at the upper end. The postcard invitation asked, "Are you lured by the beam of the Light House to the fellowship and fun of the Friendly conference at Cape May? There will be group discussions by folks who are frank and fearless." Since the accelerating wave of bank failures did not occur until later that year, the full impact of the crisis was not yet felt when Friends met in early July.

The Conference opened with a Quaker "reception to themselves." Philadelphia Yearly Meeting Friends sang "In the Good Old Conference Time." There was also a "Conference Song" composed by Russell Hayes for the occasion, sung several times during the Conference (and at subsequent Conferences). A sense of tradition, rife with affects, was growing, and Cape May seemed to elicit it especially well. This year's pageant was "Our Conference Story," going all the way back to the founding of the First-Day School Conference in 1867. This story was told in rhymed couplets like the ones quoted in the epigraph to this chapter.

As with Chautauqua in the preceding century, women outnumbered men—even if most of the speakers were still men. A conversation between two non-Quakers on the boardwalk was reported: "What's all this crowd here?" "The Quakers." "What are they?" "Dunno, but they must be some kind of Mormons. There's about nine women here to every man." *Friends Intelligencer* Supplement editor Anna Curtis added that the anecdote might be apocryphal, but "there were many more of the one-time 'gentler sex' in attendance" (FI 7/26/1930). Overall attendance continued to swell, with 1,201 registered and perhaps four to five hundred unregistered. The Junior Conference burgeoned under the leadership of Vesta Haines, with 111 children between the ages of three and fourteen.

The Conference continued to elaborate. An exhibit room, initiated at the previous Conference, rapidly expanded with displays and literature from Quaker schools and other organizations. A book display featured a variety of Quaker and other titles for examination and sale.

Curtis also commented that group singing had become an important feature of the Conference, with a half-hour of hearty vocalizing before each evening's plenary sessions. Since the publication of its first hymnal of 39 hymns and songs in 1919, FGC published supplements between 1929 and 1940 that brought the total to a little more than 200.[204] Local meetings and first-day schools were also singing more. This was a feature of the wider peace movement as well. Hymns and other songs bridged traditional Christian and newer pacifist identities, strengthening the affects of solidarity.[205]

A record number of resolutions were presented and approved by the Conference. Friends urged the Senate to ratify the second Naval Treaty (limiting the naval arms race), protested the continued lynchings of African Americans, and challenged the government's requirement that applicants for citizenship promise to bear arms in military service. By now, the Social Service Section (the new name for the old Philanthropic Union since the 1924-27 reorganization) had seven "Departments": Peace, Inter-Racial Conditions, Industrial Relations, Child Welfare and Proper Publications and Amusements, Temperance and Anti-Narcotics, Social Morality, and Prison Reform. Clearly, the concern for moral and social "purity" was still alive among Friends.

Norman Thomas, the Socialist Party's candidate for President in 1928 (and five more times after that) and director of the League for Industrial Democracy, spoke on "Ethics *versus* the Profit Motive." He asserted that ethics apply beyond the usual sphere of individual and family life, into social and economic realms as well. "It is the glory of the Society of Friends that they have taken their ethics so seriously." For that reason, Quakers were once as difficult to deal with as Communists today. Thomas found the profit system as corrosive to ethics as war itself. But "the Golden Rule challenges landlordism, exactly as it challenges war." Ethics are not just "a system of bright

CHAPTER 5 An Expansive Depression

ideas." They become operative through "effort based on the desire for the common good" (FI 8/16).

Jesse Holmes spoke on "Reasonable Religion." Two years before, he had published an article, a public letter "To the Scientifically Minded," in *The Friends Intelligencer*. It was endorsed by four other academics besides himself. This popular piece was reprinted as a leaflet by FGC and many thousands were distributed.[206] In his usual fashion, Holmes used mainstream Christianity as his foil, while presenting Quakerism as a faith in step with scientific enquiry and progress. Against set creeds, Quakers offered friendliness and reasonable conversation: "We demand no unity of opinion and we find both interest and stimulus in our many differences." He maintained the pragmatic definition of truth we found emerging among mid-nineteenth-century Progressive Friends: "There are differences among us as to details and methods, but not as to the desired end." The *goal* suggests what is right and wrong: "RIGHT is what serves the common purpose, WRONG is what hinders or thwarts it." Thus, war is wrong because it "hinders the development of the world family; yet we do not exclude from membership those who do not have that conviction." Meanwhile, "Many of us feel that our Industrial system is in need of changes, but we have not arrived at unity as to what should be done about it."

Notwithstanding his earning PhD in chemistry many years before, Holmes had perhaps forgotten that the search for truth in the scientific world is much more argumentative than the friendly relativism that had overcome liberal Quakerism. And the concern for appropriate methods of investigation (the "operationalist" definition of truth) are just as important to science as any pragmatic ends. Much as we heard Friends speak of "evolution" before World War I, we hear Holmes conveying a popularized version of "scientific" mindedness at variance with the way the sciences actually work. (The scientific community actually has more affinities with traditional Quakerism, where the select meetings of ministers and elders would test claims to new truth, much as review panels assess new findings and theories in a given field of science.)

But clearly, the popularity of the tract indicates that there were many whose worldview was at least scientistic, if not scientific: that

Clarence Pickett in 1934. Courtesy of the American Friends Service Committee.

is, they embraced science as an ideology more than as a disciplined method of investigation. The tract ends: "We believe there are many who would find a richer life in membership with us, and we know that we need the strength of larger numbers. We too need the fellowship of men and women of intelligence and courage."

Holmes's address at this Conference continued in the same vein, under the banner of rationalism. Reasonable religion "aims at a way of life which will give the most abundant experience to the largest possible number of people." It realizes that man is by his higher nature dedicated to the creation of a nobler and better civilization." Even one generation before, religion was still "the worship of a higher power from a sense of need." Now it had become "enthusiasm for the good." "We need to . . . create the Kingdom of God out of what we have, and to use the world while we do it. That's our job" (FI 8/23). Holmes's pragmatism appeared ready to "use the world" in ways we now recognize as environmentally unsustainable.

Will Alexander, director of the Commission on Interracial Cooperation, spoke on "Building Good Will." He observed, "There are no more child races to look up to and depend upon the whites. The colored peoples are demanding to be treated as equals the world

CHAPTER 5 An Expansive Depression

around. That is one difficulty today: the other difficulty, of course, is the white man" (FI 8/2). Alexander also worked with Rachel Davis DuBois in leading a round table on race relations at this Conference.

Clarence Pickett brought prophetic clarity to the 1930 Conference with "The Place of Friends in Making a Better World." His portrayal of Friends and their role was humbler than the bloated rhetoric of the 1912 Conference. He cautioned that Friends were not the only people concerned for a better world, and that they needed to discern better their place in creating it. "I only wish that the Society of Friends had the enthusiasm of the Russians for the task to which they have set themselves." The war had changed everything. There was too little religious thinking. Very few in Europe went to church anymore, because the churches had spoken no word against the war. European nations were falling apart through political and racial animosities amid "a slowly disintegrating economic order."

"So we have no right to an easy expectation of a better world. If we dare to hope for a better world, we will have to be prophetic in our use of new and living forces to bring it about." At home, he said:

> Friends should be working unitedly in the peace movement.... We have a great chance to train the peace leadership, not only of the Society of Friends but of other denominations. The Peace Institute for our own Peace Caravaners is being increasingly attended by members of other church groups.... This summer alone thirty-three young people have been given places for volunteer service in Negro schools, summer camps, in rural social work.

Pickett observed that a "better world" meant to most Americans a higher standard of living. Instead, "it is a world where the spirit transcends and uses the material, but is always master of it." Technological advances "only make a better world in so far as they help make for enriched personalities. And the political world must be likewise person-centered." But the dictatorial methods of communism and fascism were leading in the opposite direction. (There are touches here of the personalist religious philosophy that influenced a number of Quaker leaders at this time.) He concluded:

> We have come to a crucial time in these days after the war, when we lose our sustained ideals, and get impatient with them. Yet we need

more than ever now, renewed idealism and spiritual vigor. We may object to the methods of Russia, but we need the zeal, the willingness to die for an object that we find in Russia today [FI 7/26].

Clearly, an important new voice was emerging on the FGC Conference stage.

The Closing of the Woolman School, the Beginnings of Pendle Hill

Despite the encouraging report by Caroline Norment in 1926, the John Woolman School closed the summer of 1927 for lack of sustainable enrollment. That same summer Rufus Jones and other AFSC leaders convened a group of Hicksite and Orthodox Friends at Haverford to explore another venture, this time fully sponsored by both branches. They shared the desire for an adult learning center to ground the Service Committee's long-term social engagement in Quaker spirituality and principles, as well as a center to nurture new leadership among Friends in all branches. They hoped to attract a leader with wide credibility among Friends and beyond. In 1928, British Friend Henry Hodgkin, founder of the FOR, then heading the YMCA in China, agreed to become the new school's founding director. A property with potential for future expansion was purchased near Swarthmore, in Wallingford. The new experiment was named Pendle Hill, in reference to George Fox's visionary experience in 1652. It opened in September 1930.

Henry Hodgkin spoke at the July Conference on "The Light That Leads to Service." He affirmed Rufus Jones's contention that mysticism leads out into the world. Tragically, many men had entered the trenches in the recent war, believing they were following the light. He suggested three tests for the light, to discern where it may be colored by human conventions. The first is to compare our light to the light of Christ's life; love is the key criterion. Second, the light is not only the light of Christ but the light of the human mind; it can be tested rationally. Finally, "we must test our ideals in regard to other races, our Communist friends, all sections of the world." He ended with the assurance, "The light will come if we but open our hearts, if we are willing, like Christ, to pay the price of illumination" (FI 8/30).

CHAPTER 5 An Expansive Depression

Henry Hodgkin. Pendle Hill files.

Both Pickett and Hodgkin reintroduced the theme of personal sacrifice to Friends yearning for a better world. AFSC workers had sacrificed much in Europe. New sacrifices had been made in working with coal miners in West Virginia and western Pennsylvania since 1922. Hodgkin had experienced it starting the FOR in 1914 and on the mission field in China. This was an important chord to strike among middle-class Friends enjoying a week of relaxation and ideals on the Jersey shore. In addition, we hear Hodgkin introduce tests for

Poster for the 1932 Conference. Friends General Conference Records, Friends Historical Library of Swarthmore College.

discerning the light—a *method* or *means* to balance the pragmatic *ends* pressed by progressives like Jesse Holmes. And significantly, both Pickett and Hodgkin made positive references to Russia, where a more revolutionary commitment stood out so clearly. During Pendle Hill's first year, Hodgkin taught a course, "Seeing Ourselves through Russia," a collaborative study of both the accomplishments

CHAPTER 5 An Expansive Depression

Postcard for the 1932 Conference. Friends General Conference Records, Friends Historical Library of Swarthmore College.

and disasters of the Russian revolution, seeking what might be usefully applied to the American situation.

Postcards and leaflets promoting conferences in this period include a pen-and-ink drawing of a young Quaker maiden with bonnet standing on the boardwalk, curtseying to a young Quaker gentleman who has taken off his hat. The message appears to be "Come to the Cape May Conference and find a Quaker mate."

The theme of this Conference was a quote from Albert Einstein: "Man is here for the sake of other men." There were two devotional meetings each morning at 9:15, the traditional one in the convention hall on the pier and a separate young Friends meeting at the Star Villa hotel. A different generational dynamic was starting to assert itself.

In her "Story of the Conference" (FI 7/23-8/13/1932), Anna Curtis noted that the deepening Depression had not impacted attendance, with 1,050 officially registered, nearly as high as two years before. The Junior Conference had drawn 108 under the age of fourteen and was credited with bringing more parents to the Conference. Orthodox Friends were increasingly sitting in. She suggested that good attendance at devotional meetings in the mornings raised the level of succeeding deliberations. But in other ways, the ethos was changing. Traditionally, a deep silence had followed addresses. "Now we are completely converted to the manner of the world. The generous applause which followed every address lasted long enough in several cases to have brought a matinee idol back on the stage for his third bow." Meanwhile, a mixture of old-fashioned and new-fashioned bathing suits were seen on the beach. Singing and dancing continued to expand the affective space.

The exhibit area was more popular than ever, with book sales, Quaker school exhibits, and free literature. An American Indian exhibit and an AFSC exhibit offered crafts for sale, made by Native Americans and by mining families. The two exhibits enjoyed combined sales of over $600.

In his opening address, Chairman Arthur Jackson expanded on the Conference theme:

> If religion is a way of life, it should be developed through words of righteousness and brotherly kindness; it should bring the human spirit into immediate relationship with the Divine Spirit. This should lead to a fellowship which cannot recognize class, creed, citizenship, nor color, but must be concerned with the great issues of life [FI 7/30].

This Conference addressed "great issues of life" with large doses of academic expertise. Addresses were given on the Depression by

CHAPTER 5 An Expansive Depression

Clair Wilcox, professor of economics at Swarthmore College; on the growing attacks upon Prohibition by Thomas Carver, professor of economics at Harvard University; and on work with the unemployed by Hornell Hart, professor of sociology at Bryn Mawr College.

But young Friends and the AFSC spoke closer to the heart of Quaker concern. A panel of young Friends addressed the theme, "The American Friends Service Committee is leading us in the right direction." Preston Davies spoke on his experience as a Peace Caravaner the preceding summer. Fourteen teams of two fanned out across the country in second-hand cars, spreading the gospel of peace, meeting every kind of reaction. They distributed banners and posters decrying war and advocating the beauties of peace. They gave an average of five talks per day at occasions including family reunions, schools, clubs, churches, and WCTU meetings. Some of their best opportunities were with Kiwanis and Rotary club luncheons, where their talks were met with intelligent discussion. On the other hand, an American Legion meeting expelled them before the second Caravaner had a chance to speak. He wondered, "Were we doing any good?" He decided that "speaking for our principles in the face of opposition and indifference . . . to stand against that horror that is War" could only be useful. Margaret Paxson spoke about working with the AFSC in the coal fields of West Virginia and Kentucky. The average mining family consisted of seven or eight people trying to live on $2.50 a week. In April 1932, AFSC was feeding forty thousand children, with hopes to increase the work in the fall and add more work in occupational rehabilitation for unemployed miners (FI 8/6).

Young Friends' participation at this Conference was the largest yet, and their input weighed in more than ever before. They sent the following minute to the Central Committee:

> We, the young Friends who are attending Richmond Miller's Forum on questions of right and wrong as proposed by young Friends, appreciate greatly the courtesies extended to our members who belong to another race. But we are concerned that unforeseen situations should arise which are a barrier to the fullest life of the Conference. Discrimination which has prevented members from joining us in social and recreational activities, has caused us the keenest embarrassment. We ask the Conference to share this

concern with us, and we earnestly ask the Central Committee to hold all future Conferences at a place, and with a plan that will assure the same privileges to all those registered at the Conference [FI 8/13].

The Central Committee responded, assuring that this problem would not recur. Anna Curtis concluded, "Of all the important matters discussed at the Conference, none was of higher spiritual importance than this, and no decision of policy has more far-reaching implications." Evidently, Cape May's chamber of commerce took steps to assure the continuing patronage of this major summer customer.

A round table on "The Negro Problem" was led by Henry Cadbury, professor of biblical studies at Bryn Mawr. The group concluded, "There is no use in talking about world peace so long as we have the race problem.... The Negro himself is not the problem, but the white man who is responsible for what is happening." Cadbury brought in a variety of speakers. Crystal Bird (now surnamed Fauset and a Pennsylvania state legislator) spoke at the final session on "Negro Experiences of White Behavior," drawing mostly upon her personal experiences, emphasizing that racism is cultivated, not natural (FI 8/27).

Another round table on "Indians" was led by Lawrence Lindley, secretary to the Indian Rights Association. They noted four phases in the white American approach to Indians: to destroy them; to isolate them on reservations; to make white people out of them; and finally, with the new Indian Commissioners in power, to understand them and help them preserve their own life and culture. Along with other European Americans, Friends were making progress in their perceptions and responses to race in America.

Clarence Pickett spoke on "Quakerism in the Field." Quakerism is neither theological dogma nor "nicely laid out political or social schemes," but insists on connecting exhortation with experiment. "Resolutions and minutes and statements and declarations may easily become merely 'straw battles' unless they are taken as the call to action." He noted that just ten years ago, the AFSC was finishing up its great work of feeding German children. Now Hitler's movement was taking over. Yet the abiding Quaker presence in Germany

CHAPTER 5   An Expansive Depression

was challenging Hitler's militarism and racism. The Friends Center in Vienna was promoting racial difference as an asset rather than a cause for conflict.

Pickett noted that "Quakerism has spread in two ways: by the Evangelistic method, which attempts avowedly to increase our membership; and by the drawing into active work those whose spirit responds to the kind of opportunity we are able to offer." As examples of the latter approach, AFSC's Peace Caravan teams that summer included two Unitarian boys, sponsored by their church, and two Jewish boys with Jewish sponsors. AFSC's Peace Section had conducted three Peace Institutes that year, drawing people from many religious faiths. Sixty-five young people were teaching without remuneration in Indian schools, mountain schools, camps for underprivileged children, and penal institutions. "These are attempting to extend Quakerism in its truest sense, to areas of conflict." Work in the coal fields was the most dramatic project since the war. AFSC was now working in 538 counties and had started eight centers where manual arts and agriculture were taught. (Some of the furniture produced was for sale at the Conference exhibit room.)

The significance of this work: "There is in every man something of the life and spirit of the divine.... This is the great need in these communities, that spiritual forces be practically interpreted." But Pickett cautioned, "The Society is being steadily drawn into a wider field, and our own group may need more attention to enable it to keep pace with the increased responsibilities that are falling on its shoulders ... not just money but statesmanship and spirit" were needed. Some were stepping up, others pulling back; "Which way will we go?" (FI 9/3).

The Service Committee had taken the lead in the "practical Christianity" that Progressive Friends had proclaimed nearly a century before. Pickett's conclusion challenged Friends to keep pace with an organization now moving at lightning speed. Perhaps Jesse Holmes was reflecting on this activism-gap in his address ("Religion-a Sword or a Pillow?") when he summarized, "Shall we not rather arouse ourselves into vivid and vigorous life taking the stimulating power of our religion into business, into politics—and even into our meeting-houses?" (FI 7/30).

Poster for the 1934 Conference. Friends General Conference Records, Friends Historical Library of Swarthmore College.

"Memories of Cape May" were contributed by some attenders of the 1932 Conference (FI 8/20). One reflected, "We are at home again, in cities, villages, or farms, in the low-lands, the prairies, or the hills. Our days by the sea are but memories that inspire, memories that thrill."

CHAPTER 5 An Expansive Depression

Meeting during the conference, the Central Committee received a proposal from the Unitarian and Universalist Churches, which had begun combining activities in recent years. They asked FGC to join with them in forming a Council of the Free Churches. But the invitation was declined. The Committee's letter explained that while FGC had much in common with these churches, longstanding divisions in the Quaker family were beginning to heal, and the Central Committee wished to do nothing that might aggravate them again.

Meeting the next year, the Central Committee discussed holding the next Conference at Swarthmore College, at the behest of some young Friends still smarting from their experience of Cape May's racial exclusion. But arrangements were successfully made to continue at Cape May. Friends were to have exclusive control of sections of the beach during the Conference (apparently to assure that African Americans could participate in recreation and campfires there).

The 1934 Cape May Conference

The cover graphic for the Conference program showed young Friends sitting in a circle, with the words "Idea – Discussion – Action" around the border.

The dynamic of sharing viewpoints and experiences in small circles was starting to take hold among Friends and other pacifists. Richard Gregg came to teach at Pendle Hill in 1934. He had spent time with Gandhi in India and became a major transmitter to Americans of the Gandhian philosophy and method, through his book, *The Power of Nonviolence* (published in 1934 with a foreword by Rufus Jones). Gregg described nonviolent action as a "moral jiu-jitsu" that overturns the aggressor's assumptions and forces him to rethink his moral position.

In 1937 Gregg published the pamphlet, *Training for Peace: A Program for Peace Workers*, which advocated the formation of pacifist cell groups and prescribed small-group discussion in circles, folk singing, and folk dancing to instill the "sentiments" (the affective formation) of pacifist activism.[207] As we have been noting, the Conferences were strong in group affects as well as reasoned presentations. But their large-scale jamboree dynamics slowed the adoption of the small-group processes Gregg and others advocated.

The Conference theme this year was "Reflect the Inner Light." In "The Story of the Conference" (FI 7/14-8/20/1934) Anna Curtis wrote on the second full day: "Was it indeed only the day before yesterday that we came to Cape May? Or week before last? So many things have happened, so many good words spoken since we arrived, that ordinary time calculations are useless." Rousing half-hour songfests continued before each evening plenary session. "Every year this singing becomes more definitely an accepted and appreciated feature of the Conference." The Cape May Orchestra played for a dance after the opening session.

There were 1100 Friends present by Saturday evening. The Junior Conference had 117 children on the opening day. Outreach to other branches drew in 22 Friends from the Five Years Meeting and 66 from Philadelphia Yearly Meeting Orthodox. Alvin Coates and Erroll Elliott from the Five Years Meeting spoke during the sessions. Some locals were heard on the boardwalk, wondering who these people with badges were. "Quakers? That's the funny bunch, isn't it?" Curtis reflected that Friends once called themselves "a peculiar people," but were now perceived as "the funny bunch." Living the same testimonies was all that mattered, she added.

Various speakers addressed the growing momentum toward totalitarianism and war. Frederick Libby, secretary of the National Council for the Prevention of War, saw conflicts developing in both Asia and Europe, concluding, "The blame lies with the Versailles Treaty" (FI 8/4). Hillel Silver, a rabbi from Cleveland, reflected on the growth of state authority over individual freedom, particularly under Bolshevism, Nazism, and Fascism. "We have entered an age of sanctified ruthlessness and exalted brutality. But even more dangerous ... is the tragic toll of victims of the spiritual and intellectual violence. Men are driven to terrified silence. Conformity is prescribed. Men dare not dissent." He urged, "The courageous reassertion of that liberal, generous, tolerant view of life which our unhappy age has so tragically lost" (FI 7/28).

Arthur Morgan, formerly the pioneering president of Antioch College, now head of the New Deal's Tennessee Valley Authority,

CHAPTER 5   An Expansive Depression

suggested that "Today the greatest problems and issues of mankind are ethical. Science is running far ahead of our ability to direct it for the fulfillment of human need. Business technique has developed far ahead of the ability of business to serve society ... the problem which forever confronts us is the relation of means to ends." Reflecting on President Franklin Roosevelt's new initiatives, he added:

> America is striving for a "new deal." It will not get that new deal out of the pursuit of special interests, out of legislation alone.... It will win a new deal, if at all, through the actual practice day by day of the principles which were both taught and practiced so long ago, by the great teacher we all revere [FI 8/4].

A round table on "Race Relations" led by Frank Watson, professor of sociology at Haverford College, offered a macro-analysis of current racial problems, then posed the query, "Has the Society of Friends a unique contribution to make in all this?" In the discussions, "Some shame and bewilderment was expressed over inability to feel and act toward other races on so high a plane as was believed just and right. Probably unconscious early, or present, social conditioning is responsible for this. Deepened interest in individuals may overcome it" (FI 8/25). This first expression of "shame and bewilderment" at FGC Conferences perhaps marks a deepening racial awareness among Conference-goers, a decentering of white Quaker subjectivity.

The most compelling addresses came from Clarence Pickett and Rufus Jones. In "Quaker Testimonies in the World Today," Clarence Pickett struck a balance between spiritual life and social witness:

> What the outward ordinances are to other religious groups, the testimonies are to the Society of Friends. They are the outward sign of an inward grace. Some Friends are deeply interested in activity, and others in the development of spiritual life. At times one finds a sense of competition between the expression of our Testimonies in everyday life and the interests of the meeting for worship. In an integrated religious society, there can be no such separation. Our Testimonies will be strong and vigorous in their expression in proportion to the quality of the life of the spirit in our membership, and it will be impossible for us to have a creative spiritual life except that life break forth in terms of building a new and better society.

Pickett broke through a long neglect of the theological meaning and spiritual roots of the social testimonies in the FGC Conference conversation.

He also observed that the League of Nations was by now "all but dead." But Friends must continue to press for international cooperation: "We are not now moving with the popular crowd. We may be the voice crying in the wilderness, but let us not desert our peace testimony even in its day of apparent hopelessness." Pickett probably alluded here to early signs of erosion in the mainstream peace movement in America.

Germany posed a sobering prospect. But Pickett cautioned against the popular view that the violent swing toward German nationalism revealed the true nature of the German people. It was instead the product of their utter bewilderment and hopelessness. "The most important service to be rendered is to bring calm, confidence and fellowship in every way we can." He urged Friends to visit German people in their homes. "A traveling ministry of concerned Friends was never more needed than now as an expression of the Quaker peace testimony." The Haverford religion professor Thomas Kelly visited Friends and others in Germany on behalf of the AFSC in the summer of 1938. It not only brought comfort to them; it profoundly affected his own development as a spiritual leader.

With prophetic insight, Pickett compared this period to the Thirty Years War in seventeenth-century Europe. Military conflict had ended in 1918 but "the end of the war is far off." Indeed, from the beginning of World War I, through the Great Depression, and to the end of World War II amounted to thirty-one years. This was a time for rededication and renewed vision. AFSC Peace Institutes in the past year had offered training in international affairs to about 750 leaders of public opinion. The AFSC couldn't afford to finance the usual number of caravans that year, but young people raised funds themselves to finance the work, and presently more caravans were in the field than ever before.

In terms of domestic poverty, Pickett posed AFSC's continuing relief and retraining work among the nation's most desperately poor as a renewal of earlier Quaker work to abolish slavery. The AFSC was working with the federal government to resettle 1,700 families from dead industrial towns to subsistence homestead communities.[208]

CHAPTER 5 An Expansive Depression

In the field of Quaker education, Pickett pointed to the first AFSC work camp taking place that summer in western Pennsylvania, to create a water system for AFSC's Westmoreland Homesteads. He reflected that physical work leads to an intellectual inquiry about the conditions that create social upheaval, and then an exploration of ways to create a society that avoids such violent changes. Pickett's comment on the practice-reflection-theory-action cycle anticipates Paulo Freire's *Pedagogy of the Oppressed* (1968).

He concluded:

> We shall have to constantly alter and reshape the outward form which our testimonies take, but if we have a vital spiritual life, it will always express itself in some of these basic efforts to enable human life to be normal. For those who remain at home, it may be that the nourishment of the life of the spirit in the home and in the meeting is the largest service. We can never be effective without that. The combination of the inner life and the outward expression is the religion of Friends [FI 8/18].

Pickett sounds some themes in common with a talk Howard Brinton gave at Pendle Hill earlier that summer.[209] Clarence Pickett and his family moved into a home built by the AFSC next to the Brintons at Pendle Hill in 1937.

Rufus Jones, in his first Conference address since 1904, supplemented Pickett's efforts to rebalance FGC's activism and appetite for academic expertise with stronger spiritual foundations. In "Some Quaker Ideals," he addressed the Conference theme of "Reflect the Inner Light" by using the more traditional Quaker expression, the *Inward* Light. (Jones himself tended to use "Inner Light" in his earlier writings.) He began by noting that "The inward Light is beyond question the master ideal of Quakerism." It suggests that "There is something of God about us. And we have direct relations with a world of Spirit." He defined the central mission of Quakers: to give effective testimony to "the continuous revelation of the life of God through the inner life of man. . . . God is still a vital factor in the affairs of men today. But the only way He can operate spiritually is through the lives of persons."

From these basic principles, Jones reviewed other historic Quaker "ideals": corporate worship; shared ministry and decision-making;

Rufus Jones. Courtesy of Friends Historical Library of Swarthmore College.

the inward experience of the sacraments; that of God in each person; the peace testimony. "But always at the center of their testimony lay their championship of human rights and privileges, and their protest against unfairness and oppression.... And nothing was trivial to them which affected the true unfolding of personality. *They took the way of the Cross very seriously*" (his italics in the printed text). In this regard, he quoted John Woolman:

CHAPTER 5 An Expansive Depression

It requires much self-denial and resignation of ourselves to God to attain that state wherein we can freely cease from fighting when wrongly invaded if, by our fighting there were a probability of overcoming the invaders. Whoever rightly attains to it does in some degree feel that spirit in which our Redeemer gave His Life for us.

Jones concluded, "Once more the way of peace is the way of the Cross.... The ideal of the 'peacemaker' is therefore a very costly one" (FI 9/1).

No doubt, both Pickett and Jones admired the Friends General Conference and wished to draw closer in fellowship with Conference Friends. But it appears that these two visitors from the Orthodox-Gurneyite stream also aimed to reintroduce more spiritual grounding and rigor to the high-flying rhetoric that often dominated Conference addresses, leaving Friends stimulated but too easy on the Jersey shore, while the nation wallowed in Depression and grave new specters of war loomed on horizons East and West. Conference chairman Arthur Jackson himself had said in his opening remarks, "The Religious Society of Friends has special responsibilities in this new world . . . it behooves us to make sincere effort to contribute freely thoughts, services and examples during this period of evolution even though doing so may lead to a cross" (FI 7/14). A sense of the tragic in history was starting to bear upon Friends again.

Perhaps one contributing factor was the defection of Reinhold Niebuhr from the peace movement, with the publication of his *Moral Man in Immoral Society* (1932) and his subsequent attacks upon liberal religion. He found liberal Christianity's attempts to moralize society not only futile but stupid. "I hold that the chief sin of liberalism is that it has given selfish man an entirely too good opinion of himself." He found true Christianity, like Marxism, to be both realistic and utopian; it is a tragic view of history tempered by a hope for its transformation. He described himself as theologically to the right and politically to the left of modern liberal Protestantism. He believed that only socialism could save western civilization.[210] Niebuhr's strong, public attacks on the peace movement, combined with the erosion of the mainstream peace movement in the face of looming war, put Friends and other committed pacifists on notice that a tougher, more countercultural witness would soon be required.

Howard Thurman. Creative Commons.

Jones also addressed the International Congress of Religious Liberals meeting in Copenhagen in 1934. In *Re-thinking Religious Liberalism*[211] he confronted the new, neo-orthodox attacks on liberal religion. "This is just now a bad moment for liberals. It is the open season for hunting and trapping all types of them." He defended liberalism as an "open religion" committed to an unending pursuit of the truth, rather than to a set system of thought. But he admitted that liberalism had become too one-sidedly rationalistic, individualistic, and humanistic. In true religion, man is in "conscious relationship to transcendent reality, that is, to an over-world which feels akin to himself." This corrective emphasis may have inspired his use of "inward" instead of "inner" light at the FGC Conference. (It is regrettable that there was no comparable intellectual leader from within the FGC ranks to facilitate an internal critique and renewal.) Jones's "rethinking" was not a significant change in his liberal assumptions. Gary Dorrien, historian of liberal religion in America, suggests that even the harsh neo-orthodox attacks by Reinhold Niebuhr and others against liberalism were more a corrective than a real departure from the idealistic orientation of liberal religious renewal.[212]

Other Conference addresses offered fresh perspectives on Jesus. At the preceding Conference in 1932, Alexander Purdy, Quaker professor at Hartford Theological Seminary, had portrayed Jesus as a revolutionary rather than the reformer typically portrayed by liberals. Howard Thurman, The African American devotional writer and biblical scholar who had studied with Rufus Jones in 1929, spoke at the 1934 Conference. He reflected on the temptations of Jesus in the wilderness. In rejecting the tempter's offer of the kingdoms of this world, Jesus chose instead to enact the mystery of the kingdom of heaven among his own people. He concluded that "the hope for a weary world" is to *be* the kingdom of heaven, which will draw others into the same mystery (FI 8/25).

A "Statement on Economic Objectives"

Like Niebuhr, some Friends were drawn toward more overtly socialist activism. Like Niebuhr, Jesse Holmes ran for Congress on the Socialist Party ticket in the 1930s. Holmes and Patrick Murphy Malin led the 1934 Conference round table on "Economic Conditions." In the final session they led the discussion of a "Statement on Economic Objectives" prepared by FGC's Industrial Relations Committee. It deserves some attention here.

This far-reaching four-page document was printed and distributed at the Conference. The Committee hoped the statement "might well be accepted as an ideal economic doctrine of the Religious Society of Friends, of an economy certain to come in the future." The Committee was described as "engineers," all with long experience in economic study and practical business experience.

They proposed a centrally planned economy with a national planning board to determine needs and to allocate production accordingly, "a basis with which no clear-thinking person will take issue." Living standards would be greatly raised. The board would schedule about thirty years of work for each person, in a full employment scheme with individual choice of employment and location preserved. As for wages, "We set as a goal the securing of an equal income for all, male and female, without regard to race or color, as the ultimate solution to the wage question. Such income, once started, to continue beyond retirement from active work, until the end of life." This would function effectively "in leveling social, racial, economic barriers . . . foster Brotherly Love and a spirit of good-will . . . the Christian conscience should be satisfied with nothing less." Since wealth is the product of many brains and bodies, "it results because of common endeavor and should be owned in common."

Further, "We believe it possible to eliminate entirely the necessity for money, by broadening the use of credits now so well established in business transactions." Banks would be eliminated, leaving just one central national treasury with two functions: a clearing house for the distribution of national income and a bank for payment of international balances. The Statement concludes:

> What could be more fitting than that the group which fostered the abolition of Negro slavery, sponsored prison reform, gives testimony against war, initiated European Reconstruction, carries on American Friends' Service Work in the coal fields, should once again advance the outpost of civilization by carrying an easily understood message of economic reform to the world?[213]

This may be the most radical document ever presented to a major Quaker body for approval. It appears to have gone no further than a lively discussion at the round table. (I found no records of discussion or decision about it in Central Committee or Executive Committee minutes.) A remarkable Quaker document died a quiet death and was soon forgotten.

From another viewpoint, Deborah Haines reflects that by the 1920s:

> Liberal Friends were willing to tolerate differences of opinion and even welcome challenges to traditional wisdom. Some of the credit for this shift probably belongs to the existence of the structured forum for discussion provided by FGC's biennial conferences. The morning "roundtables" at these conferences routinely addressed controversial issues. Although the conference as a whole could and did issue statements on social policy from time to time, their

pronouncements were not binding on Friends, and failure to reach agreement had very little impact on the organization.[214]

Still, in June 1935 the Executive Committee instructed subcommittees not to issue controversial statements except on letterheads that listed the name of the sub-committee first and the name of Friends General Conference in smaller type below. There should also be a statement that the editor is solely responsible for the contents. Clearly the Industrial Relations Committee had ruffled some Quaker feathers.

This was the year that Robert LaFollette headed a reformulated Progressive Party which called itself "not liberal" but "radical" and advocated a "cooperative society." The Socialist Party enjoyed its zenith of popularity, and the Communist Party proposed a Soviet-style reconstruction of American society. Historian David Kennedy suggests that through his moderate tinkering with the capitalist system, Franklin Roosevelt was able to fend off more radical proposals from the left, as well as more reactionary elements on the right.[215] Both were intensifying during the mid-1930s.

A Query from a Young Friend

The 1934 Conference is surely among the most notable. Still, soon afterward, *The Friends Intelligencer* (9/8) led with an editorial (presumably by editor Sue Yerkes) titled "After the Conference—What?" What permanent value would come from the gathering? Lasting friendships were valuable, but what more? The addresses and discussions were stirring, but how could these build up the Society of Friends? "Are they just to evaporate into thin air?" These questions were posed as an introduction to an article by a young Friend, the twenty-four year-old Elizabeth Furnas: "Is There a Better Way?":

> A great concern in regard to the Friends General Conference has gripped my mind since before this last one which was so excellent of its kind. I feel we are in danger of repeating them of their own momentum without seriously considering what they are meaning to the life of American Quakerism as a whole. [The Conferences have been beneficial.] But our liberal religious tendencies have been

accentuated by dwelling on less controversial matters than belief, and we have concerned ourselves chiefly with the more general aspects of Quaker concerns and activities. By our actions we have said, "Other things matter more than our relationship to God." Yet a religious experience is certainly the source of spiritual power.

Consequently, Furnas found a serious lack of spiritual vitality among Conference Friends. She cited two indicators: no numerical increase in membership and a lifeless character in many meetings. Concentration upon testimonies and social concerns had neglected the religious message and experience basic to true Quakerism. Conferences didn't emphasize living in the love of God, the basis of all Quaker testimonies. She acknowledged that others would disagree, but it was clear that the Conferences were not producing lasting benefits. She suggested that smaller, regional summer schools, with real study and intimate fellowship, might prove more useful.

She also referenced the mood building among young Friends for reconciliation among the branches of American Quakers. "We must lose the life of the separate branches to find the life of American Quakerism. This is no idle play on words. It is a spiritual law, full of significance for us." At a recent seminar, young Friends had concluded, "The bringing together of the Orthodox and the Liberal points of view will be along lines of fresh experience and not of adjusted beliefs."

Furnas had met with the Central Committee during the Conference and shared her concerns with them. She urged that future Conferences be smaller and "held in a place where the resort features are less prominent and where it will be easier to hold real Friends Meetings for Worship. We need a Conference that will help make clear to us in a personal way the burning reality of our Quaker faith."

"Much sympathy was expressed with the concern of Elizabeth Furnas," but the Committee felt that the large Conference format was too popular to abandon. Perhaps round tables could become smaller, and more meetings for worship could be scheduled. They encouraged young Friends to organize smaller group meetings in preparation for future Conferences.

CHAPTER 5   An Expansive Depression

The Committee thus seized upon questions of format, not the more critical issue Furnas had raised regarding declining clarity and vitality of faith. We have heard brief, oblique criticisms before (such as "less information, more inspiration"), but Furnas articulated the concern more fully and pointedly. We shall hear this concern raised again, in the aftermath of the World Conference of Friends.

The Growing Influence of the AFSC

At an Executive Committee meeting in May 1936, Hannah Clothier Hull, Chair of the Social Service Section, expressed discouragement. Recent reports from yearly meetings either padded or understated the work being done by Friends. Three out of four yearly meeting chairmen wished to resign, feeling they were not accomplishing much. Other organizations were obviating their work. Deborah Haines points out that the Section had a small budget and no staff support. Moreover, lack of consensus over social testimonies was eroding the basis of action.[216] But AFSC's trail-blazing renown was no doubt a major factor, drawing the attention and support of many Friends.

The Executive Committee also pondered what FGC's relationship should be with AFSC's newly formed American Friends Fellowship Council (AFFC). They saw potential to broaden advancement activity by working with the AFFC "in the effort to extend Quakerism to the greatest possible degree." Some even wondered if FGC's Advancement program should be taken over by the AFFC. But it was clarified that the AFFC was less interested in "Advancement work as such" than to promote inter-visitation among Friends and to create interconnections among AFSC-inspired independent meetings.

Meanwhile, the AFSC and AFFC were initiating plans to hold a World Conference of Friends at Swarthmore and Haverford Colleges in the summer of 1937. Gregory Barnes suggests that the World Conference was calculated not only to advance convergence among Friends but to consolidate Quaker support for AFSC programs. Some Friends, Philadelphia Yearly Meeting Orthodox in particular, complained that the AFSC sought to place all Friends under its aegis.[217]

The 1936 Cape May Conference

Partly in response to concerns raised by Elizabeth Furnas, the Central Committee (10/35) chose to provide a large number of small devotional meetings all over Cape May for the 1936 Conference, with more round tables for adults and high school Friends on religious and devotional topics, with emphasis on mutual discussion rather than lecture. In addition, invitations were sent to the executive committee of the Five Years Meeting and to Philadelphia Yearly Meeting Orthodox Friends. (Some Friends had reservations about reconciliation among Friends. During the Conference, one Committee member cautioned, "We should not lose our identity in steps toward unity, co-operation and efficiency.")

The Committee also felt Friends were becoming lax on temperance since the repeal of Prohibition in 1933 and recommended that it be a major focus of the Conference. But temperance was not strongly featured in the final program. In general, the "purity" concern, so strong in the early decades, was fading among Conference Friends. But as we shall see, song and dance flourished.

A promotional leaflet for the 1936 Conference was titled, "Why I Can't Afford to Miss Cape May." The Friends quoted were generally from Philadelphia and the wider area of eastern Pennsylvania, New York and New Jersey. Some remarked on the daily opportunities for worship, song, and play. Others thrived on gaining new knowledge of social needs, combined with friendly fellowship. One recalled her first Conference in 1928, in particularly the opening procession with each yearly meeting's representatives marching across the stage. "For those of us who are members of outlying meetings there is a feeling of unity with the rest of the Society." Another chirped, "I'm 95 and I can't afford to miss these Conferences." Others mentioned the open sea, morning walks on the beach, and singing around a bonfire on the last evening. Hence, it appears that motivations were at least as much affective and recreational as devotional or informational.

Cape May was hard-pressed to provide enough spaces for all the small-group discussion and devotional opportunities planned for this Conference. In her "Story of the Conference" (FI 7/18-8/2/1936),

CHAPTER 5   An Expansive Depression

Anna Curtis noted that 900 had registered by the second day, with 134 in the Junior Conference. There were so many high-school-aged Friends that the two round tables originally planned for them had to be expanded to four. She marveled, "This may become a Young Friends Conference."

There were seventeen round tables in all this year, counting the four high-school ones. Ten of them focused on subjects of Quaker faith, in anticipation of the next year's World Conference of Friends. Chairman Arthur Jackson described this as a "preparatory Conference" for that purpose. Since the 1920 All Friends Conference in London, half a dozen new yearly meetings had sprung up in Europe, and international conferences among European Friends had been held annually since 1930. Eight languages would be spoken next year at the World Conference. Curtis reflected, "We have long been accustomed to say (most of us), with a vague internationalism, 'Our field is the world.' We must learn to realize that this is literal truth." (Her perspective was still Anglo-American, but starting to open out.) She concluded, "1937 will probably influence Quaker thought and action for years to come. Our Conference this summer and our later deliberations [studying advance materials in local meetings] will help shape that meeting. The responsibility lies heavy on every one of us to share in that study" (FI 7/18).

Conference book sales continued to grow, with more than $300 in receipts in the exhibit room. Furniture made by AFSC's Mountaineer Craftsmen's Cooperative Association in West Virginia was also sold.[218] This Conference featured dancing in the convention hall every night—except Sunday—after the evening lecture. The good orchestra drew almost everyone in.

The Conference strove to clarify a distinctively Quaker faith with addresses by Patrick Murphy Malin, professor of economics at Swarthmore, Harold Speight, dean of men at Swarthmore, Bliss Forbush, executive secretary of Baltimore Yearly meeting, George Walton, principal of George School, Jesse Holmes, now retired from teaching at Swarthmore, and Brand Blanshard, his replacement there. None offered a compelling statement. Three different speakers emphasized "We have no creed." One called Quakerism more "a philosophy of life." For all their efforts, it seemed that these weighty

Jane Rushmore. Courtesy of Friends Historical Library of Swarthmore College.

Quaker men only confirmed the concern young Elizabeth Furnas had expressed two years before.

A more engaging talk came from Jane Rushmore, general secretary of Philadelphia Yearly Meeting. It was her first appearance as a Conference plenary speaker, though she had been an influential Friend in FGC circles for many years by now. We noted her in Chapter 1 as an emerging leader among young Friends in the 1890s. She was already assistant clerk of the FUPL in 1900 and was then hired by FGC's Religious Education Committee to advance their work. The same year as this Conference, FGC published her *Testimonies and Practice of the Society of Friends*. Much of the material had developed out of her many years (1916 to 1945) of writing FGC's First-Day School Bulletins for both adults and children. The book's 172 pages

CHAPTER 5   An Expansive Depression

probably provide the best normative statement of FGC Quakerism in this period. As the title suggests, it is not a statement of faith, but of testimonies and practice. In her Foreword, Rushmore explains:

> Since our religious profession is based on experience with the doctrine of the Inner Light as its center, no one is commissioned to speak for the entire membership except with historical statements.... The lack of [creedal] statements is an essential corollary to any non-authoritative religion.... We do not deny any doctrine not in accord with our experience but we do not accept formulated historical creeds which, in general, do not accord with the experience of Friends, and are often outdated by modern reverent scholarship. We base our religious profession on a direct and first-hand knowledge of God and its expression in conduct, commonly called "a way of life."

In "Quakerism Faces the Future," Rushmore addressed the Conference in terms both promising and admonitory. She noted that "the barriers which separate the divisions in the Society are crumbling." Friends were becoming more tolerant toward one another and toward the world. But she warned of attendant dangers:

> It is easy to become tolerant because we do not care, rather than we care so much.... [For example, in] abolishing special symbols of simplicity, the testimony for simplicity may get into the discard. ... In our desire to be active we may spend our energies in poorly coordinated effort to be busy about something.

She also countenanced the rising profile of young Friends coming into maturity. "We should furnish them with compasses and familiarize them with the guide posts for experience. They must be free to explore. They will change the Society of Friends no doubt. Our concern is not that they shall not change it, but that they shall change it for the better." Meetings for worship needed revitalization. She wondered if there was some "technique of worship" that Friends no longer understood. Moreover, "We discourse much about vocal ministry, but have little to say about the conditions out of which vocal expression comes, except that we meet on a basis of silence."

Like many FGC leaders of this era, she spoke as a rational Friend, confident in the advances of science and technology. "The mystical approach will always remain more or less incomprehensible to them whose spiritual equipment comes through explicable means." It may come through "the channel of directed thought." Henry Cadbury made a similar point that same year in a lecture at the Harvard Divinity School titled, "My Personal Religion." He suggested that while Quakerism has a "large mystical strain" in its history, "I am quite convinced that it has never been general and that a large number of nonmystics have enjoyed religious life under its auspices and have contributed much that Friends have done for human good."[219] He was unwilling to claim anything in his own experience as mystical.

Rushmore concluded with a challenge to Friends: "Are we prepared to be pioneers in our generation? Or are we satisfied to adjust to prevalent ideas and customs in the name of tolerance and liberality to such an extent that our distinctive mission as a religious society is largely lost? . . . A confused world needs us" (FI 8/22). Jane Rushmore offered a balance of affirmation and criticism with the credibility of a Friend with long years of service among Friends.

With an eye toward the World Conference, Clarence Pickett continued to advocate international visitation among Friends. He suggested that the past twenty years had renewed the international outreach of early Friends. He set the world Quaker population at 160,000 with 130,000 living in the US and Great Britain, and eight thousand in Africa. Smaller groups had spread around the world. (In her talk, Rushmore counted fifty-six yearly meetings of Friends on four continents. The six yearly meetings of FGC had slipped a little lower in numbers, to 16,222. Most of the shrinkage occurred outside Philadelphia Yearly Meeting, which now accounted for 55 percent of all Conference Friends.) But Pickett emphasized that inter-visitation was not just about Anglo-Saxons carrying the message abroad. It also included receiving with humility the message from Africans, Asians, Arabs, and Europeans. "We stand in need of the fellowship and courage that can come to us from Friends in other lands" (FI 8/22). Pickett moved beyond the Anglo-American perspective more clearly than any other Quaker speaker in Conferences to date.

Henry Cadbury spoke on "The Quaker Concern for Academic Freedom." He found academic freedom under attack in Europe and the US. (Cadbury himself had been forced out of teaching at

CHAPTER 5 An Expansive Depression

Henry Cadbury. Pendle Hill files.

Haverford College during the war, after he had written an editorial for a local newspaper lamenting popular prejudices against German-Americans.) Some colleges and universities were firing professors for their socialist or pacifist views. He added, "You all remember the experience of Rachel Davis DuBois." (We noted earlier, in Chapter 4 that she had left teaching at a high school in New Jersey in 1929 due to controversy around her teaching of interracial respect.) Cadbury found that 15 percent of adult Quaker members were presently teachers. He described education as one of the slow, peaceful methods Friends utilize to work for social change, boosting liberal public opinion and showing the futility of suppression (FI 8/1).

Cadbury also announced during the conference that Anna and Howard Brinton had agreed to come to Pendle Hill in the fall, as Director and Director of Education respectively. This began the golden age of Pendle Hill's collaboration with the AFSC, which continued to the end of the 1940s. Pendle Hill offered the spiritual grounding for AFSC's wide-ranging work in the world, while the AFSC kept Pendle Hill's community from becoming too inward-looking. In 1940,

Cadbury called the AFSC and Pendle Hill "the obverse and reverse of the same good currency of American Quakerism."[220]

The Friends World Conference of 1937

Nearly a thousand Friends from twenty-four countries attended the event on the Swarthmore and Haverford campuses in early September 1937. Eight countries not represented at the All-Friends Conference at Oxford in 1920 sent representatives: Cuba, Mexico, Austria, Czechoslovakia, Germany, the Netherlands, Sweden, and Switzerland. These gains represented not only British and American Friends Service Committee outreach in Europe but also Five Years Meeting missions to Latin America and the Caribbean. At least twenty-three of the twenty-five yearly meetings in the US had representation. American Friends accounted for 754 of the 985 delegates, British Friends 118. It was still a strongly Anglo-American event. But given a worldwide Depression, the growing international representation was significant. The total number of official delegates were almost equally men and women. The Conference approved establishing a worldwide committee to promote ongoing international contacts and cooperation among Friends.[221] By the following year, the Friends World Committee for Consultation was founded. That same summer, the founding conference of the World Council of Churches was held at Oxford. Thus, in the face of growing nationalism and the threat of war, religious internationalism and ecumenism also surged.

Rufus Jones was asked to preside over the Conference, to which he reluctantly agreed. In a letter the preceding July to Violet Holdsworth, he confided:

> In regard to the World Conference, I sincerely hope for good results, but I have become a good deal disillusioned over "big" conferences and large gatherings. I pin my hopes to quiet processes and small circles, in which vital and transforming events take place. But others see differently, and I respect their judgment.[222]

This comment may explain why Jones spoke at only two FGC Conferences. In any event, he gave the "Broadcast Message" for this Conference. Jones set Friends apart from the larger ecumenical movement; Quakerism is not as a sect cut off behind "the Protestant body, entrenched behind theological parapets. It is a spiritual movement, at heart mystical, i.e. seeking fellowship with God, and in its practical purpose dedicated to the realization of a universal Kingdom of God in the world of men." He referred several times to "the Quaker philosophy of life."[223]

Fellowship-worship groups were a prominent feature of the event. The whole Conference was divided into groups of about forty, intentionally mixed according to geographical and religious backgrounds, meeting for ninety minutes each morning. Two leaders facilitated each group, which spent time in worship first and then devoted the remaining time in discussion, with no set topics. The method succeeded in a variety of ways and produced high levels of group unity. Sympathetic consideration for opposing opinions was reported, though groups faced the usual problem of "the professional talker with his set piece." Sharing personal histories was effective in breaking down barriers. Some found these groups the best part of the Conference. Although these groups of forty were still large, they demonstrated results along lines Jones suggested in the letter quoted above.

"The Contribution of Negroes to the Education of Friends"

As the American Quaker frame of reference slowly became more international, it also struggled to become more interracial. Later in 1937, Henry Cadbury published an article in *The Friend* (12/16) with the above title, an ironic inversion of the commonly held satisfaction that Friends had contributed to the education of negroes. He suggested that African Americans had quietly educated Friends all along in advancing their attitudes toward slavery, race, and discrimination. The final two paragraphs of the article are particularly arresting:

> Taking the Society of Friends as it is today, its education by the Negro is still quite incomplete. In some ways we are less open to their useful influence than we were generations ago. We understand less imaginatively their less spectacular sufferings, and we no

longer invite upon ourselves the same persecution, ostracism and loss that our grandfathers did who worked for the slave or freedman. In spite of their growing culture we are not intimate with them in any level, not even of intellectual fellowship or of worship. The mores of the dominant white group tend to suppress that inherited independence of democratic Quaker fellowship and vigorous social conscience which should be the cherished birthright of every Friend.

As we look back over our past we do well to appreciate what we owe to them. How often have they summoned us to courage and action from self-complacency and ease. How often they have reinforced our faith in man, how often they have justified the trust we have reposed in them, and how often they have taught us the very tenets of our own religion. Whatever the future may hold in store for the African race, may we share their joys and sorrows, their successes and defeats. May they admit us into the fellowship of their problems and may the Society of Friends be teachable and quick to receive the contribution that the Negro race has yet to make to our education. In that lively hope for the future the Quaker says to the Negro, "we thank you for what you have already made us learn."

As noted occasionally in this book, as Friends entered the liberal-progressive mainstream, the same mainstream entered Friends, expanding their vision in some ways, limiting it in others. Cadbury's trenchant comments take their place alongside the dialogical round tables led by Rachel Davis DuBois and the AFSC's Interracial Section during this passage in the long Quaker struggle toward greater racial awareness and engagement.

CHAPTER 6

War Without, Reassessment Within
FGC Conferences 1938–1944

The Quakers have worked throughout the world to make the teachings of Christ in their inner reality effective in actual life.

— Albert Einstein,
1938 commencement address, Swarthmore College

But let us make no mistake. The Society of Friends as you and I know it is very far from this kingdom which we dimly see and seek.... The wide breach between our notions of fellowship and our conduct concerning race may be one of the emerging signs of our decline and lack of significance unless we face it squarely.... We shall suffer from anemia and weakness... until we discover these deeper levels of human nature, for the lack of which we so often live a superficial and meaningless existence.

— Clarence Pickett,
address to the 1942 Cape May Conference

World prospects continued to darken in 1938. Franklin Roosevelt's New Deal programs had eased the worst effects of the Great Depression for many, but they had not revived the American economy. By 1938, the New Deal was floundering. In Europe, the Spanish Civil War precipitated the first clash with Fascist nationalism, with more serious threats rising in Italy and Germany. In American politics, Roosevelt held an uneasy center against restive elements on both the left and the right.

Meanwhile, three-quarters of African Americans remained bottled up in the South, the poorest population of the nation's poorest region. Nearly 90 percent of black families there lived below the poverty line. A third were sharecroppers or tenant farmers; three-quarters had not finished high school. With Jim Crow still regnant, less than 5 percent of African Americans could vote.

Rumbles of Liberal Discontent

The 1937 Oxford Conference of Christian churches that led to the founding of the World Council of Churches, and the World Conference of Friends the same summer near Philadelphia (treated near the end of the preceding chapter) were expressions of faith communities rallying together as never before, to face these sobering prospects. Both were largely the fruits of liberal renewal in Christian churches and in the Society of Friends. The World Conference of Friends was predominantly positive in mood, uniting Friends behind the pioneering work of the American and British Friends Service Committees. But the Oxford Conference countenanced the growing threats more gravely. Right after the 1938 Cape May Conference had concluded, *Friends Intelligencer* editor Sue Yerkes chose to publish two articles by Lewis Benson in successive issues (FI 7/2 and 7/9), an alarm to Friends starker than the one Elizabeth Furnas had issued following the 1934 Conference.

At that time, Lewis Benson was the meeting secretary to the Evanston Friends Meeting near Chicago, helping them transition to a non-pastoral basis. He had previously been at Pendle Hill building their library. Before that, he had studied early Friends for several months with H. G. Wood at Woodbrooke, the Quaker study center in Birmingham, England. He was also influenced by the neo-orthodox theology of Emil Brunner and others, which led him to question the liberal gloss Rufus Jones and others had placed over the early Quaker message and movement.[224]

In the first article, "The New Orthodoxy," Benson characterized the mood of crisis set by the Oxford Conference. Christians were discovering that their faith and its culture were no longer the foundation of western civilization, and "the weakness of liberal Christianity's

CHAPTER 6   War Without, Reassessment Within

Lewis and Sarah Benson. Courtesy of Friends Historical Library of Swarthmore College.

optimistic activism" had become clear. He quoted from recent editorials from *The Christian Century*, the standard of liberal religion in America:

> There can be no Christianity without a theology. Those who most loudly decry theology do so in the interest of a theology they stupidly refuse to examine. For the Christian church to follow the lead of those who advocate practical religion at the expense of sound thinking on the great realities of faith is suicidal.
>
> What the church testifies to, what it does, merely by being itself, is not only primary, but far more important in the saving of civilization than anything it can ever do in direct social action.

Benson commented, "This is an astonishing statement from the editor of a religious journal which has so long been preoccupied with programs for Christian social action." After a quarter-century trying to "apply" Christianity, liberal Christians were starting to search for the faith itself. "What was the gospel?"

That question served as the title of Benson's sequel in the *The Intelligencer*'s next issue, as he brought these wider Christian concerns to bear upon the Society of Friends. He began by noting that liberal Friends had largely followed the trend of liberal Protestantism.

"We have shown many of the characteristics that are now seriously questioned by leading liberal thinkers." Shrugging off theological questions as irrelevant and focusing instead on social reform had led to a loss of vitality in group worship. He found it "remarkable that our Society shows so little alarm."

Comparing current Quaker trends with the witness of early Friends, Benson concluded, "There is really little in common with Fox's distrust of school theology and our contempt for theology in general." The social conduct of early Friends as testimony to the power of the gospel "is scarcely the equivalent of our feverish efforts to improve the world. . . . We have been more than ready to accept uncritically the dictum of William James that modern Christian liberalism is merely a reversion to essential Quakerism." Modern Quakerism and liberal Protestantism are much more alike than either is with early Quakerism:

> Soon or late our program of good works will also become bogged and we will be forced to ask ourselves "What was the gospel?" What was that gospel for which the Boston martyrs were hanged for trying to preach? What was the "good news" for which the early Friends were willing to spend the best years of their lives in prison? What seeker on coming to our meetings today will hear this good news or feel his heart secretly touched? . . . Our strategy for world peace has rested on ideologies that were partly Christian, but very largely secular ideologies. Now these secular ideologies are disintegrating.
>
> We are told that "theology and belief are unimportant as long as you have the real spiritual experience." But any concept of "spiritual experience" which does not affect our religious convictions is a sub-Quaker conception of spirituality. Real spiritual life does not thrive where there are no religious convictions.

The decision by Sue Yerkes and her editorial board to publish articles by Lewis Benson and Elizabeth Furnas along with Conference proceedings suggests that they found these Friends articulating a concern among FGC Friends that did not find representation in Conference programming. Perhaps a liberal-progressive orthodoxy had taken control of Conference planning in a manner similar to what Progressive Friends had deplored in the select meetings of ministers and elders in the preceding century.

CHAPTER 6   War Without, Reassessment Within

Other rumbles of a more intergenerational discontent can also be heard. In 1937, the Religious Education Committee of Philadelphia Yearly Meeting asked FGC's Central Committee to create more programs for adolescent Friends. A High School Section was created "to use up their very abundant energy" (Executive Committee, 10/1937). Minutes do not mention whether there had been behavioral problems at the 1936 Conference. In any case, restive energies among young Friends were contained but also focused and intensified in new directions over the coming decade by this addition to Conference programming.

The 1938 Cape May Conference

The advance publicity brochure for the Conference was titled "A Typical Day at Cape May" and began, "Here we gather strength and help to do that clear thinking which we all want to do. Conflict is everywhere—personal and social, industrial, racial and international." The Conference day began with a plenary lecture at 9:30 followed by round tables at 11:00. Some were for the usual discussion of issues. But others would be "worship-fellowship groups combining discussion and silent meditation as at the World Conference." (These served as the main opportunity for worship at this Conference.) The brochure also mentions the new section for senior high school Friends. Meanwhile, "the sea beckons from dawn 'til moonlight. In the afternoon it holds full sway" with opportunities for socializing on the boardwalk, play on the beach, tennis, and so on. Evenings would feature singing before the lecture, followed by social events at the hotels, music, dancing, games, or beach bonfires with old-fashioned songs.

Notes from one of the worship-fellowship groups[225] testify to the value of worship, sharing of experiences, and small-group dynamics in working for peace and justice: "We need training in the ethics of sharing." Small groups form "a basis for the right understanding of our problems," through listening for the voice of God "beyond what words can utter." Topics for discussion were chosen by the group itself, as facilitated by its two leaders. Some of these comments about small-group work are much along lines Richard Gregg advocated in

Poster for the 1938 Conference. Friends General Conference Records, Friends Historical Library of Swarthmore College.

Training for Peace (1936). In "The Story of the Conference" (FI 7/9-8/6/1938) Anna Curtis noted that the ten round tables and eight worship-fellowship groups made for the most small groups ever, spread all over Cape May. Clearly, the World Conference left its mark on this gathering. Small groups attained greater spiritual intimacy than was possible in the large early morning devotional meetings of previous Conferences.

The Conference theme was "World Conflict Tests the Way of Love." Chairman Arthur Jackson opened the first session with a reading from Romans 12: "Present your bodies as a living sacrifice, holy, acceptable to God," intimating the challenging times ahead for pacifists. Nevertheless, the usual festive reception followed the session, with the "grand march" of Friends snaking around the hall, greeting one another. Then the dancing.

Frank Aydelotte, still president of Swarthmore College, spoke on "Education for Peace." Citing the challenges of a rapidly changing society, he concluded, "The task of training men and women to meet these demands ... is indeed a staggering one. Perhaps it is impossible. As to that no man can say, but ... it is the only true education for peace" (FI 7/9). Aydelotte's Sisyphean overtones were answered by Alexander Purdy of Hartford Theological Seminary in terms more akin to Lewis Benson's. In "The Distinctive Contribution of Religion to Human Conflict" he countered the pragmatic definition of religion often heard from Jesse Holmes and others: "Testing of religion by its human consequences must not be confused with superficial talk about 'using' religion for social ends. ... If religion is 'for' anything, it is only for itself–that is to achieve the meeting, colloquy and mutual love of God and man." It has its own validity. First, it "nourishes the dignity of human personality;" second, it "nourishes a unique kind of human fellowship;" and third, it may "contribute in a nervous world, centers of light rather than heat" (FI 7/16).

Round tables such as "Revitalizing the Quaker Message" and "Quaker Ministry" seemed to spark no new fire, however. Reports of the discussions repeated the usual tropes: It is a mistake to say we have no ministers, we are all ministers; Friends *do* believe in the Inner Light; ministry must be based upon experience; the AFSC is a model for all of us to emulate individually; do we need more publicity? (FI 7/30).

Three Friends spoke in the final session in "Evaluations of the Conference." George Walton, principal of the George School, enthused:

> What a contrast ... between the tangle of insoluble conflicts and the amazing joy, sheer happiness, in being together. Oh! the power that there is in enjoying life as God means us to enjoy life! We are not going home this afternoon bowed down with fear. Grim forebodings of disaster are not supreme in our minds and feelings [FI 8/13].

This was not an outstanding Conference in terms of plenary addresses. I found little worth mentioning from what appeared in the *Intelligencer*. But the growing small-group dynamics and the broader affects of reunion and mutual encouragement offered respite, at least, from the melancholy of a devastating outlook. For some, the Conference would transmute melancholy to the spleen of renewed service and a more robust pacifist resistance.

To Be or Not to Be Ecumenical

Later in 1938 the Central and Executive Committees began what proved to be a decade-long journey into membership in the World Council of Churches. They were approached at that time by both the WCC and the International Association for Liberal Christianity and Religious Freedom. Initially, Bliss Forbush suggested that "our place" was with the latter, an organization Friends (particularly Henry Wilbur and Jesse Holmes) had helped to found. Membership in the organization had lapsed due to some technicality.

In November 1939, FGC received a formal letter of invitation from the World Council in Geneva. Arthur Jackson responded, stating FGC's "hope that their creedal statement and formula would be omitted or changed so that we might unite with them" (Executive Committee, 7/40). The WCC described itself as churches that "accept our Lord Jesus Christ as God and Saviour." Ultimately, the decision would have to be made individually by the six constituent yearly meetings (Ohio Yearly Meeting had been laid down a decade earlier). The Five Years Meeting was clear to join the WCC in October 1940. The WCC responded with at least a provisional acceptance when FGC suggested an alternative basis of membership: inward experience and love of God and neighbor. In September 1941, Forbush recommended to FGC's Central Committee that they proceed with the WCC and become a financially contributing

CHAPTER 6   War Without, Reassessment Within

member, until or unless they were formally rejected. That uncertain status continued until FGC's membership was finally confirmed in 1948, when the WCC held its first formal assembly in Amsterdam.

In 1941, Arthur Jackson retired from FGC's chairmanship after twenty-one years, succeeded by Bliss Forbush, now teaching at the Baltimore Friends School (he became principal there in 1943, serving until his retirement in 1960). Forbush represented FGC at the 1948 WCC Assembly in Amsterdam.

Meanwhile, inter-Quaker *rapprochement* progressed. The Central Committee had invited new and independent meetings to send a visitor or unofficial representative to the 1938 Conference. Indeed, several independent meetings (somehow) already had members serving on the Central Committee. The Five Years Meeting Executive Committee and Philadelphia Yearly Meeting Orthodox were also invited to the Conference.

War: Crisis and Opportunity

As war broke out in Europe in 1939, interest in the Society of Friends grew. Albert Martin of the Executive Committee urged, "This crisis that faces the world today is our opportunity, and we should grasp it." One response was William Hubben's booklet, "Who Are These Friends?" published by FGC that year. It had already sold 1,500 copies by November. FGC also distributed AFSC's *Handbook for Conscientious Objectors* "to help educate our membership" in making decisions about military service (Central Committee, 9/39).

The Central Committee also drafted a minute of protest against the Congressional bill to authorize renewed military conscription, calling it

> A negation of the right of conscience, and a denial of religious freedom. It is a violation of the fundamental concepts of democracy. It tends to a system of life and type of government in which the individual becomes subservient to the state. We appreciate the duties and responsibilities of citizenship, especially in these times, and are eager to perform constructive service for the community, but are unwilling to grant the right of the state to conscript its citizens for services which they hold to be morally wrong.

The minute was approved at the 1940 Conference.

The year 1940 was decisive for the peace movement. That year the peace evangelist Kirby Page traveled seventeen thousand miles speaking against war. The Quaker FOR activist A. J. Muste gave ninety-eight talks in three months. But as the mainstream movement buckled before the compelling threats in Europe and Asia, more committed pacifists drew together into a decidedly resistant and countercultural mode. Patricia Appelbaum, in *Kingdom to Commune: Protestant Pacifist Culture between World War I and the Vietnam Era*,[226] charts this transformation, the influence of Richard Gregg, and the rising profile of FGC Quakerism. In the process, pacifism became less a broadly Christian movement and more a sectarian, folk culture in resistance to society's larger movements and institutions. Quaker meetings and particularly Pendle Hill became beacons of encouragement to pacifists who felt increasingly censured by their mainstream peers. Pacifism, and with it liberal Friends, became more subversive and marginal in profile. Along the way, ties with the wider Christian churches weakened. Pacifism was measured less by Christian standards than Christianity by pacifist standards. Pacifism came to be viewed as inherently universalist.

The three Historic Peace Churches—Mennonites, Brethren, and Friends—were able to negotiate conscientious objection status and alternative service provisions with the federal government. The Civilian Public Service was formed in 1940 through their intense lobbying. Bliss Forbush, who had been a conscientious objector in World War I, organized one of the first camps. Nearly twelve thousand men participated in them, about half of them Mennonites and Brethren. Quakers accounted for 951 of them. One-eighth were mainline Protestants from eight different denominations. Of these, Methodists were the largest group at 673.[227] Friends administered twenty of the camps, with 3,400 men. The camps included some nonreligious conscientious objectors, who sometimes brought more conflict and alienation than the organizers anticipated. But the camps also served as intensive centers for radical pacifism and social change thought. Muste, Gregg, and Douglas Steere of Haverford College taught nonviolent theory and practice in at least one camp. By the end of the war, a cohort of new pacifist leadership emerged from the camps, to be influential for decades to come.

CHAPTER 6   War Without, Reassessment Within

Poster for the 1940 Conference. Friends General Conference Records, Friends Historical Library of Swarthmore College.

The 1940 Cape May Conference

As war engulfed Europe, the wider peace movement crumbled. FGC stubbornly chose to look beyond the war before the US had even

Cover graphic for the High School Section program. Friends General Conference Records, Friends Historical Library of Swarthmore College.

entered it. The theme this year was "Building for the World of Tomorrow." The optimistic ideology of "evolution" was now long gone, and the rhetoric of "progress" largely implicit. But the commitment to human betterment was still abundantly clear. The advance brochure for the new High School Section had a modernist graphic of a family of four climbing up steps to "The World of Tomorrow" with sun breaking through the clouds. If the "escalator of progress" had stalled, Friends would take the stairs.

The advance program for the General Conference featured a drawing of a small group studying together on the beach: "All ye young and old come to Cape May and work together for a world at peace."

Frances Hart Burke replaced Anna Curtis in reporting "The Story of the Conference" (FI 7/20-8/10/1940). World crisis brought 1600 Friends to Cape May, perhaps the largest attendance since FGC's first decade. Chairing his last Conference, Arthur Jackson opened the sessions by noting, "We are meeting under darker skies than at any time in the twenty years I have been your presiding officer." Accordingly, Alexander Purdy took Hebrews 12:25-29 as the basis for his opening address, "Foundations That Cannot Be Shaken" (FI 7/20). In a time of crisis, religion needs to be affirmative: declaring faith in a moral power that holds the course of history; upholding the supremacy of personal values against the

Cover graphic for the advance 1940 program. Friends General Conference Records, Friends Historical Library of Swarthmore College.

totalitarian state; finding the supremacy of love beyond all conflicts. These foundations cannot be shaken. Purdy's affirmations were an insistence upon a historic faith applied to changing circumstances, rather than the progressive revelation of new truths.

Frank Aydelotte, recently retired from Swarthmore College and now director of the Institute for Advanced Study at Princeton, spoke on "Federal Union" (FI 7/20). For the second time in the century, the future of democracy was seriously in question. Either the crumbling world order would be replaced by despotism, or international democracy might accomplish for the world what the Constitution of the United States brought on a smaller scale to the confusion and conflicts among early American states. The opportunity for such a federal union might yet come. The United States would need to discard short-sighted isolationism and take the lead. Aydelotte's comments anticipate developments soon to come. At the start of 1942, Franklin Roosevelt announced the Declaration by United Nations, already approved by some world leaders, to begin the process that would create the United Nations after the war. Then in July 1944, a conference of forty-four Allied nations at Bretton Woods, New Hampshire mapped out the economic arrangements for the postwar world, including the World Trade Organization, International Monetary Fund, and the World Bank.

Patrick Murphy Malin, economics professor at Swarthmore College, had taken a leave of absence earlier in the year to work for the government's aid to European children. In "The Moral Equivalent of War," he anticipated the temptation many young Friends would feel to join in military service against palpable evil. He reaffirmed the peace testimony of Friends: "We must serve not by inappropriate ways disapproved by our consciences but by hardship and difficulties and danger. For those with eyes to see, there is the moral equivalent of war." Elton Trueblood, professor of religion and chaplain at Stanford University, also reflected on the challenges for Friends. "Inasmuch as we have no creed to which we can appeal and no hierarchy to decide for us, we need to come together for practical help in mutual counsel" (FI 7/27).

Clarence Pickett continued to balance inward and outward, as he had done at the preceding Conference. The recent notoriety of

CHAPTER 6 War Without, Reassessment Within

Quaker work had led some to view the Society of Friends as "a kind of social service agency." But present work built upon the conviction of Quaker ancestors that "the primary fact of human beings is that they are children of God and are of inestimable worth." That perspective would be vital at a time when Americans were torn between allegiance to government and allegiance to conscience. "Are Friends bad citizens?" Some thought so. (Appelbaum comments on the turn from heroic to ironic overtones in pacifist rhetoric at this time. After World War I pacifists had viewed themselves as torch bearers of a future world. Now they embraced the world's judgment upon them as misfits and subversives.) Pickett answered that perception with a query:

> Do you put your dependence in the army and navy for security, or do you find ways of becoming the instruments of the power and the spirit so that you can meet situations which the army and navy try to meet? . . . More than we need money or any kind of recognition, more than anything else, we need a deepening consciousness of our religious faith.

In AFSC's work, "Almost miracles sometimes happen. Hearts and spirits of military men and dictators soften. This comes true largely in proportion to the depth of our religious faith."

Pickett accentuated the *prophetic* aspect of this faith. "Isaiah and Jeremiah [were] two young men who stood pretty much alone within their own groups." They believed that God is in this world and that we can be instruments for the interpretation of divine purposes. Jeremiah could see even the fall of Jerusalem and the exile of his people as an *opportunity* to share their faith with a wider world. That kind of insight requires strong foundations:

> I do not know whether you feel keenly what a loss it is not to get to meeting. . . . I have no disposition to dictate as to what people should do on Sunday morning, but we are talking of things that need to concern us as a Society of Friends. . . . When I miss [meeting] I miss something needed to face the decisions and perplexities of the next week. . . . We must feel always the need to readjusting our "sights". . . . We need to prepare ourselves to express in *words* as well as in *deeds* what is the basis of the external life people see.

Bliss Forbush. Courtesy of Friends Historical Library of Swarthmore College.

Pickett consistently opted to speak in positive terms, but clearly he was concerned for the spiritual foundations of a Society of Friends entering a time of testing. "I covet for Friends that kind of poise in life" like Jeremiah's, to find opportunity even in disaster. He concluded, "We cannot say which comes first—works or worship."

Pickett also reflected, "I have a notion... that we have only served in a rather crude and unscientific way." AFSC's work thus far was "really a prelude to the service we may render on a wider scale and on a more intelligent basis" (FI 8/17). Gregory Barnes[228] notes that the AFSC grew in complexity through the 1930s and was starting to professionalize during the war, partly in order to meet the challenges of negotiating with hostile nations. In the long term, that

CHAPTER 6   War Without, Reassessment Within

trend would contribute to a drift in relations between the AFSC and the Society of Friends. But for the present, the AFSC had become the gold standard of liberal Quakerism in America. At a round table on "The Friends' Message," one Friend described the local meeting as "a community outpost of the Service Committee."

Bliss Forbush spoke more bluntly than Pickett, in a direct critique of the state of the Society. With Conference membership sinking to 16,007 he asked, what hinders growth? Some factors were *class-bound*. Friends had lost the ability to speak to all conditions:

> Today we have become a middle-class group reaching merchants, semi-professional and professional men in the cities, and the farm owners in rural areas. We do not reach lower income groups. This may be ... due to the manner in which we express our religious faith. I hope it is not due to an unexpressed but real denial of the inherent worth of *all* men. Sometimes Friends act as though a Meeting should be made up of one social class or type of individual. Some Friends are concerned over admitting into membership recent arrivals from Europe, and others act on the assumption that all Friends should belong to one political party. We have unconsciously developed an exclusiveness which repels.

This is the first time these issues of economic class and social status were directly confronted in a Conference address. The advent of new meetings in cities and in campus towns accentuated trends that had been growing for decades.

Forbush then confronted the state of Quaker *worship and ministry*. Newcomers needed to hear the great truths of the Christian faith and their relation to personal experience and to the times:

> Too often there is not a single person, to say nothing of several persons, willing to accept the responsibility and to use what talents and training they have, to think through the great problems of life, to become acquainted with some of the material that has been accumulated through the ages in effort to answer these problems, and to express the resultant ideas for the benefit of the group. We believe that God may speak through any individual member of a Friends Meeting.... But in many areas Meetings will dwindle unless more of our members accept the responsibility of preparation of mind and spirit for vocal ministry.

We have heard this concern growing over the decades. But Forbush more compellingly placed it in context with other issues. In regard to the *social testimonies* and other areas of Quaker practice, "We recognize the statements in our Discipline as goals toward which we should strive, but we fall so far short of their attainment that it is possible to question whether we have in any sense come as close to their realization as could be expected of us." Liberal Quakerism had turned testimonies into ideals, which could be praised without practice, the very thing that early Friends had criticized about "professing" Christians and their creeds.

In terms similar to those we heard from Henry Cadbury at the end of the preceding chapter, Forbush also pressed the issue of race:

> There was a time when the Society of Friends stood in the first rank in the matter of inter-racial betterment. We still hold in theory to the belief in that of God in all men and we profess that in all human relations God's universal Fatherhood should prevent our making any distinction of class, station, wealth, color or race. And yet we are not leaders in the movements of our time which seek to free the Negro from political, economic, and social handicaps, and it may be said that the attitude of the average Friend toward minority groups is little different from that of his non-Quaker neighbor.

Forbush then went after the most cherished Quaker ideal, peace: "Matters pertaining to peace and war received full attention during the Conference." Each meeting had a strong peace "bloc." And young Friends were often the most loyal to the peace testimony:

> But we often hear rationalizations of war among us today such as "This war is different, civilization is at stake. . . ." Can we say, in the words of the Discipline, that we stand for "an inviolable peace" when so many of our members are as confused and hesitant as at present? . . . It would be no disgrace for an individual to be forced to admit to his inability to live up to the requirements of the Sermon on the Mount. . . . The danger lies in becoming complacent or in assuming that we have achieved a greater degree of success than is the case.

As an FGC insider, Forbush could press the case more plainly than Gurneyite visitors like Rufus Jones and Clarence Pickett dared.

CHAPTER 6 War Without, Reassessment Within

"We are a RELIGIOUS Society of Friends. We are more than an organization for humanitarian deeds, and what is done for the good of humanity is done because of religious motives." Without spiritual nourishment, spiritual sensitivity was blunted. Friends were missing the finer distinctions between right and wrong, making compromises, and were overcome by the world:

> The Bible is one of the means of nourishing the soul, yet it may be said with fairness that this generation knows less about it than any generation in the past, in spite of the tools of literary and historical study which are now available.... How many Friends are able to turn at will to those eternal and sublime passages which have been the spiritual meat of mightier men than we?

Perhaps it was his attention to wider ecumenical relations, combined with the crisis of war, that accentuated Forbush's perspective on the Quaker condition. In any case, he finished with a stark assessment:

> If the Society of Friends is but another sect, made up of individuals who have certain peculiar ways of doing things, and who give lip service to the ideals of their high-minded forerunners, it is not needed in a world already overcrowded with denominations. But the Society of Friends can be a channel through which God can work [8/31].

Ironically, Forbush repeated in slightly altered form the same critique liberal-progressive Friends had made of the quietist tradition. Instead of prescribing idiosyncratic behaviors like the quietists, these Friends reverenced high ideals. Friends had become a liberal sect while numbers continued to decline.

A panel of three speakers addressed "Our Conference—Its Work Now and for Tomorrow" (FI 8/31) to mark FGC's first forty years of existence and to take its bearings in wartime. Jesse Holmes, in what proved to be his final Conference (he died early in 1942) offered an overview of FGC's beginnings. But he concluded that the Quaker message is not just the message of a small religious group but of hundreds of groups: "The real Society might consist of millions of people, most of whom do not know they belong." Holmes, ever the activist and agitator for good causes, repeated once more his lifelong commitment to that "invisible church" we found articulated in the proto-liberal strain of Seekers in the pre-Quaker milieu (see the start of Chapter 1). His remarks stood in sharp counterpoint to Forbush's warnings that Friends had become too invisible in their white, middle-class surroundings.

Elizabeth Bartlett, secretary of FGC, described its current organization and work, reminding Friends that these biennial gatherings were just the most visible aspect of year-round work. She praised the leadership of Barnard Walton as executive secretary in preparing the Conferences and for his wide travels among yearly meetings: "He is a rare spirit." She also commended Jane Rushmore's work for the Religious Education Committee: "A clearer thinker cannot be found." She noted that one of the founding Conferences, the Education Conference, had been instrumental in founding the Friends Council on Education in 1931, bringing all Friends schools together as "an integrating force in Quaker education in an advisory and consultative capacity." Barnard Walton spoke of the continuing work of the Advancement Committee, offering an FGC version of history: Henry Wilbur had started the Friends Meeting at Cambridge; Pendle Hill was founded originally under the name of Woolman School; and the AFSC grew out of initiatives by FGC's Social Service Committee. All these assertions were partly true. Looking ahead, Esther Holmes Jones affirmed the earnestness and vitality of young Friends, who were becoming a force for renewal and change in FGC. She quoted a high-school-age Friend's comment: "Older Friends who speak in meeting make things so complicated."

As often in these Conferences, many addresses were by non-Quaker academics and other "experts" on world events, foreign policy, economics, and so on—problems "out there" to be discussed.

The exhibit room continued to expand, with twenty displays this year. Burke reflected, "Most of us are eye people, and we are glad the exhibit idea has taken hold." But the liberal book culture also thrived. Sales burgeoned, with a number of fresh Quaker titles for sale. "We came to the Conference hungry in mind and spirit. We left with courage and knowledge, renewed for the tasks ahead in helping to build the world of tomorrow." This was indeed a useful Conference, both for mutual encouragement and as a sobering "gut-check" for Friends wading into crisis.

CHAPTER 6   War Without, Reassessment Within

The summer of 1940 also saw the eighty-eighth and final session of the Pennsylvania/Longwood Yearly Meeting of Progressive Friends, held at Cheyney College with Jesse Holmes as its clerk. The last, semi-organized vestige of the Progressive Friends movement disappeared without much notice. Yet the movement had greatly affected the founding and course of Friends General Conference, and of liberal Quakerism more generally. While many Progressive Friends resumed membership in the Hicksite yearly meetings in the latter nineteenth century, we could equally say that Hicksites joined the Progressives—and that the Orthodox would eventually follow.

The 1942 Cape May Conference

In early 1942, with the US now in the war, the Executive Committee discussed whether to hold the Conference. Holding it would serve the mutual encouragement of Friends, but the military might take over parts of Cape May as a base. The government might even forbid holding the Conference; it forbade holding the Rose Bowl that year (an amusing comparison). Barnard Walton sent out 900 questionnaires to Friends and received a strong response in favor of holding the Conference, which was held July 6 to 13. The Admiral Hotel had been taken over by the military as officers' headquarters, so the High School Section was moved to the Star Villa, along with the older young Friends. Otherwise, FGC had its usual run of Cape May.

This Conference celebrated fifty years since the founding Conferences began meeting together at Chappaqua, New York in 1892. The theme, "Toward a Free and Generous World," sustained the previous Conference's determination to look beyond the war. The advance program unpacked the theme: "What is a FREE and GENEROUS world? Why do we have faith in it? What are the obstacles? What methods shall we use? How can we begin now? What undergirding of the spirit is essential? . . . We will meet with an open mind as seekers for light and guidance." The language of *seeking* had become common in the FGC conversation in recent years. Also, "free" and "generous" offered more basic definitions of liberality that avoided the more confident liberal ideology of progress, amid modernity's most catastrophic setback yet.

Poster for the 1942 Conference. Friends General Conference Records, Friends Historical Library of Swarthmore College.

Round tables included The Friends Message, Religious Education, Economic Problems, Education, International Peace and Justice, Social Problems in the Community, and the Work of the AFSC. These topics parallel much of the curriculum of Pendle Hill in 1942, where post-war reconstruction was already being planned in conversation with the AFSC. (After the war, Pendle Hill served as AFSC's training center for volunteers going abroad for relief and reconstruction.)

CHAPTER 6   War Without, Reassessment Within

Among the records of the Conference Planning Committee, a three-page document of proposed questions for discussion groups focused on the question, "Dare we live our Christianity?"[229] For "Christianity," the document used Carlyle's definition of religion: "What a man practically lays to heart and knows for certain concerning this mysterious universe and his duty and destiny here—that is man's religion, and the most important thing about him for it creatively determines all the rest." It is not clear what these "discussion groups" were, since they do not appear on the Conference program as such. But the document's use of Carlyle is revealing. What was still tactfully labeled "Christianity" was migrating toward a universalism, even a nontheism, that in 1942 still "dared not speak its name," to repurpose Oscar Wilde's famous phrase.

This year's "Story of the Conference" (FI 7/18-25/1942) was written by Edith Reeves Solenberger. She noted a good turnout, even if not comparable to 1940's total of 1600 (the final count was 1132). Fewer men in their twenties were present (though she demurred from spelling out the reason). War conditions mandated a "dim-out" at night, which made the stars shine brighter. There was much talk of the reorganization of the world. New books such as Janet Whitney's *John Woolman* and Elizabeth Gray Vining's *Penn* were stimulants to fresh thinking. The late Thomas Kelly's *Testament of Devotion* (1941) articulated the unity of contemplation and action. This Conference returned to the practice of large devotional meetings in the morning to set the tone for the day. Singing at evening sessions continued robustly, with hymns followed by old popular songs. One evening Bayard Rustin led Friends in singing "Swing Low, Sweet Chariot." Both he and Friends were surprised at how well they sang. The 1940 supplement to the *Friends Hymnal* finally included one spiritual, "Study War No More."

Patrick Murphy Malin was becoming a favorite Conference speaker. He continued on leave from teaching economics at Swarthmore, now working for the government's wartime price-control administration and serving as vice-chair of the AFSC. Malin spoke of "Our Home in the Wilderness." Moral progress is "terribly slow," he said. Humanity keeps having to learn the same moral lessons in new technological and social circumstances. In the 1920s,

Patrick Murphy Malin. Courtesy of Friends Historical Library of Swarthmore College.

Friends and others had been called alarmist and radical for warning of the present catastrophe. Now in the 1940s, their role was to be encouragers of a better world. Augustine wrote *The City of God* as Rome crumbled. It became his home in the wilderness and a home for future generations. Two key principles must be kept in mind: first, do not become attached to any attainment, as it is imperfect and corruptible; second, there is always "the mercy of possibility" to begin again. Standing at the cross, we see this; bearing the cross, we make it real. Malin finished by remarking, "Our home within the wilderness has for its foundation the fact that creation may be somewhat redeemed, and for its superstructure the fact that truth may be found and proclaimed even in the midst of power" (FI 7/18). *The Friends Intelligencer* noted that Malin's message moved Friends more deeply than the text itself might suggest. His modifications on the concept of progress were useful for a challenging time.

CHAPTER 6   War Without, Reassessment Within

In his first Conference as Chairman, Bliss Forbush reframed FGC within a wider, ecumenical perspective in "One Household in the Family of God." "No man liveth unto himself, nor does a religious society. Both the individual and the group are acted upon by the total environment, and in turn react to that environment, shaping it to some degree by their own conduct, and being shaped by it far more than they imagine." Where did FGC fit among the more than two hundred religious groups in the United States? The US was a melting pot of religions as well as races and nationalities. While schism had been a strong tendency in American religious history, the current trend was toward reunion and amalgamation. Recent examples: Lutherans, Methodists, and the United Church of Canada. The World Council of Churches, still in formation, already consisted of seventy-six churches in twenty-seven countries.

Forbush observed Friends reflecting these trends on a smaller scale. Cooperation was growing between the Quaker branches, moving toward reunion. And FGC had joined the WCC. New meetings and independent meetings were welcoming a wide variety of seekers. Some new meetings were united meetings, dually affiliated. Three factors would promote further cooperation: first, increased fellowship and work on common projects; second, recognition that the truth has different aspects, and no body of Friends successfully holds all the values of Quaker faith and practice; and third, Friends can cooperate without insisting upon conversion. He concluded, "A household suggests a haven of peace and quiet and refreshment, but it is only a household in the family of God if from it men and women go forth to do His will in the world about them" (FI 7/18).

Clarence Pickett returned, this time speaking more plainly, in "Toward a Significant Religious Society." He defined significance not as numbers, influence, or theological dogmas but as a religious society that builds and preserves persons and motivates society toward creative ends. He sketched examples from ancient Israel, the early Church, and early Friends. He concluded soberly (in words also included in this chapter's epigraph):

> But let us make no mistake. The Society of Friends as you and I know it is very far from this kingdom which we dimly see and seek. I say this not as one who condemns from the outside but who in speaking

frankly criticizes his own life and conduct. The wide breach between our notions of fellowship and our conduct concerning race may be one of the emerging signs of our decline and lack of significance unless we face it squarely.... We shall suffer from anemia and weakness ... until we discover these deeper levels of human nature, for the lack of which we so often live a superficial and meaningless existence [FI 8/8].

Thomas Jones, president of Fisk University and director of the Friends sector of the Civilian Public Service, spoke candidly on the early progress of CPS camps, only six months old at the time. In "Creative Pioneers," he acknowledged that the wide variety of conscientious objectors in the camps had brought with it some demoralizing influences. Moreover, the US military viewed the conscientious objector not as a creative pioneer but as a negativist in the guard house. Men trained for overseas service were denied passports, and thus kept from doing dangerous and heroic work, and then criticized for not doing it. Despite this, an important movement was underway, performing conservation work and social service. Morale in the camps was improving (FI 8/18).

Rachel Davis DuBois returned to lead the round table on race relations, showcasing the Neighborhood Home Festival and Group Conversation techniques she had developed working in troubled neighborhoods and schools of New York. The Festivals brought twenty to forty individuals together from diverse backgrounds to recall childhood memories, touching on universal themes like the change of seasons, work holidays, home customs, and so on. She observed that people don't act according to what they know, but how they *feel* about what they know. She developed the Festival as a method to reach that emotional component in racial attitudes and help people find their commonalities. She published her findings in *Get Together Americans* (1943). Bayard Rustin spoke at the round table on methods of nonviolent direct action. The group also devoted attention to Japanese and Native Americans. They reported feeling "a deep sense of sin" over the new internment camps for Japanese Americans. "During the week at Cape May we became more deeply aware than ever before of the struggle of Negro, Oriental, Jew and Indian for equality in our American life" (FI 8/15).

Notable presentations on social and economic issues included "Cooperatives" by Samuel Ashelman. A growing phenomenon in American life, "Consumer cooperatives are a practical tool for working toward a free and generous world. They are undramatic and peaceful, [but] they have forced monopolies to lower prices to all consumers" (FI 8/22). Bennet Schauffler of the National Labor Relations Board spoke on "Labor's Contribution to the Well-Being of Society," bemoaning that propaganda makes people forget that "'Labor,' 'Management,' 'Ownership,' 'Government,' and 'Consumers' are all made up of *people*." He commended Friends for stubbornly resisting this pattern. He posed labor organizations as a modern extension of democracy, drawing competent leadership forward and improving the quality of the electorate (FI 8/1). (Pendle Hill was a focal point for Quaker engagement with these issues 1941-51, through the work of Haines Turner with local labor groups and cooperative organizing.[230])

Managing Disagreement and Growth

Before this Conference, *The Friends Intelligencer* (6/20, 27) had published two controversial articles by Brand Blanshard, former professor of philosophy at Swarthmore, titled "Non-Pacifist Quakerism." Writing as an ambivalent Friend, he observed "Quakers have no formal creed; in its place we have put one great central doctrine, the doctrine of the Inner Light.... *What* the Light reveals is left to the individual conscience." He described pacifism using that most damning word in the liberal vocabulary, "dogma." The pacifist's motives are pure but misled:

"The kindest heart may in practice be cancelled out by a muddled head...." "Of course it follows from all this that if pacifism is a requirement for membership in the Society of Friends, I have no right to remain. But *is* it a requirement?" Blanshard thus opposed pacifism with an individualistic relativism in which the light might lead anywhere. He went on to argue that this war must be fought, and after victory, a system of world government with irresistible force must be instituted.

Brand Blanshard. Courtesy of Friends Historical Library of Swarthmore College.

Frederick Libby. Courtesy of Friends Historical Library of Swarthmore College.

Blanshard was answered in the 7/18 issue with "Pacifist Quakerism," by Frederick Libby. The 8/1 issue featured a boxed statement over the masthead:

> The ancient testimony of the Society of Friends against war continues to express the Society's fundamental position. Articles and letters are published by the *Intelligencer* which give the diversity of views always existing in a living society, but it should be understood that these opinions are those of the writers and not necessarily those of the Society of Friends as a whole or of the editorial board of the *Friends Intelligencer*.

On other fronts, FGC continued to work with the American Friends Fellowship Council to manage the growth of new and independent meetings. FGC's Executive Committee (1/43) and the AFFC approved a minute describing current practices and intentions. To summarize, many new meetings had sprung up across the country over the last quarter-century. Both organizations were working to "gather this new life into the fabric of the whole Society of Friends, and in turn the strength of the Society of Friends made available to new meetings." The new Friends "have come into the Society because of various Friends' testimonies and the spiritual life which they found there."

The AFFC helped new meetings develop connections with nearby yearly meetings, while also encouraging the yearly meetings to confer with the new meetings. If the new meeting chose to affiliate with the AFFC and not with a yearly meeting, the AFFC should work to counter any resulting feelings of disharmony. The AFFC would continue to nurture the new meeting under its auspices until a comfortable relationship formed with a yearly meeting, or the meeting became a "united meeting," joining two or more yearly meetings. As we noted earlier, Friends from the new meetings were already gravitating to the biennial Conferences, some even participating with the Central Committee's meetings. The unpredictable, rhizomatic growth of new meetings stimulated creative responses like this.

The 1944 Cape May Conference

The final program featured a pen and ink drawing of young Friends talking on the boardwalk, no longer retro-Quaker but looking rather fashionable.

Notwithstanding the D-Day invasion earlier that month and desperate combat in both Europe and the Pacific, the Conference (June 23-30) theme was "Reconstruction: Inward and Outward." The AFSC was already negotiating with the US government and making contingency plans for relief and reconstruction work in Europe and Asia. Pendle Hill was preparing to serve as a training center for Friends and others recruited for that work. But the theme intimated more than the physical rebuilding of battle zones: a reconstruction of American society and the world order, founded upon spiritual renewal. The promotional brochure unpacked the theme:

> Friends feel that this is a time of opportunity. What are the reasons for coming together? There is a call to gather in closer fellowship, with each member taking a significant part to recognize the bigness of our share in meeting the world situation: to give and receive clearer perception of the light within; to gain strength for our individual lives and for the life of the community.... Outside of meetings, we will live and play and visit together as we have always done at Cape May, happily and with rich reward.

Poster for the 1944 Conference. Friends General Conference Records, Friends Historical Library of Swarthmore College.

For its part, Cape May was happy to see Friends return for the eleventh time and even donated $800 for Conference publicity that year. FGC spent less than $100 on publicity, helping to keep registration costs very low: $3 per person, $5 per family, $1 for young Friends under eighteen without family present; Friends were asked to give more if they could.

CHAPTER 6   War Without, Reassessment Within

Cover graphic for the 1944 final program. Friends General Conference Records, Friends Historical Library of Swarthmore College.

Under its new managing editor William Hubben, *The Friends Intelligencer* had a smart new format. Edith Reeves Solenberger and Hubben wrote general accounts of the Conference (FI 7/8-25/1944). Solenberger reported a resurgence in attendance (the final count was 1,382), and a widely shared sense of responsibility for Quaker action during the war "and its possibly more difficult aftermath." A larger proportion of women than usual attended. Young men over eighteen were few, except for some CPS men and some in the military who got furlough to attend. The High School Section was at capacity with 250 again this year, and a record 199 attended the Junior Conference. Fully one-third of Conference attenders were high-school aged or younger. Most Friends were from the general region, but a few came from the "western states" of Illinois and Indiana. Waynesville, Ohio Friends had no less than twenty-nine present (owing largely to the local influence of Elizabeth Furnas, who remained a supporter of the Conference all her life).

Chairman Bliss Forbush commented that the Conference fulfilled "the need widely felt among Friends to see others with similar concerns and hopes for the immediate future." The tone of the gathering was serious but not gloomy. Solenberger noted that "family parties of two or three generations continued to provide one of the unique and delightful features of this Conference." Exhibits grew, with Friends schools filling one room by themselves.

Themes of inward and outward reconstruction were woven together in the Conference program. Forbush gave the keynote, "We Know in Part." Clearly influenced by his continuing ecumenical engagement on behalf of FGC, his address might be called a reconstructive Quaker theology. He observed that while Friends are generally suspicious of theology, George Fox shared many of the theological doctrines of his day, even if he rejected creeds as such. While Friends have no creed, he said, "We do feel it is imperative that each individual shall have his own personal faith." The Latin *credo* means "I believe." Every seeker must grapple with four elements that show up in traditional creeds: a concept of God and of human nature, and an interpretation of the person of Jesus and of the problem of suffering. When one takes time to withdraw from the confusion and chaos of the day, certain fundamentals of faith become clearer and one can say, "I know in part, but this I know" (FI 7/8). Older forms of Christian faith will continue to affirm older and more authoritarian versions of faith, but the same eternal truths may be expressed in newer phrases and a simpler manner. While he spoke in less overtly critical terms than Lewis Benson wrote in 1938, Forbush consistently sought in these Conferences to help Friends regain a theological

CHAPTER 6 War Without, Reassessment Within

sense of themselves and their work in the world. The mantra, "We have no creed" could only take them so far.

The burgeoning High School Section focused on racial concerns. They read a statement, "Young Friends and the Race Question," at the closing session of the Conference. They wished to:

> Express our good will toward the young people of all groups, particularly the Negroes of our own country. We want those who feel separated from us by race or color to know of our realization that racial discrimination, hate and pride will never lead to peace and the kind of world in which we want to live. We have been thinking of you and have been trying to find ways in which we can show our feeling of kinship with you.... We want to understand and value your contribution to our common culture. We need your help to do this, as we cannot do it alone [FI 7/15].

The statement shows the influence of Bayard Rustin's and Rachel Davis DuBois's time with the group. It also bodes the formation of a generational cohort that would be prepared to ally with the civil rights movement a decade later. An older Conference attender commented, "The Conference brought to me fresh hope and faith in the future. The many young people in attendance showed such earnestness and interest in the questions of the day that one felt ... there would be sincere souls to carry on. I felt this meeting together gave strength to all."

Worship at the Conference included both plenary and small-group occasions. At the plenary worship Sunday morning, the trend appeared to be more "democratic," with a better balance between speaking and silence, fewer "sermons from weighty Friends," and more messages coming from the floor than from the platform. Forbush likened Quaker worship to "a jigsaw puzzle as we come to it with our varying concerns, but gradually a pattern takes form." One high school Friend was quoted saying, "We want things said in meeting for worship which are shorter and better." The dynamics of Quaker worship were changing.

Nine round tables were held during the week: International Peace, Community Relations, Race Relations, AFSC Work, Economic Relations, Education, Religious Education, Inward Reconstruction, and a Young Friends Group.

James Gordon Gilkey, a Congregational minister and popular author, asked "Has Christianity Any Real Help for the Postwar World?" A deeper faith would be needed to answer the horrors of two world wars. He felt that the leaders of the Church were adequate to the challenge, but that the Church in general was growing weak. "Will the young Christian leaders of tomorrow secure from their own generation the backing they need? As I watch the typical young Americans of our time, particularly young parents . . . these well-mannered young pagans fail to see what is at stake as the postwar era approaches" (FI 7/22). We have heard similar concerns voiced among Friends at these Conferences. Middle-class life was generating its own atmosphere, buffering the more rigorous affects of religious community, while the sociology of professionalization—not just among clergy but among academics and service organizations—would engender a more passive "client" posture among the postwar population.

Clarence Pickett offered another report from the front of Quaker service and peace action in "Post War Planning and the Effect on Friends." He saw many discouraging signs on the horizon. The churches were losing influence. There was a growing sense that the war would not accomplish anything more than a military victory. "We are clearly in the midst of a revolution and the war is only one incident." Friends must "take stock and try to find our position in this fast moving scene." Like Friends, many groups were engaged in feverish postwar planning. At times it looked like an escape from the present horrors of war. But it was also a sign of hope that "an orderly life can be found."

America would emerge from the war as the largest military power, with almost all other countries owing it money. In the nineteenth century, Britain had used its economic power to foster a century of relative peace, 1815 to 1914. How would the US use its power? If it opted to dominate weaker nations, peacetime conscription would be inevitable. In that case, Friends would need to "give much more attention to the development early in life of convictions concerning war among our young people."

In addition, Friends would need "to emphasize more strongly than ever before the warm and intimate fellowship of community living ... the fellowship of the Meeting and community needs to be strengthened and shared in order to maintain a sense of direction, of purpose and steadiness to our membership." He found the hunger for community most acute among young Friends and conscientious objectors.

Given their past work, it was likely Friends would be enlisted by the government to aid in relief and reconstruction after the war. "The hand of Providence has to a wholly unprecedented degree prepared the way for this development." All over Europe, people were eager for Friends to begin the work (FI 7/29). Pickett sounded a number of prophetic notes in this address we will find confirmed in our final chapter on postwar Conferences and related developments. Howard Brinton (his next-door-neighbor at Pendle Hill) wrote similarly in *Pendle Hill Bulletins*.[231]

Katherine Lenroot, chief of the Children's Bureau of the US Department of Labor, spoke on "Youth in Transition." She commented on the unprecedented numbers of young people serving in the military. And many fourteen- to seventeen-year-olds were balancing heavy schedules of school and work to meet the need for productive labor. There were almost nine hundred thousand fewer boys and girls in school than there were in 1939–40. "Our youth of today have had to grow up very fast. ... Many are carrying burdens beyond their strength and maturity." Headlines about a juvenile crime wave were worrying, but millions of youth were meeting the challenge of the times. Meanwhile:

> Racial tensions have been heightened in some communities as a result of war-time migration and war-time pressures. Americans must find a way in which children of all races may be assured freedom to develop their full capacities, without humiliation, ostracism, or other forms of social injustice ... the years ahead will be one of the most exciting and challenging chapters of history [FI 8/22].

Notwithstanding the idealism of young Friends at this Conference, Lenroot's assessments of the wider social scene foretell youth alienation and rebellion, appearing soon after the war. The phenomenon was portrayed in novels such as J. D. Salinger's *The Catcher in the Rye* (1951) and films such as *The Wild Ones* (1953) and *Rebel*

Without a Cause (1955). The racial impasse would be confronted by books such as Gunnar Myrdal's *An American Dilemma: The Negro Problem and Modern Democracy* (1944) and Ralph Ellison's novel, *The Invisible Man* (1952).

Editor William Hubben reflected that this Conference had particular appeal

> to the seeker who hoped for guidance and the fellowship of like-minded friends. . . . From the large meetings and the round table discussions there spread a wholesome kind of uneasiness that was as much valued as the fellowship of those days and the assurance which was the gracious gift of our meetings for worship [FI 7/15].

Friends and America at the End of the War

World War II was a massive mobilization in every sense. One-fifth of the US population moved during the war, predominantly from south to north and east to west, often in search of wartime employment. Much of the excess labor in the Midwest and South was urbanized along the way. Immigrant populations were mainstreamed. With Roosevelt's 1941 executive order requiring defense contractors to hire black applicants, another wave of the Great Migration, approximately seven hundred thousand African Americans, left the South. Two million more left over the next twenty years. By 1970, a majority of black families lived outside Dixie. Membership in the NAACP increased ten-fold during the war, auguring the civil rights struggle to come.

Women entered the workforce during the war as never before. Nearly nineteen million were employed for some period of time during those years, reaching a high of thirty-six per cent of employment-aged women in 1944. But that quickly receded to twenty-eight per cent by 1947. Half cited "family responsibilities" as their reason for leaving their job. Three-quarters expressed positive feelings about moving from employment to motherhood.[232] The baby boom was underway.

Friends had experienced their own mobilization, with nearly a thousand Friends in CPS camps and hundreds more serving as conscientious objectors in other forms of alternative service. Another mobilization of Friends into relief and reconstruction work overseas awaited the end of war.

We have heard FGC's rising consciousness regarding issues of racial inclusion and justice. But after women's suffrage was achieved, we heard little or nothing on women's issues. The war remixed the nation in ways that would play out dramatically in the decades to come, for the nation and for Friends in particular.

Historian David Kennedy summarizes, "World War II left the American people energized, freshened, and invigorated."[233] The same energy came to Friends General Conference. Membership among the six surviving yearly meetings had bottomed out in the 1930s at just over sixteen thousand. As new independent meetings found their way into wider affiliation with yearly meetings, FGC statistics began to rebound. The Friends Meeting at Cambridge sought and received direct membership with FGC in 1945. An Advancement Committee report to the Central Committee (10/45) found growth each year after 1937:

- 1936: 16,174
- 1937: 16,161
- 1938: 16,225
- 1940: 16,460
- 1945: 17,598

But a qualitative resurgence is also notable, despite an unprecedented degree of critical self-assessment, at least from leaders such as Forbush and Pickett. One strength of the liberal Quaker tradition is its willingness to tolerate serious criticism from within its ranks. Perhaps this is a corollary to the renunciation of disciplined unity on the testimonies and permissive attitudes toward most norms of faith and practice. Serious questions are bound to arise. Self-criticism may also be seen as a by-product of academic influence since the latter nineteenth century; the free inquiry and debate of the classroom had permeated the meetinghouse.

The liberal Quaker enterprise escaped solipsism through continuing outward focus on service and reform. To some degree, that steady influx of "social capital"[234] staved off the spiritual bankruptcy Lewis Benson and Bliss Forbush warned against in this period.

Wider engagement also sustained the progressive Quaker "constitutionalism" we noted in Chapter 1, as originally theorized in William Penn's political writings. Conference Friends engaged in a continuing quest to move America into a fuller realization of its written US Constitution, especially in regard to race and gender. This entailed a deep discernment of the "living constitution" as it evolved among the American people. Moreover, Clarence Pickett's reflections on the advent of a global society suggest that a living constitution was taking shape not only among the American people, but among the human race in all its variety. Many Friends hoped that the coming peace would find written constitutional form in some form of world federalism after the war.

CHAPTER 7

Pax Americana and the End of FGC's Heroic Era
FGC Conferences 1946–1950

We pray that out of the suffering of our day One World will surely come, and that in it we shall be prepared for fruitful citizenship. But we are fearful as we stand trembling before a new dawn. Which way shall we go and what shall we do to aid the new dawning? Have we the power with which to aid in the new birth?

— Bliss Forbush at the 1946 Conference (FI 7/20/1946)

At the end of the war, the United States was the world's greatest military power, with a near monopoly on capital liquidity. In contrast to the rejection of Woodrow Wilson's Fourteen Points at the Versailles peace conference, the US could now dictate a generous peace. Franklin Roosevelt's Marshall Plan to rebuild war-ravaged nations and their economies was a Keynsian project to extend New Deal economics around the world. The policy was motivated in part by the fears that America and the world could slump back into depression again after the war. But the foundations for the new global economic order set at Bretton Woods in 1944 created the mechanisms for circulating trade and investment. The Marshall Plan jump-started those mechanisms. Meanwhile, the new United Nations would manage political conflicts in FDR's one-world vision.

But after Roosevelt's death in early 1945, Soviet territorial expansion across Eastern and Central Europe, followed by the Chinese communist revolution, quickly changed the outlook. President Harry Truman, influenced in part by Winston Churchill, shifted from Roosevelt's one-world vision to a two-world policy that set the tone for a long cold-war era. The Truman Doctrine motivated a fearful Congress to recycle still more surplus liquidity back into the world economy through the largest rearmament campaign ever seen in peacetime. Military aid kept flowing into Europe well after the Marshall Plan ended and kept Europe tied to US economic and political interests. Then, as the political consensus for such expenditure began to fall apart, the Korean conflict stampeded Congress to renew military aid as well as direct US military spending. Concomitantly, sustained anticommunist propaganda and military conscription kept militaristic affects flowing among the American population.

Much as arms spending in Europe at the end of the nineteenth century helped stimulate the *belle epoque* of the British regime of capitalist accumulation, so this sustained militarization put the US-led global economy on steroids, fueling "the most profitable period of economic growth in the history of world capitalism."[235] The economic, political, and affective provisions of *pax Americana* were firmly in place by the end of the Korean war.

Labor grew in power during the war and the early aftermath. But further unionization was increasingly blocked, especially in the South and West. Corporate public relations campaigns began to turn public opinion against unions, whose social agenda narrowed during the 1950s to better wages and benefits for members. Still, the labor movement was a major factor in doubling the size of the American middle class over the next generation to roughly half of the US population.

Much as the Roaring Twenties blew away the pall of World War I and the moral astringency of progressive politics, so postwar prosperity and its baby boom shook off fifteen years of depression and war with a new, consumer-driven economy, suburban expansion, an explosion of car ownership and travel, and a new wave of consumer electronics, particularly the television. A confident, fun-loving, acquisitive, family-oriented surge of American affects put Friends and other liberal reformers back on their heels. Historians of pacifism Peter Brock and Nigel Young remark that it took a decade after the end of World War II for the peace movement to regroup with focus and strength.[236]

CHAPTER 7   Pax Americana and the End of FGC's Heroic Era

In the preceding chapter, we heard forebodings from Clarence Pickett and others regarding postwar challenges for Friends and other pacifists. The Society of Friends became a rallying point for pacifists and other social idealists feeling bereft in the new era. FGC grew by 3 to 5 percent per year from 1948 to 1955.[237]

The hunger for community Clarence Pickett mentioned in 1944 continued to grow among pacifists discouraged by mainstream American trends. A number of Friends joined neo-Hutterite Bruderhoff communities in the late 1940s and early 1950s. Others founded new communities or took to farming. Rural life attracted the increasingly countercultural pacifist movement, something like the Christians who withdrew into the deserts after Constantine began to imperialize the Church in the fourth century.

FGC's Growing Confidence and Influence

New meetings were finding their home with FGC. Fifteen had joined FGC yearly meetings or joined FGC directly by the end of 1943. The Central Committee reported seven more by October 1945—mainly urban or campus meetings. The Finance Committee saw the opportunity to increase funding, programs, and influence:

> The growing power of the Conference and the appeal which it makes to ever widening circles seems to warrant encouragement of increased gifts—even inspires the very young to contribute. Friends vitally interested in the Conference might be asked to help explain the need for more funds in terms of religious activity and wider social service. Perhaps the Yearly Meetings should accept the responsibility of helping with some of the current expenses of our committees. They receive and use the services of the committees and appear to appreciate them.

The Central Committee (6/46) found unity to act upon these recommendations.

The 1946 Cape May Conference

Cape May suffered extensive damage from a hurricane toward the end of 1944, but the beach and boardwalk were being repaired and

Poster for the 1946 Conference. Friends General Conference Records, Friends Historical Library of Swarthmore College.

CHAPTER 7   Pax Americana and the End of FGC's Heroic Era

the town was anxious for FGC to return, even willing to help finance the next Conference in 1946. Cape May's hotels continued to offer special rates to Conference attenders, ranging from $20 to $50 per person in double rooms for the week.

The Conference theme for 1946 (June 21-28) was "Religious Foundations for Citizenship in One World," clearly aligning Friends with Roosevelt's vision. The promotional brochure explained:

> People everywhere are longing for a lasting peace. They hope for the advances in science, culture and human welfare which can come only in times of peace. They know that cooperation among the peoples of the world is essential to progress in any of these lines. They are hurt by the conflicts and evils that hold us back. They are searching for the basis upon which we can build a united world. Friends believe this basis is found in religion. At the Conference this year we aim to present the faith of Friends in confidence that by following the guidance of God within, men can move toward the solution of the present world problems.

A special issue of *The Friends' Intelligencer* (7/20) summarized nearly all of the Conference. Its cover reproduced that year's Conference poster, a high-modernist, almost Soviet-style graphic of a heroic family looking up and out together.

Round tables included International Peace; Cultural Democracy in our Homes, Neighborhoods and Schools; the AFSC in Europe; Economic Relations; The Importance of Stimulating Teacher Growth Through In-Service Training; The First Day School's Responsibility for the Religious Nurture of Our Children; the Seeker and the Message; The Old Teaching in the New World; and a Young Friends Round Table.

Plenary speakers included Ira Moomaw of the Church of the Brethren on "The Church and the Future of Rural Life," Andrew Cordier, executive assistant to the secretary-general of the United Nations, on "Building One World," and British Quaker Vera Brittain on "The Road to Spiritual Renaissance."

Eleanor Starr wrote "The Story of Friends General Conference" for this special issue. She noted that it was a rainy day as Friends arrived at Cape May. But as the group gathered at the pier convention hall, the sun broke through and a rainbow appeared. "Was it too much to hope that it could be an omen?" The beach and boardwalk were still in bad shape from the hurricane. "Unlike two years ago, only a few army and navy uniforms were in evidence."

The troubled affects of uncertainty and misgiving are quite evident from the addresses and reports. But in tune with the nascent baby boom, troubling thoughts about the past and future were at least partly displaced by the continuing surge of young Friends' participation. The Junior Conference boasted a record 255 children from nine states. The new Junior High group had eight-five and published a *Junior Friends Intelligencer* in mimeographed form during the Conference, featuring their artwork. It was a hot item on the boardwalk, selling for ten cents a copy. Young Friends were 125 in all. The final total for the Conference overall was 1,717, another high since the early Conferences. Friends clearly sensed the need for mutual encouragement and fresh insights on a postwar world still less than a year old and only beginning to take shape.

In this new format, the *Intelligencer* published the "gist" or "abstract" of addresses, rather than full texts. These do not always give a coherent sense of the speaker's message.

Bliss Forbush gave the opening address, "What Is That in Thy Hand?" drawing upon the Exodus story of Moses performing wonders with the staff in his hand, to liberate his people from bondage. He asked what staff Friends held "as we face the task of building religious foundations for One World. What have we in our hands with which to confront the problems of personal and group living?" Like the ancient Roman lictor's staff, Friends hold a staff composed of several rods. He developed these under the headings of basic Christianity, mysticism, quietism, religious humanism, and social gospel activism. (It is surprising to find quietism presented as a positive attribute here, after decades of progressive excoriation. But Forbush, probably influenced by his study of Elias Hicks, clarified its basic meaning: seeking God and turning away from everything that might hinder that pursuit.)

He observed that during two world wars, Friends had offered sympathy and counsel to members who chose military service:

> This does not mean that the Quaker testimony against war has changed. We continue to hold that war is, in the words of the

CHAPTER 7 Pax Americana and the End of FGC's Heroic Era

Discipline, "contrary to the spirit, the life, and the teachings of Jesus." We see that the problem of eliminating war is more complex than we had supposed, and that it is evident from our action that in time of conflict we expect the individual to follow his best guidance. But we accept the responsibility of positive action in every channel which we believe will restrain the use of violence and help build One World in which brotherhood will reign.

Forbush articulates well the ambiguous realm where FGC (and most other Friends) had settled. War continued to be contrary to the *ideal* that Friends (and, well, most decent people) cherished. But the corporate sense of a united, existential resistance to participation in war, which would seriously challenge and presume to teach individual consciences, was now too weak to stand. Friends were basically in line with Jesse Holmes, who we recall saying in 1914, "We're against war, even if we go into it" (see Chapter 3). Such a peace position or principle was not far different from the emerging *Pax Americana*.

Clarence Pickett spoke of "The Quaker as Citizen." He set a countercultural tone by portraying early Christians as a "colony of Heaven" under a Roman imperial dictatorship and offering that image for Friends to consider in their present circumstances. In one world, things that happen anywhere will have waves of influence everywhere else. For example, the AFSC currently has young men and women serving around the world from China to Finland in a selfless desire for a peaceful world. "To think of the world as one whole tends to elevate the significance and value of the individual. ... We dare not yield to petty, inept, unworthy, or evil impulses. We must start growing those forces that will overcome evil with good in this total world."

One evil impulse was fear. The war was supposed to end fear, yet the most powerful nation in the world is more afraid now than ever. Pickett describes what we now know as the beginnings of a permanent war economy, and the military-industrial complex:

> We shall be appropriating more than half of the current national revenue this year, more than 16 billion dollars, for building and maintaining our Army and Navy in peace time. We are not sure of our selves. We have indulged in practices which we know do not bring in their wake soundness, integrity, and honor.

So how should Friends respond to fear? "Venture in applying the practice of love and good will even to the least responsive ought to be the heart of this little colony called the Society of Friends."

Famine was another challenge: "But the discipline which we as the little colony of Heaven exercise in sharing our food, our clothes, our culture and our services, will be a telling test of our faith." Finally, there was ongoing racial exclusion:

> We shall have to learn far better than is now our practice to rise above those distinctions, and it will not be easy. It is a high calling that comes to Friends these days. Our assets of privilege... are all now at our command. It remains to be seen with what dedication and abandon we join as members of a colony of Heaven, living out the good life in a world that has glimpsed these better things but which all too often has been unwilling to pay the price that they will cost.

Once again, Pickett offered cutting-edge insights, from the perspective of the frontlines of Quaker service around the world, but always grounded in the deep structures of Quaker faith and practice.

Frank Aydelotte spoke from his experience of a visit to Palestine with the Anglo-American Committee of Inquiry. He described it as "an armed camp, the theater of a bitter struggle between Jews and Arabs, in which both groups have at different times taken the law into their own hands and attempted to impose their will by armed violence." The West wanted to perform some act of "atonement" for the death of six million Jews in the Nazi Holocaust. Zionists wanted it to take the form of a national Jewish state. Arabs responded that they had lived in Palestine for 1,200 years and should not be asked to make atonement for a persecution they had no part in. Instead, the US and Great Britain should open their own doors. He concluded:

> In a certain sense the problem of Palestine is unique. In another sense, it is only an illustration on a small scale of the kind of problem which must be solved in India, in Africa, and in the Far East if relations between nations of varying degrees of achievement in civilization are to be placed upon a satisfactory basis. From this point of view our success in dealing with Palestine will be an indication as to whether or not we are likely to be successful in the future in preserving the peace of the world by international action.

CHAPTER 7   Pax Americana and the End of FGC's Heroic Era

Aydelotte's analysis is cogent. He presciently viewed Palestine as a litmus test for world peace in the new era (and by implication the destiny of the United Nations). But his phrase "varying degrees of achievement in civilization" betrays an abiding Eurocentric viewpoint, one obstacle to world peace in the decades to come.

Kermit Eby, director of education and research for the Congress of Industrial Organizations (CIO), addressed "Labor and Religion—What They Have in Common." Both organized labor and organized religion faced a common crisis, the disintegrating influences of war. Postwar "moral schizophrenia" posed an even greater danger: holding ideals without practicing them:

> Old ways and vested interests block our prophetic insights. We have become the bulwark of the middle class, our churches the symbols of the status quo. We ... stress the little sins because we are afraid to mention the all-consuming ones and the injustice which is all around us. The time has come, if we would have influence, to stand and be counted, to fight with every energy the injustices which grow out of intolerance, out of greed, and out of war.

Eby also spoke to the High School Section and at the round table on Economic Life. He faced questions and criticisms from both young and older Friends on labor methods such as strikes, closed shops, and picket lines. With the emergency production needs of wartime past, the press had begun to side more with management. Some Friends were shifting their sympathies as well.

Bayard Rustin spent time with the High School Section. He also held an audience of 800 adult Friends spellbound as he described his experiences of twenty-eight months in prison (ending a mere two weeks before the Conference) for draft resistance. His singing continued to enchant as well. Jean Toomer, African American Friend and Harlem Renaissance writer, also spent time with the High School Section.

Esther Holmes Jones led the International Relations round table, as she had done for many years. The final session featured no speaker. Jones instead led an open discussion, which participants found to be "a much appreciated opportunity to thrash out points raised in previous sessions and to ask other questions on their own initiative. The session was as successful as those with visiting speakers." Again, one can hear a desire for less presentational, more participatory modes.

The AFSC round table was chaired by Eleanor Stabler Clarke, assistant executive secretary. The group heard of the rapidly expanding relief and reconstruction work in Europe and Asia, work for Negro employment, summer Peace Institutes for young people, and the challenges AFSC faced in a time of rapid growth. With 480 workers and staff now, the Service Committee was stretched to remain sensitive to Quaker concerns, to cooperate with other church groups, to personalize relief work, and to raise a foreign service budget of nearly six million dollars. (Amazingly, the AFSC still had only eight staff working at the central offices in Philadelphia in 1946.[238])

William Hubben led the round table on The Seeker and the Message. The Quaker message today is "God is a friend to all" and "every man has a particle of the divine." Concerns were raised that "we need to become more literate in basic religious concepts. We also need the mystical approach and ought to be able to interpret the Quaker message to the seekers of our time." Seekers had lots of questions and looked for kindred spirits to share their experiences with. Through such a fellowship in seeking, "Another foundation may be laid for 'Citizenship in One World'." We can hear Friends beginning to define themselves as fellow-seekers.

Eleanor Starr's report on the Conference concluded:

> When one looks back to the last Conference in 1944, it almost seems that aeons of time has elapsed. Then we were longing for the end of the war and the rehabilitation of all that had been devastated. Now we question whether we and the world are at peace although the warring has ceased. That to this reporter was the powerful undertow which, during the Conference days, was pulling at us in spite of all we could do. Every speaker's address was tinged with a note of caution or discouragement. Some were pessimistic, some mildly optimistic about the future. But all agreed that as Friends we must exert our strength as never before to cooperate with other religious groups all over the world to save God's children from the abyss toward which they are heading. Plans must be formulated quickly to bring our world back to sanity. What about the rainbow? Dare we ask of it more than just good weather for one short week?

CHAPTER 7 Pax Americana and the End of FGC's Heroic Era

While FGC Conferences usually tended to transmute the melancholy of the times into the spleen of renewed courage and action, this year's gathering seemed to confirm the anxieties Friends brought to it. Perhaps the graphic ruin of Cape May's beach and boardwalk before them caused Friends to register the world's disorder more acutely.

The Nobel Peace Prize

The 1947 Nobel Peace Prize was awarded to the Religious Society of Friends in Britain and America for 300 years of relief work in wartime. The British and American Friends Service Committees, currently awash in the largest Quaker relief work in history, were appointed to receive the Prize on behalf of Friends. Henry Cadbury represented them at the ceremony in Oslo. He later quipped that "Friends in my meeting are bursting their buttons with humility." It was indeed a high-point for a Religious Society now strangely inured to the approval of a world they had once renounced—and which had once scorned them. Once again, the paradoxical qualities of a "liberal sect" apply.

The Future of Quaker Journalism

The board of managers for *The Friends Intelligencer* had for some years periodically approached FGC's Central Committee to see if the latter would take the journal under its wing. The *Intelligencer*'s board was shrinking and so were contributions in support of its work. But the Committee believed the journal would function best if it remained organizationally independent of FGC. At its September 1947 meeting the Central Committee learned that some Friends were urging the *Intelligencer* and *The Friend* (the journal of Philadelphia Yearly Meeting Orthodox) to explore some form of merger, to create one new journal representing all non-pastoral Friends, including the independent and Conservative meetings. The ensuing discussion was positive but inconclusive.

The following November, the two Philadelphia Yearly Meetings began holding an annual joint "General Meeting" to begin melding the two bodies together. They already had some joint committees in operation. A process for "organic union" was underway.

By the next Central Committee meeting the following June at Cape May, *Friends Intelligencer* managing editor William Hubben was chary of merging the two journals. It would be a mismatch. *Friends Intelligencer* represented six yearly meetings and *The Friend* only one and was in worse financial condition. The matter was laid aside, with the feeling that the merger of journals would more appropriately ensue from the reunification of yearly meetings, rather than precede it. (The creation of *The Friends Journal* out of the two existing journals was effected in 1955, as the Hicksite and Orthodox yearly meetings of Philadelphia, New York, and Baltimore were reunited.)

The Death of Rufus Jones, Heroic Friend

Rufus Jones died in his Haverford campus home the morning of June 16, 1948, aged eighty-five, just nine days before the start of the Cape May Conference. He died in his sleep after making some corrections to an address he had planned to deliver later that summer at New England Yearly Meeting. That text, "A Call to a New Installment of Heroic Spirit," was published in *The Friends Intelligencer* (7/17). He began:

> I have a feeling that nothing is more important in our Quaker world today than a recovery of that heroic spirit which was a striking feature of early Quakerism. The most frequent phrase in George Fox's Epistles to his followers in all parts of the world is: *"Be valiant for the truth."* And he himself was valiant before he called upon his followers to be valiant.

By contrast, Jones recalled the Quakerism he grew up with in rural Maine as "the least heroic feature of our town." Repeatedly, messages in worship warned against action, innovation, even thought. Based on his childhood reading of the Bible and early Quaker literature, he learned that Friends had developed their testimonies as "heroic principles" that were costly to those who lived them. "I resolved as a boy to be a heroic Quaker."

CHAPTER 7 Pax Americana and the End of FGC's Heroic Era

Among his own heroic accomplishments, he mentioned the creation of *The American Friend* journal in 1894 serving Five Years Meeting Friends, founding in 1914 with Henry Hodgkin the American chapter of the Fellowship of Reconciliation, and establishing the American Friends Service Committee in 1917. This was "a heroic type of Christianity more like the heroism of primitive Quakerism than anything else that has appeared since those first years." And since the AFSC started them in 1934, work camps had drawn together seven thousand young Friends, "and a great many of them have *found themselves* and have built their lives on a new pattern while they were in these work camps."

He concluded, "I believe that our next heroic effort will be a concerted movement to recover our rural communities and bring back to full production the abandoned farms.... The moral fiber of the nation has come from the farm." Those returning from rebuilding war-torn cities in Europe should begin rebuilding villages and rural areas at home. "We must discover a new skyline, new frontiers of life and creative faith. I believe this can best be found in a concerted effort to recover our rural communities." (We heard some expression of this concern for rural renewal at the 1946 Conference. We will hear more in 1948.)

Jones ended the address, "The only way to be good in this crisis is to be *heroically good*." He remained irrepressibly positive to the end. But this final encouragement to Friends was also a veiled warning.

A Response to Conscription and Militarism

Earlier, we heard concerns that the US might continue military conscription beyond the war. Those concerns were well founded. The Central Committee approved (11/47) a minute to the House Armed Services Committee, expressing deep disturbance at "the passage of the Draft Act for peace time conscription and by the vast increase in military manpower and expenditures." They stated further:

> We consider this draft law is a vote of no confidence in the United Nations, at a time when we should be giving energetic support to this organization and its efforts to regulate and reduce armaments. This law substitutes the threat of violence for methods of

international cooperation and the establishment of a reign of law. We deplore the wastage of human and economic resources in the whole militaristic program.

Much as the European victors in the first world war had undercut the development of the League of Nations, American military dominance of the new world order threatened the UN's potential.

The minute also urged monthly meetings to counsel their young men about the draft. Based on the conviction of "that of God in every man," Friends believe "that it is wrong to destroy human life under any circumstances.... We urge young men to consider prayerfully their responsibilities to their God and to mankind and to act according to the dictates of their conscience."

This minute went further than we have heard earlier in suggesting what the Quaker's conscience dictates. Further erosion of conscientious objection among Friends might jeopardize the rights that Friends and the other Historic Peace Churches had struggled to secure during the first world war. It could also make it more difficult for Friends to advocate broadened definitions of conscientious objection:

> The exception granted our young men by this law obligates us all to be deeply concerned about those sincere conscientious objectors who may not be so classified because of the limited definition of conscience or because of possible misinterpretation of the intent of the law by draft officials. It is the responsibility of all Friends to dedicate themselves to the building of a world in which national armaments are abolished and nations submit to World Government.

This robust statement articulates the growing realization that militarism would no longer be the exception in American society; it was becoming a chronic malignancy that Friends must counter in sustained, determined ways. The minute was brought to the following Conference.

The 1948 Cape May Conference

The Central Committee received invitations from Ocean Grove and Ocean City, New Jersey. But they opted to meet again at Cape May, June 21-28, 1948. They instructed the planning committee "to have

CHAPTER 7   Pax Americana and the End of FGC's Heroic Era

Poster for the 1948 Conference. Friends General Conference Records, Friends Historical Library of Swarthmore College.

it clearly understood that negroes or members of other races attending the Conference be given hotel and entertainment privileges while at Cape May" (9/1947). The next gathering should focus on religious dedication and its product in service. It should

> provide youth with dedicated and able leadership, making youth interests a central and important part of the Conference. The kind

of social and cultural influence found in literature, radio and film should be recognized and something done to combat its evils. We have a duty to take a strong stand and not lose sight of the importance of the arts and their influence. Old and young should seek together and the Conference should offer opportunity for them to do so.

The "purity" concern among Friends had been largely attenuated, after Prohibition had turned a moral concern into public policy and then dropped it. But we can hear it still stirring among Central Committee members here, perhaps an expression of the wider public concern about postwar morality. It is balanced by an affirmation of the arts and their influence, something not heard earlier in the FGC conversation. By the early 1950s, the arts as channels of wholesome personal expression finally found their way into Pendle Hill's curriculum. We will also hear more of the language of seeking at this Conference. No longer shall the older teach the younger; they shall seek together.

The Planning Committee (11/1947) responded to the surge of young Friends by expanding the number of groups. The Junior Conference included children up to the sixth grade. The Junior High Section, grades 7-9, the High School Section, grades 10-12, and finally, the young Friends group, college age and older. High School Section teens would be housed in separate hotels for boys and girls. The brochure advertising the High School Section featured a drawing of black, white, and Asian youth (all male) facing the future together.

This year, young Friends organized their round tables and other activities themselves. These included a work project at a Cape May negro community center for four afternoons. In addition, "Low-Cost, Cooperative Living" in a local high school and grade school would be offered as an option, keeping down costs ($15 for the week), making for greater attendance and wider participation. "The Committee feels this project follows the testimony on simplicity and at the same time offers an opportunity for group cooperation and personal comradeship." This is a rare mention of the testimony of simplicity up to this point in FGC records. The dynamics of a new generational cohort were rapidly developing.

CHAPTER 7   Pax Americana and the End of FGC's Heroic Era

The Planning Committee also felt that "two years is too long a break between one Conference and the next," and asked whether Conferences could be held on alternate years as well. This is the first time I find this concern raised. It would be another fifteen years before that step was taken, partly in order to hold some Conferences outside the Philadelphia region and attract the growing number of FGC Friends living elsewhere.

The Conference theme for 1948 was "A Living Faith for Today's Needs." The preliminary announcement unpacked the title:

> Hunger stalks the world today, but all its pangs are not physical. The deeper, more pervading hunger is spiritual. It weighs heavily upon many who are well-fed, well-clothed and well-housed. It is a hunger that is bred of confusions, uncertainty, frustrations and fears. That hunger can be assuaged. Friends believe, by recognizing its cause and supplying the fundamental foods of the spirit—which are religious clarity, faith and courage—men ... will find their way to peace of mind, to a wider understanding and more comprehensive brotherhood.

The coming decade indeed manifested widespread spiritual hunger in America. Religious participation soared. Whereas membership in churches and synagogues was a robust 49 percent of the US population in 1940, it rose to 55 percent by 1950, and reached 69 percent in 1959, the highest level in American history. Social conformity was a strong factor in this period, but as historian James T. Patterson suggests, people joined religious groups mainly to feel safe and comfortable amid rapid social change and anticommunist fears.[239] As noted earlier in this chapter, FGC Friends garnered some of this influx into religious life, mainly from the more left-leaning and pacifist sectors of American society.

Eleanor Starr again supplied "The Story of Friends Genera Conference" for the special issue of the *Intelligencer* (7/24) containing most of the proceedings:

> How uplifting it was to meet together again at the Cape May Conference! The Conference of 1948 will be one of the long remembered gatherings in this hospitable seaside resort. There was a shadow, however, which could not be dispelled: Rufus M. Jones

has left us. That gallant spirit had slipped away, and American Quakerdom does not seem the same. He wrote of luminous trails and if ever a man left a luminous trail behind him in this unhappy world, it was Rufus Jones. As the Conference went on, it became apparent that his influence permeated our gatherings more compellingly than when he was still alive.

To savor the memory of Rufus, Chairman Bliss Forbush opened each plenary session with a reading from his many works.

Starr continued, noting that the weather this year was perfect and that all signs of the destructive hurricane of 1944 were now gone. The convention center on the pier had been expanded to accommodate 1,200.

The opening address was given by William Hubben, managing editor of the *Intelligencer*, on "Faith in Our Time." He offered a progressive-humanist definition of faith as "spiritual impatience to see our ideals realized." He defined the supreme task of the time as "the spiritual and moral regeneration of man." Thus, we can hear the heroic impulses of moral idealism and questing activism resilient through the many changes we have seen in this half-century of FGC Conferences, holding at bay melancholy and the tragic sense.

Marking the bicentennial of the birth of Elias Hicks, Bliss Forbush shared from his extensive study of Hicks in "Light Hath Broken." (His work would eventually be published in 1956 as *Elias Hicks, Quaker Liberal*). In his day, Hicks had warned that in wider associations Friends would be "swallowed up in the mass of people, and be numbered among the unstable multitude who have no sure and solid foundation to rest their hopes upon." Friends had been set apart to make a peculiar contribution to the world. That vocation was discerned through "the complete subjugation of the human will to the divine will, and a renunciation of self, the closest obedience to the Inner Light." Most Friends at the Conference probably preferred Hubbens' idealist definition of faith to Hicks's quietist one. But Forbush insisted that Friends not forget these deeper registers of their tradition.

Henry Cadbury spoke of his work with the team of New Testament scholars producing a fresh translation of the Bible (their work was published as the Revised Standard Version in 1952). Cadbury worked on the Book of Acts, his area of specialization. But he suggested that the larger task, shared by all, is to translate the New Testament into life, not just into modern English. Cadbury also led a round table on the apostle Paul, which drew the largest attendance with "good jokes" and "rich stores of information."

Patrick Murphy Malin, a favorite Conference speaker, was gifted at bridging traditional and contemporary Quaker sensibilities. The enlarged convention hall was filled to overflowing for his address, in which he reminded Friends of the definition of faith found in Hebrews 11: "The Substance of Things Hoped For." He defined Quakers as "a people who are committed to a theology of search. They have integrity and justice, and are not cruel or fanatical, and are not too often greedy. But they are moderately indifferent. The hardest thing to do is get outside the inertia that besets us." He praised Rufus Jones as a Quaker Moses who had broken that inertia for many. One attender remarked, "This young man is following in the footsteps of Rufus Jones more closely than anyone else in our midst."

Dorothy Tilly of President Truman's Civil Rights Committee commented that "Politics have made capital out of the rights of the people. Civil rights are a political football." Meanwhile, the war years had seen not only the internment of Japanese Americans but the lynching of African Americans in all but six states. The Civil Rights Committee's report called urgently for new legislation. (Truman was able to desegregate the armed forces by executive order during the Korean War. The Supreme Court was able to overturn some Jim Crow laws. But the larger political impasse was broken by faith-based civil rights initiatives from the grassroots in the years to come.)

Allan Freelon, assistant to the director of fine arts for Philadelphia's public schools, spoke on "Art as a Means of Communication." He acknowledged the positive and negative potentials of art. Commercial artists serving the purposes of advertising and profit flooded the public with images "to make life appear happy." Blonde women and six-foot men had become the ideal, while darker people became villains. He urged that "Quakers should make greater use of the arts to share their ideals with the rest of America. The use of every avenue of communication is of imperative importance." As noted earlier, Friends were at last ready to embrace the arts. In the next decade, the Quaker artist Fritz Eichenberg made the case for socially engaged art and contributed more than a hundred woodcuts to *The Catholic Worker*.[240] But art as self-expression often served more narrowly personal purposes beginning in the 1950s, as Friends were influenced by the expanding affects of private life in American culture.

William Biddle, director of community studies at Earlham College, amplified Rufus Jones' concern for rural America in "Rural Roots of Democracy." Rural life had been the "laboratory of democracy" through most of American history. Yet the balance had swung toward cities:

> Why is democracy deteriorating at the grass roots, and why do we all increasingly depend upon the central government to solve our problems for us? . . . Friends should be peculiarly challenged by the possibilities of rural life. They are essentially a rural sect. Their historic witness fits into methods for releasing good will.

The progressive agenda to enlist government in effecting social reform had achieved many successes. But the urban focus of centralized government had largely neglected rural America. As liberal Quakerism became increasingly urban and campus-oriented, it manifested some of the same social dynamics. Biddle and Jones sounded a call to rural renewal that few Friends followed beyond the rapidly expanding suburbs.

The Conference featured eleven round tables plus four more for young Friends. The language of "crisis" was pervasive, whether the focus was on education, international relations, race relations, Quaker renewal, or rural life. "Seeking" had also become a Quaker meme. A round table titled "Audacious Quakerism" affirmed that "We can all share in welcoming into membership fellow seekers." One might conclude that Friends had joined the seekers as much as seekers were joining Friends, in an indeterminate search. That tendency was queried by Gilbert Kilpack, extension secretary at Pendle Hill, in another round table, "What Is Our message?" Kilpack asked, "Have we a message other than the power of the Inward Light and the necessity for every man to work out his own salvation? Does even this need amplification?"

CHAPTER 7 Pax Americana and the End of FGC's Heroic Era

Rachel Davis Dubois continued to offer her workshop-style round tables, teaching the method of spontaneous intercultural conversation she had created. She had by now founded and directed the Workshop for Cultural Democracy in New York. (Later, after a time of retreat at Pendle Hill, she created a version of her technique for Friends, called Quaker Dialogue. Backed by FGC's Advancement Committee, she introduced Quaker Dialogue to over four hundred Friends groups. Meanwhile, her growing reputation beyond the Society of Friends led Martin Luther King, Jr. to invite her to bring her methods to the civil rights struggle. She joined the Southern Christian Leadership Conference staff in Atlanta in 1965. She then taught her methods at Earlham College in the early 1970s.[241])

A round table on "The Rural Friends Meeting Today" looked at population trends in rural areas versus cities, suggesting that rural Friends meetings could build local community by linking with other organizations such as the Grange, Future Farmers of America, 4-H, and others.

A total of 1,683 officially registered at the Conference, from twenty-two states and three other nations. Perhaps as many as two thousand attended at least a session or two. The usual preponderance of Friends from the immediate region led one speaker to remark on "the fatherhood of God, the brotherhood of man, and the neighborhood of Philadelphia." The tenth Junior Conference boasted 250 children from fourteen states. Besides producing and selling *The Junior Intelligencer* again this year, the Junior High group also studied drama, nature, and art. The High School Section had 233 and largely followed its very successful 1946 program. A high point was a meeting for worship on the beach, in which only two or three messages were spoken (again, evincing a distaste for the older generations' wordy ways). Finally, young Friends were more process-oriented than the older Friends in organizing their round tables; the four round tables reported back to the entire young Friends group at the end of the week.

Afternoons continued to be free for recreation and relaxation, but many Friends instead attended various "side-shows," as Starr dubbed them. For example, the American Friends Fellowship Council held a well-attended meeting on outreach. The AFFC had created the Wider Quaker Fellowship in 1936. The WQF now had 33,600 members in one hundred cities. The AFFC also worked to encourage inter-visitation among meetings, which was particularly helpful to new meetings. To further that work, a new *Directory of Meetings* was now available. Two large exhibit rooms accommodated the growing number of organizations wishing to make Friends aware of their work. Book sales were stimulated by short book reviews at the start of morning plenary sessions. Finally, Conference finances were also healthy in this period. The 1948 gathering totaled $4,576 in expenditures and $5,424 in income.

Emboldened Vision amid Major Transitions

During the 1948 Conference, the Central Committee formed a committee to explore "widening the influence" of FGC. The following September 1949, the Central Committee asked this ad hoc committee to explore drawing other yearly meetings into affiliation with FGC, in particular Philadelphia Yearly Meeting Orthodox, the recently formed Pacific Yearly Meeting, and the recently united New England Yearly Meeting (Gurneyite and Wilburite Orthodox Friends in New England reunited in 1945). They were further asked to explore what changes in FGC's constitution and organization would facilitate this expansion. Larger questions were also raised: "Where shall FGC look in the future?" "Where shall the emphasis be laid?" These confident affects generated new initiatives by the time of the 1950 Conference.

Shortly after 1948 Conference, Bliss Forbush represented FGC Friends at the first Assembly of the World Council of Churches in Amsterdam, a convergence of 130 churches from forty-one nations. The following November he reported to the Executive Committee that the Council had decided for certain that FGC "may remain a member basing membership on the spirit rather than the letter of the Council's interpretation." The Committee concluded that it was better to remain in the WCC than to withdraw over a theological technicality. "Friends are in the stream of Christianity and belong to such a world fellowship." FGC also remained engaged with the Federal Council of Churches and the International Association for Liberal Christianity and Religious Freedom.

CHAPTER 7   Pax Americana and the End of FGC's Heroic Era

Barnard Walton on the boardwalk at Cape May. Courtesy of the Walton family.

After eight energetic years as chairman of FGC, Bliss Forbush resigned in November 1949, but remained active as one of the vice chairs. His tenure was much shorter than those of his two twenty-year predecessors, but Forbush was both a capable organizational leader and a powerful voice for reclaiming the historic, normative definitions of Quaker faith and practice.

Clarence and Lilly Pickett in 1949. Courtesy of Friends Historical Library of Swarthmore College.

Six months later, Barnard Walton asked to be relieved as FGC's Executive Secretary, after thirty-five years of service (he had replaced Henry Wilbur). In addition, Vesta Haines, who had organized the first ten Junior Conferences, asked to be released from that responsibility. All three received warm accolades from the Executive and Central Committees for their faithful, innovative leadership. FGC thus embarked upon a major transitional phase. Marshall Taylor of the Advancement Committee remarked that "The Society of Friends seems to be in the hands of the younger generation" (Executive Committee, 1/1950).

The AFSC was also in transition as its historic work in postwar relief and reconstruction came to an end. Suffering health problems from twenty-one years of self-expending service, Clarence Pickett resigned as executive secretary in April 1950. He and his family moved from Pendle Hill to Haverford, but Pickett remained active with the AFSC on an emeritus basis. Friends were already a minority of AFSC staff, and the dynamics of bureaucratization and professionalization would continue to work against the tradition of inspired-amateur, short-term Quaker service. Barnes summarizes that as the Service Committee edged out further into the world, it "inevitably became worldly."[242] The Nobel Peace Prize probably also stimulated the organization's ambitions.

These are not necessarily criticisms of the AFSC, but a realistic assessment of the way a successful experiment institutionalizes and generalizes. The same dynamics can be seen in many other path-breaking Quaker initiatives in history. Indeed, the success of the Gurneyite evangelical renewal in the latter nineteenth century and the eventual success of FGC by the mid-twentieth century demonstrate how even denominational membership organizations metamorphose into institutional arrangements that might be called para-Quaker. The dwindling numbers of "real" Quakers, the Conservative Friends, continued to subsist in rural America, where Rufus Jones had grown up, and where his heart gravitated during his last days.

The 1950 Cape May Conference

The Conference theme for 1950 (June 23-30) was "Bridging the Gaps of Misunderstanding." The preliminary announcement suggested that, like building a material bridge, bridging gaps of misunderstanding requires activity on both sides. Like civil engineers, the Conference speakers would submit specifications for the bridges to be built and suggest ways Quaker religious faith could contribute. "Gaps Which Must Be Bridged": interpersonal, generational, racial, East and West, communism and democracy, labor and management, faith and works, religious profession and practice, the church and the common man, man and God.

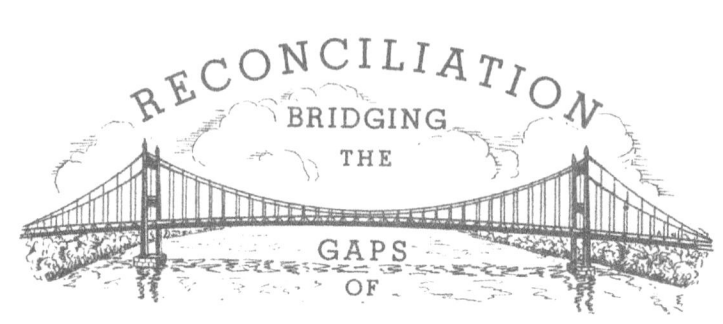

Poster for the 1950 Conference. Friends General Conference Records, Friends Historical Library of Swarthmore College.

Liberal Friends before World War I had confidently heralded a new world they believed all would soon join them in entering. They now confronted stubborn, pervasive conflicts, but still with a liberal

CHAPTER 7 Pax Americana and the End of FGC's Heroic Era

confidence that differences are mainly misunderstandings to be overcome through more study and dialogue.

The theme also addressed a social and spiritual malaise that soon found various expressions in the coming decade. For many, the shattering dissonances of the war—massive destruction, twenty million lives lost, including genocidal horrors, had destroyed their faith in both God and humanity. Many of those who had come of age during the war were alienated and confused. The baby boom and the surge in religious participation sought to stabilize reality in foundational norms and values. Psychology and psychotherapy took hold among the middle classes. The personalist psychology of Carl Rogers was especially popular. But catch-phrases of the 1950s—"the lonely crowd," "alienation," "individualism," "loss of community," "identity crisis"—expressed the anomic affects of postwar America. French existentialism, declaring the raw absurdity of life, became popular in intellectual circles.

This year, the Publicity Committee produced fliers, posters, programs, invitations, news releases, and publicity articles. After the Conference, they also sent the texts or abstracts of some addresses and reports of the Conference to *The Friend* (Philadelphia), *The Friend* (London), and *The American Friend* (Richmond, Indiana). Clearly, FGC was working to extend its influence across borders that were becoming more porous.

Registration fees were low: $4 for adults, $6 for a couple, $10 for an entire family, $2 for high-school teenagers. Even these rates were voluntary, but larger contributions were also invited. A total of eighteen Cape May hotels offering a range of rates were open to Conference attenders. Each hotel had an FGC host to facilitate accommodations. FGC's youth movement continued. The Junior Conference was broken down into two groups, Juniors (fourth to sixth grades) and Primary (first to third grades). Young Friends repeated their cooperative living experiment. The High School Section program was loaded with stimulating speakers including Bayard Rustin of the FOR and sociologist Ira Reid from Haverford College.

The Conference was summarized in one issue of the *Intelligencer* (7/22). "Sidelights from Cape May" began with the news of Barnard Walton's retirement announcement, "everywhere received with universal regret." But his plan to continue serving as "ambassador-at-large" would "more than guarantee the continuity of our tradition." Walton's extensive travels among Friends had not only encouraged existing meetings but also drew new meetings into affiliation with FGC. The use of the word "tradition" is noteworthy, as we have not often heard it used with positive connotation among liberal-progressive Friends. Perhaps at this high-point (and turning-point) of FGC's first half-century, Friends were sufficiently confident in their identity and purpose to reclaim the word.

Meetings for worship continued to be a point of intergenerational friction: "Many meetings for worship became occasions for practicing forbearance with some of our all too vocal Friends." Young Friends held an alternative daily worship "guaranteed to be a silent meeting," obviously in protest. The author (uncredited) wondered, however, "whether this assurance of silence was not doing an injustice of another kind to the character of an unprogrammed worship hour."

Nine Friends schools and sixteen Friends organizations and committees displayed visual materials and literature, suggesting the broad scope of Quaker activity. "Many samples of art and handicraft from Friends schools showed an unusual level of achievement." Book tables featured a total of 469 titles this year. Authors of new Quaker books were on hand to autograph their work. Group singing continued to be a high-point. This year, Luther Saxton sang solo renditions of spirituals, strengthening affective connection across racial lines.

Fully 1,900 Friends registered at this Conference. *The Intelligencer* called it "one of the most auspicious gatherings in its long tradition." Even more impressive, however, was the evident

> determination to see present-day realities as basic spiritual needs in the realms of politics, social conflict, and racial tension. We are sensing the urgency to find our place in the large family of ecumenical Christianity without compromising our beliefs, and to inject into the blood stream of the Christian Church our specific testimonies.

First "tradition," now "beliefs."

In "The Spirit of Friends General Conference," editor William Hubben offered apt remarks about plenary addresses, "but many

CHAPTER 7 Pax Americana and the End of FGC's Heroic Era

Friends felt even more enriched by the Study Groups" (a new terminology for small-group work). Meanwhile the Central Committee held soul-searching sessions on future "unity among Philadelphia Friends." It was made clear that in any move toward union, FGC "will maintain its present organization and be open to even more inclusive and flexible affiliation with other bodies of Friends." The movement toward "organic union" was now fully on the table and in public. (At Pendle Hill, Howard Brinton was persuaded to delay his retirement as director for two years, to help foster the process among Philadelphia Friends. He and Anna Brinton left in 1952 for two years in Japan.) Hubben summarized, "We are entering the fourth century of Quakerism with a new vision."

Notwithstanding all these encouraging indicators, Gilbert Kilpack's opening address offered a sobering assessment of the challenges facing Friends at midcentury. He spoke of "the poisonous flowering of our secular humanist renaissance. This renaissance started positively by affirming human values and ended by denying them in the name of statism and of collectivism of all forms." Without the eternal perspective, humanism collapses into sheer pragmatism and meaningless freedom, "a new dark age." He warned Friends against "the inward seduction" of good intentions without strong moral character, of settling for false unity. "Friends, we have nothing to be proud of except that we are called of God to do something particular in this world." Hubben characterized Kilpack's astringent message as a "critical diagnosis of much of our religious thinking as vague and noncommittal theism with only a weak Christological core."

Friends were probably relieved to return their attention outward to the world's problems. Cornelius Krusé, a New England Friend and one of the drafters of AFSC's recent report, *The United States and the Soviet Union*, commented that cold war developments were in such flux that some details of the report were already dated. Meanwhile, he placed the ideological sparring between the US and USSR within a wider perspective:

> There is the rest of the world, far outnumbering both in population, hoping for peace, but desiring neither *pax Americana* nor *pax Russiana*, in fact fearful of a conflict between both in which they

would be helpless victims; hoping to emerge from want and undernourishment to a sufficiency for life and health, eager too for a place of dignity in the world—all of these are watching our every move.

Thus, Krusé shifted focus to what was later named the "third world." He urged that the forces of democracy should "make friends rather than allies" among the nations of the world.

At the end of the Wednesday morning session, Raymond Wilson of the Friends Committee on National Legislation brought news of the invasion of South Korea by the North, aided by China. He stressed the need for world law. The next morning, novelist Pearl Buck asked, "Can We Be Friends with the Chinese?" (Two of her children were starting at George School in the fall.) She observed that, with the new developments in Korea and President Truman's plans to occupy the island of Formosa, relations with China would become still more challenging. She urged Friends to use their world-wide credibility to work for better East-West relations. Hubben remarked that Buck's address was enough "to antagonize anyone who has surrendered to anti-Russian hysteria."

Bayard Rustin made his first FGC plenary address: "The dominant note of our time is fear. We are afraid of each other and ourselves. We behave as though we were afraid that the truth were not true." The new prophetic voices were coming not from the Church but from scientists speaking against the atomic bomb. Answers would come not from institutions but from "individuals who are so completely responsible, so revolutionary, as to be able to cut themselves off from dead practices and to develop on their own." Security springs from insecurity. When we hold onto security, we become insecure. Rustin had recently traveled in the South, sitting at the front of the bus. He told of a friendly conversation that arose out of one of these confrontations. He concluded:

> If you would win your life, you must be willing to lose it, to gamble it, to throw it away. Nonviolent resistance to injustice will first of all establish your self-respect. Then you can go about loving others.... We cannot feel love if we have not self-respect. In the face of all our difficulties, there is always a way out, through God. We are not alone in what we do.

CHAPTER 7 Pax Americana and the End of FGC's Heroic Era

Bayard Rustin with the lute he learned to play while in prison for draft resistance. By permission of The Bayard Rustin Estate.

Rustin closed by singing "There Is a Balm in Gilead." Grounded in concrete nonviolent practice, Rustin could tell illustrative stories rather than rely solely upon the general, idealistic statements common among more traditional pacifists. As Hubben remarked, "the fresh air of action was breathing through his courageous testimony." Besides his twenty-eight months in prison for draft resistance, Rustin had already been arrested more than twenty times for various nonviolent actions before he began working as a nonviolent strategist for Martin Luther King, Jr. in 1955.[243]

William Simkin, a Quaker labor arbitrator, spoke on "Arbitration and Mediation." He noted that hundreds of strikes were being settled by arbitration. A good mediator must be fearless and tireless in order to build bridges between management and labor. He had arbitrated more than 1,600 cases between companies and unions, and could count on one hand the number of cases where parties didn't live up to their agreements. He found compulsory arbitration unhelpful; both parties must agree to arbitrate. David Henley, economics professor at Earlham College, spoke on "The Impact of Organized Labor on the Social Order." He saw the US changing from a capitalist society to a labor society. Organized labor would prove a stabilizing force and a key to preserving freedom in American society. (That was not an unrealistic assessment in 1950; but consumer-driven capitalism privatized labor's gains over the next decade.) Hubben commented that ten to fifteen years earlier, some Friends might have protested such favorable portrayals of organized labor; they were now "accepted in a spirit of fairness and realism."

That evening, William Visser 'T Hooft, general secretary of the World Council of Churches, spoke on "Diversities of Gifts but the Same Spirit." He observed that the ecumenical movement was rediscovering what is already true: there is only one body, religiously speaking. The Church has been impoverished by not taking this truth seriously. The particular gifts of each branch of the Church must be shared with the others. (For example, in the years ahead, Friends worked with Mennonites and the Church of the Brethren to press the Christian vocation of peacemaking upon the wider Church, through the WCC and other channels.[244])

The Conference's twelve round tables and study groups (the difference between the two is not clear) covered a wide range of issues, from First-Day school teaching to international affairs. "Problems of International Peace," chaired by Esther Holmes Jones, drew the largest numbers, more than 200 daily, to ponder the hot-button issues of the day. The First-Day school round table drew the smallest at thirty-seven.

"Unity in Faith," led by Hale Sutherland, found the differences between evangelical and liberal beliefs trivial. The psychological insights of Carl Jung and Fritz Künkel (a personalist psychologist who taught that summer at Pendle Hill) had put myth in a new light:

> Actually, the inner man, the subconscious, is at one with the Universal Self, with God, and it is the mission of religion to "save"

man, to awaken him to the truth of his being, to bring subconscious and conscious under the domination of the superconscious, the Christ within. Too often the liberal is unaware of his psychological bondage and drifts along in drab mediocrity without inner experience of the divine renewing. Other liberals, aware of the lives and teachings of the great mystics, experience the same inward work of grace and come easily to accept the evangelical as brother Christian in spite of semantic differences.

This is an important first sighting of the new interest in psychology, which would sweep across liberal Quakerism and much of American society. In this case, it was employed in the service of Christian faith; but psychology became a spirituality in its own right in the years to come.

"The Religion of Jesus" was led by Mary Blackmar. Reading among the synoptic gospels, they found Jesus to be a "keen searcher for the truth." Bigotry and hypocrisy were to him the greatest sin. Jesus stressed that all are free to choose; no one is coerced into the kingdom. From the preceding Conference, we noticed that Friends were joining the new seekers, as much as seekers were joining Friends meetings. Now we find Jesus a seeker too, with liberal values. In 1941, Reinhold Niebuhr had snidely characterized the liberal Christian's Jesus as "a very, very, very good man."[245]

Reports of the round tables and study groups seem to indicate more participational modes replacing the strongly presentational style that had dominated for so long. But while more perspectives were shared, the diffuse understandings of participants also became more noticeable. And the broadening scope of Friendly inquiry diffused Quakerism further in the decades ahead.

The Central Committee Looking Ahead

George Walton (see photograph on p. 104) became FGC's new chairman by the time of the 1950 Conference. He took hold of a Central Committee at full gallop. A record seventy-five Committee members attended its sessions during the Conference (attendance typically averaged forty-five to fifty-five). A Survey Committee had been appointed earlier to evaluate the state of FGC. Its work was still in progress, but concern was already expressed that "our efforts are far too often utilitarian ... we should rather consider ourselves part of the creative process of God, ready to work as His tools and work in the mysteries of His creation."

Still, in view of the movement toward unity among unprogrammed Friends:

> it seemed to be the sense of the meeting that it would be unwise for the General Conference to try to write or publish any statement of religious belief but rather to adjust their thinking to the growing movement of unity that now exists in the whole Society. We must continue to keep away from theological statements.

We have heard this caution before. It was a sensible concern but tended to forestall any attempt to bring more religious focus to FGC, notwithstanding calls for it. The conversation shifted briefly to an article by Bliss Forbush that month in the *Intelligencer*. He had found that George Fox and even Elias Hicks followed the traditional theology of Jesus as both human and divine. In response, someone reflected, "It is hard to see why some Friends want to deprive Jesus of every divine attribute when they stress 'that of God in every man'."

The Survey Committee's six-page progress report advocated a restatement of the fundamentally religious purpose of FGC:

> A more direct religious emphasis by FGC would clarify the misunderstanding with which some Friends regard the Conference.... The Conference was founded as a religious organization. It deals with the religious concerns of Friends and should foster inward, personal, spiritual growth. Members of the Conference need such growth just as much as their neighbors do.

These discernments among Survey and Central Committee members, largely Friends with long-term experience and commitment, identified some serious points of concern. Yet the large influx of new meetings and Friends who had been attracted by AFSC's programmatic Quakerism boded a continued momentum toward pragmatic activism.

The Central Committee also struggled to absorb the news of Barnard Walton's retirement as general secretary. One member remarked, "He can cross any barrier with ease." Walton would

CHAPTER 7 Pax Americana and the End of FGC's Heroic Era

continue on staff, however, and planned to organize a nucleus of visiting Friends to multiply his efforts, much as the "Valiant Sixty" had multiplied the effectiveness of George Fox.

The next general secretary would hopefully "lead us into a deeper religious life and contribute to the growth of unity among Friends." (In the next month, it was announced that Earle Edwards, a Swarthmore and Union Seminary graduate heading the AFSC's Chicago office, had accepted the role.)

New Directions

Later that same summer (8/5), the *Intelligencer* published an article, "New Directions," by Preston Roberts, a member of Philadelphia Yearly Meeting teaching with the Federated Theological Schools of the University of Chicago. He began by noting:

> The American Friends Service Committee has in a sense and to a degree established its life and work once and for all. For a generation it has enabled a concern for peace and social service to stand at the center of Friendly interest and attention. By virtue of the excellence and permanence of its achievements, it is now possible to say that never again, or at least not for a long time, will the Society of Friends be unable to provide its ethical and political testimony with an effective witness. And yet many young Friends are beginning to look, and I think quite rightly, in new directions. The Service Committee is something their fathers and mothers did or are doing. In their eyes, it already has the status of a living tradition—a *living* tradition, but a tradition nonetheless. They are quite rightly asking: What is to be the new creature and the new life?

Roberts continued, noting that many young Friends were finding new life in the united meetings and work for an undivided Society. This would prove significant—*if* it meant the resolution of deep theological differences, bridged gaps between rural and urban Friends, between convinced and birthright members, and united Friends on more than a social or administrative basis.

Moreover, many young Friends realized that even this would not suffice. Internal resolutions would mean little if the Society did not relate itself to the wider Christian movement. But this would be a daunting task. "Through no fault of their own, too many members of our Society are theologically and religiously uninformed, if not illiterate." And worse, much of the wider Church was indifferent or even hostile to Quaker doctrinal, social, and political witness. The central theme of Quaker religiosity is the simple truth that the letter killeth and the Spirit giveth life. "This lack of explicitness, however, means that the Society of Friends can participate in ecumenical discussion only with great difficulty and at many crucial points and moments with small success." Roberts observed that the founders of the AFSC had faced obstacles just as great. Perhaps a sufficient number of young Friends would commit themselves to acquire the theological training required for ecumenical engagement.

Roberts's article contains significant insights. His experience with young Friends offered further definition to the generational cohort we have watched forming at Conferences over the last decade. He focused more on theological concerns than we heard from Conference reports. It is worth noting that a small cluster of young Friends did undertake advanced theological studies at this time. These include Arthur Roberts (an evangelical Friend), T. Canby Jones, Wilmer Cooper, and Hugh Barbour, all of whom went on to academic teaching in Quaker colleges. These were also among the founders of the Quaker Theological Discussion Group in the mid-1950s. Wilmer Cooper was also central in founding the Earlham School of Religion in 1960.

Roberts's references to the AFSC also ring prophetic. Gregory Barnes notes that by 1950, with Quakers already a minority of its staff, the era of AFSC as a Quaker stronghold was coming to an end. In 1945, Clarence Pickett had remarked that while the AFSC sought to foster the Society of Friends in every way, it also benefitted from the presence of non-Friends on staff. He hoped it would become more socially diverse: "We wish to avoid becoming sectarian, but we would lose our significance as an agency functioning in our chosen fields if we did not represent the spirit of the Society of Friends at its best." The Service Committee struggled with that tension the rest of the century.[246] Meanwhile, as Roberts notes, many young Friends were exploring new channels of service and witness for new times.

CONCLUSION

At the start of Chapter 1, we observed that the early Quaker movement emerged from a fusion of two kinds of Seekers, some radical Protestants and others proto-liberals. The early Quaker message and spiritual formation confirmed the seeking expectations of both groups in some ways and disconfirmed them in other ways. Both the backward-longing orientation of the radical Protestant Seekers, looking for a way back to the purity of the New Testament Church, as well as the forward-straining orientation of the proto-liberal Seekers, heralding the imminent new age of the Spirit, were reoriented to a radical present by George Fox's spiritual counsel to "stand still in the light."

Fox's 1652 letter to his parents could be taken to summarize his spiritual counsel to these two kinds of Seekers:

> Oh! Be faithful! Look not back, nor be too forward, further than you have attained; for you have no time, but this present time: therefore prize your time for your souls' sake. And so grow up in that which is pure, and keep to the oneness; then shall my joy be full.[247]

But that personal spiritual counsel was also accentuated by a sense of a historic moment in Fox's proclamation that "Christ is come to teach his people himself and take them off the world's religions and ways." That sense of moment made the Quaker movement more than a new mysticism, but a prophetic confrontation with a religiously hypocritical, socially inequitable, and physically violent English society. This second-coming announcement of Christ's return *via* the light in each person's conscience was *apocalyptic* in the sense of the word's Greek root (*apokalypto*, "to reveal"): it was the *present revelation* of the end. It deconstructed the false self and the world it construes around itself. So, it was grounded in inward experience but moved outward to confront and challenge an unjust, alienated society. The fulfillment Seekers had only dreamed of became real as they became radically present in the present moment to the divine Presence. Looking backwards or forwards only fostered wishful idealism in either direction.

It is commonly supposed that early Christians and early Friends were mistaken in their apocalyptic message. The world didn't end after all. But the end-time had indeed begun with these movements. It was simply rebuffed by the human alienation and violent persecution of a society inured to the meantime's mean comforts. God respects the human freedom to reject divine invitations and to postpone the kingdom of heaven.

As Friends accepted defeat, both in England of the latter seventeenth century and again in America a century later (as described early in Chapter 1), they settled into the meantime, but in ways that preserved and codified their utopian impulses and countercultural ways. The hedged, sectarian mode of the "quietist" period sought to preserve a life Friends knew was a divine gift. But the longer they drifted into the meantime, the world's categories of thought slowly reasserted themselves. We traced in Chapter 1 the ways the original Seeker outlooks reasserted themselves, polarizing into divergent evangelical and liberal streams.

From this perspective, the nineteenth-century trajectories of evangelical and liberal Friends can be recognized as more than random drift through the wider culture. Just as radical Protestant Seekers had longed for a visible Church re-founded in the New Testament pattern, Orthodox Friends renewed their Quaker faith through a hybridization with the evangelical movement and its biblical moorings, resulting in a large growth in numbers. They renewed the covenant as understood in the Hebrew-Christian tradition. Evangelical renewal also manifested itself in various forms of social service and work for reform: abolition, prison work, poor relief, education.

For their part, Hicksite Friends were unsuccessful in numerical growth, but they were less focused on that kind of visible manifestation. They were more attuned to the invisible church as a universal human project, framed sometimes in terms of common humanity and other times in terms of all persons and groups that follow the light in the human conscience. Like many proto-liberal Seekers of the seventeenth century, these liberalizing Friends took civil, constitutional polity, rather than biblical covenant, as their framing for understanding where the light was leading.

In many respects, both streams of Friends can claim as their spiritual parent William Penn, who could think and write one moment like a Protestant sectarian and the next moment as an early liberal. George Fox and the other leaders of the first Friends, though just one generation older, represent another, not quite yet modern, species of the Spirit. We tend to appropriate their words in sound-bytes but miss their very different mindset.[248]

So, our story of Hicksite developments through the nineteenth century in Chapter 1, followed by the evolution of Friends General Conferences up to 1950 in Chapters 2 through 7, has traced the reincarnation of liberal Seekerism. By the latter 1940s, we even heard FGC Friends starting to reframe themselves as seekers. All along the way, we found them strongly exercised, some of them actively engaged, for the full realization of the US Constitution in American society, particularly in terms of women's suffrage and racial justice, but also including greater economic equality in various forms. We also heard, in the aftermaths of two catastrophic world wars, a concern rising for the expansion of constitutionalism into some form of world government.

In the early decades of FGC, we also heard a strong concern for moral purity, the personal discipline that undergirds family life, which in turn grounds a healthy society. But we also saw the purity concern fade after the federal government turned the moral concern for temperance into a Constitutional amendment, and then repealed it. (See the Appendix, "A Quaker Moral Compass," for more background regarding the concern for purity and how it intersects with the concern for equity and justice.)

Our story has also followed *affect* as a key to understanding a Quaker renewal with a strong orientation to the Spirit. In the Introduction, we defined affect as the realm of human sensibility below the level of cognitive thought. Affects include subjective emotion, but also float more broadly in the culture, "affecting" whole classes, groups, nations, and so on. Affect theory has proved useful to our story of FGC Conferences, for gauging the dynamics of a middle-class religious group meeting in a resort environment for a week. As suggested in the Introduction, FGC Conferences serve as a valuable "registering instrument" for following what has inspired and disturbed liberal Friends over time. The affective registers of the Conferences, to the extent we can glean traces of them from the records, are as revealing as the cognitive content of the presentations and discussions. In particular, this book has focused on melancholy, grief, and mourning as a key affect for a group that entered the twentieth century with such high expectations for human progress, but then found itself buffeted by modernity's catastrophic setbacks.

We saw how the hubris of inflated confidence expressed in the early Conferences was blind-sided by the irrationality of World War I. We then followed ways in which the founding of the American Friends Service Committee helped transmute Quaker grief into creative service and advocacy. We saw how that renewed energy enabled Friends to expand creatively into the Great Depression, even as they clearly saw a second global conflict looming in Europe and Asia. We also observed how the collapse of the mainstream peace movement in the 1930s repositioned Friends as a countercultural force for peace and drew other bereft pacifists to FGC Friends in the 1940s. We can conclude that forward-looking progressive Friends got ahead of themselves in the early years of FGC; then the shock of crisis of war focused their minds more productively in the present, which then unfolded in unexpected patterns of renewal.

In terms of racial justice, we found Friends in a sustained melancholy of sympathy with African Americans in their oppression. Their sympathy was rather paternalistic in the early decades, owing to the lack of social contact, especially on a peer basis. But we watched it mature slowly by midcentury toward a truly dialogical relationship, aspiring to partnership. That shift was facilitated in particular by Rachel Davis DuBois's pioneering group-process methods and Bayard Rustin's personal charisma and teachings in nonviolence. Again, grounding in here-and-now relationship across racial barriers prepared Friends to be partners with African Americans in the 1950s.

We also kept an eye on generational dynamics over more than half a century. For example, the Young Friends Associations spawned a cluster of new leadership in the 1890s that included Jesse Holmes and Jane Rushmore. Both made long-term contributions to Conferences and other FGC work. Toward the end this book, we saw another notable generational cohort form through the the growing presence of young Friends at Conferences and the development of the High School Section in the 1940s. This new cohort began to challenge the group processes, especially the worship style, of the older generations. They also evinced determination to take part in new work for racial justice, which would soon find traction.

I have called this half-century of FGC liberal Quakerism a "heroic" era. That word had occurred to me well before I found Rufus Jones's last missive to Friends in 1948, calling for a renewal of heroic spirit in the postwar era (see Chapter 7). The Quaker "ideals" we have heard vaunted throughout these chapters bespeak a heroic outlook. Friends shared this outlook with the wider progressive and social gospel movements, but we have heard them articulate it in their own idiomatic way as a "liberal sect."

In the 1930s, the "Christian realism" of Reinhold Niebuhr and other neo-orthodox theologians posed a brusque challenge to the heroic idealism of liberal religion, as the world drifted from one horrific war toward the next. Fortunately, the work of the AFSC at home and abroad helped Friends ground their idealism in concrete service. Clarence Pickett's addresses in the 1930s and 40s are telling markers of that process. In addition, Bliss Forbush pressed some uncomfortable questions upon FGC Friends, inspired in part by his study of their patron saint, Elias Hicks. Lewis Benson's neo-orthodox articles in *The Friends Intelligencer* shortly after the 1938 Conference may have been too blunt to penetrate the liberal Quaker consensus. In any case, the heroic spirit can still be seen portrayed in Conference posters and program covers of the 1940s.

Posters and other graphics also express the changing affective atmosphere of the Conferences. Early promotional literature featured pen-and-ink drawings of Friends in retro-plain dress, long after the traditional Quaker dress codes had been abandoned. By the 1930s and 40s, poster and program cover graphics portrayed young Friends stylishly dressed and having fun. The shift in graphic representation accompanies the rise of singing and social dancing at the

Conferences. Friends inevitably moved into the expanding affective spaces opened by radio, motion pictures, and the phonograph.

These new aesthetic registers diffused the ethical imperatives of the traditional Quaker testimonies. This shift was most striking in the rising tide of young Quaker men going to war in this period. Academic education also expanded Quaker social analysis, ethical inquiry, and political theory in all directions. Forging united Quaker perceptions and commitments became almost impossible. The testimonies became ideals to be revered in unison but enacted only in individualized directions and degrees. The refreshing resort atmosphere of Conferences and the mutual encouragement that such large gatherings enabled tended to obscure the drift in Quaker faith and practice.

The Introduction cautioned that the Conferences functioned as a kind of Greek chorus, registering the affects of the age and lamenting the tragedies of race, poverty, and war, while also singing the praises of courageous Quaker actors in the world. How broadly these Friends followed their leaders into creative witness and action is beyond the scope of our story. But as we heard Clarence Pickett reflect, the spiritual work of individual devotion and ministry in the local Friends meeting was crucial counterbalance to Quaker work in the wider world.

We noted in Chapter 2 the influence of the Chautauqua phenomenon on the progressive movement in general and on the development of FGC in particular. We heard William James's highbrow mixture of admiration and revulsion after his week-long immersion in Chautauqua's middlebrow intelligence and affects in 1896. Perhaps the creation of a middle-class consensus that could have social and political impact required a middlebrow intellectual medium. At the end of Chapter 4 we noted the advent of middlebrow liberal religious book culture, of which Rufus Jones was a pioneer, and its efflorescence at Conference book tables.

Perhaps the strong democratizing impetus that began with Progressive Friends in the mid-nineteenth century tended to repress intellectual leadership. The specter of a Quaker intelligentsia, as embodied in the select meetings of ministers and elders, still haunted many FGC meetinghouses long after those fusty old Friends had died off. Henry Wilbur's enthusiasm and sustained energy made him a paragon of the "consecrated common sense" he extolled, even if some of his comments at Conferences were painfully parochial. We briefly noted in Chapter 5 Jesse Holmes's 1928 public letter "To the Scientifically Minded." While he rightly compared the liberal Quaker ethos of open inquiry to that of modern science, he neglected the key balancing trait in modern science: the review of scientific findings by panels of scientists to assess the validity of new claims. That function, which the select meetings had once embodied (and which they surely over-exercised in many cases) had dropped out of liberal Quakerism. With intellectual rigor weakened, affects were left to gather or scatter Friends according to the prevailing *geists* of the *zeit*.

Cape May provided an optimal space for affects to expand and intermix. Friends could literally turn their backs on the bustle and blights of Philadelphia, New York, and Baltimore, and contemplate the open sea while engaging in friendly conversation or probing discussion. The Atlantic's open expanse was an evocative correlate to the silence of Quaker meeting for worship. It is revealing that while the older generations gravitated toward wordy ministry in the large devotional sessions inside the convention hall, young Friends gravitated toward more silence—actually forbade vocal ministry one year—and occasionally held worship in smaller groups on the beach.

Perhaps in that way the Jersey shore, as a liminal (threshold) space between nature and culture, provided an ideal site for Friends to reassemble every two years, bring assorted ideas and affects from their various cultural settings and social activisms, hold them up to the open horizon, and let the sea breeze blow the chaff away from the kernel of genuine discernment. That of course is the imagery behind the traditional Quaker practice of a "threshing meeting." It does not aim to arrive at a definite decision on a matter but creates the space for a free airing of viewpoints and concerns. Real decisions may be made at other times and in other settings, but the threshing meeting is a useful preparative step in the process. So, Friends could return from Cape May cleansed by the catharsis of a week of mutual encouragement and wide-ranging inquiry, clarified in their understandings and intentions, and thereby renewed in their Quaker faith and practice, whether it was on the front-lines of peace and service work or in the quieter internal life of the local Friends meeting. The week might also add clarity and resolve to decision-making and implementation for FGC's year-round programs, or even influence the work of AFSC and other Quaker institutions represented at the Conference.

A Peek into FGC's Future-Past

In the final chapter, we heard the quip by a 1948 Conference speaker that the gathering affirmed once again "the Fatherhood of God, the brotherhood of man, and the neighborhood of Philadelphia." The second half of the twentieth century found FGC Conferences deconstructing all three of those affirmations. We will close with a brief sketch of those later developments.

First, "the Fatherhood of God," emblematic of a Christian theology, was already under revision well before 1950, when we heard Jesus described not as the Father's Son but as a fellow seeker after truth. As the "one world" thematic of the 1946 Conference portended, a more interfaith perspective would soon overtake the ecumenical Christian exploration that Bliss Forbush and others had advanced. The full, universal dimensions of "that of God in every one" found greater expression among Friends in concert with the liberalized US immigration laws of 1965 and the cultural circulation concomitant with a globalizing economy. Future decades witnessed growing interest at Conferences in eastern, Native American, and neo-pagan religious teachings and practices.

In connection with this, the baby boom generation moved into the expanded affective spaces induced by television, stereo sound, FM radio formats, headphones, Panavision films, and so on, to press a vast expansion of spiritual exploration. The ends-oriented pragmatism that energized FGC's earlier, activist generations was balanced by a more means-oriented emphasis upon spiritual techniques, alternatives, and combinations to help Friends live through the thrilling/alarming *anomie* of a world undergoing accelerating change. By the 1970s the outward-activist impetus of FGC Quakerism turned more inward and restorative. The expression of this change in Conference (renamed "Gathering" in 1978) programming was a vast expansion of a dozen "round tables" to fifty "workshops" on a wide range of spiritual, religious, social, and environmental topics.

Along the way, a growing concern for the care of the earth led to a surprising return of the purity/pollution axis of the Quaker moral compass (again, see the Appendix). We watched the early concern for moral purity, foundational to family and society, fade after the repeal of Prohibition. The other axis, the extension of compassion and justice in ever-widening circles, became dominant. But as industrial society's pollution and resource depletion reached crisis proportions, the purity/pollution code returned, not only in terms of environmental activism, but in an intensified concern for the human body and its vulnerability to a polluted environment. Eclectic practices, including yoga and Native American sweat lodges, appeared in FGC Gatherings and grounded environmental and health concerns in spiritual practice, with or without religious framing. Perhaps the planet replaced a heavenly Father as the transcendent horizon within which Quaker faith and practice were being renewed.

Second, and intimately interwoven with the first, "the brotherhood of man" emblematic of a patriarchal society and androcentric worldview, underwent deconstruction from several different angles in the second half of the century. First, we noted how feminist concerns dropped out of the programmatic focus of Conferences after the Nineteenth Amendment finally achieved women's suffrage. That does not mean that FGC women became quietly docile in the heroic era. There was no more powerfully influential Friend in the FGC orbit in this period than Jane Rushmore. Anna Jackson was a force in New York City social reform and a powerful voice on behalf of African Americans in the early Conferences. Many women were outstanding in the early decades of the AFSC. But two world wars and the drama of conscientious objection may have delayed an advancement of women's issues among Friends in this period.

Much in the way progressive Friends took many of their cues from the wider progressive movement, the deep feminist impulses of the Quaker tradition were reactivated by the wider women's movement arising at the end of the 1960s. It is indicative of those latent impulses that when they were reactivated, FGC women were quick to respond, even to move to the vanguard of the new feminism. And drawing from the Quaker tradition, these Friends were quick to connect the humanistic and political issues with feminism's underlying spiritual sensibilities. "Women's ways of knowing" were reclaimed in ways that further strengthened the reassertion of means and processes in counterbalance to pragmatic ends. Neo-pagan, wiccan, and other feminist streams of spiritual formation entered the mix of FGC Gatherings.

In some respects, the women's movement built upon the template of identity politics already pioneered by the civil rights movement. "The brotherhood of man" had implicit Eurocentric as well as androcentric framing. We saw the grooming of a new generational cohort in the 1940s that were ready to enter into dialogue and partnership with African Americans in the 1950s and beyond. Certainly, abiding paternalism remained to be examined and renounced in succeeding years, but that generation's advance over the rhetoric of preceding generations is considerable. Their advance was enabled in part through the influence of generational forerunners such as Bayard Rustin. Older Friends befriended and mentored younger Friends toward this new horizon. A high-point of this next phase of FGC's quest was Martin Luther King Jr's address to the 1958 Cape May Conference, arranged through the wide connections and credibility of AFSC's general secretary emeritus, Clarence Pickett. Racial justice concerns lost momentum among FGC Friends starting in the 1970s, in step with wider liberal trends.

The civil rights cause was displaced in the 1970s in part by the women's rights and gay rights movements. All these concerns operated mainly on the gift/debt axis and its principle of extension of compassion and justice to new social identities. Along the way, both the women's rights and gay rights movements challenged the traditional sexual taboos and gender proscriptions of the purity/pollution axis. So, the homophobic subtext of "the brotherhood of man" was next to be deconstructed among liberal Friends, and that project too found representation at FGC Conferences.

Finally, "the neighborhood of Philadelphia" was already in the early stages of deconstruction by the 1930s, as the growth of new and independent meetings spread slowly across the country, mostly in cities and campus towns, and as these new meetings were drawn into the FGC fold. The trend continued to grow from the postwar era, even producing new FGC yearly meetings such as Lake Erie and Ohio Valley. New yearly meetings and associations of Friends west of the Rocky Mountains resisted affiliation with FGC for reasons more geographical than theological. Still, many western Friends flocked to FGC Conferences as the century progressed. In 1963, FGC began holding Conferences every year, meeting on college campuses outside the mid-Atlantic region on odd years. Perhaps the event-driven decade of the sixties was also a factor: there was just too much happening and Quaker affects were evolving too quickly to be digested on a biennial basis. We heard an early expression of that concern already in the latter 1940s.

The last Conference to be held at Cape May was in 1968. The conservative radio evangelist Carl McIntyre bought up enough hotels in the town to make it untenable for FGC Conferences to be held there any longer. Conferences began to be held consistently on college campuses around the country (though attendance was usually strongest when they were held somewhere east of Ohio and north of the Carolinas). The Conferences thereby lost the unique affects of an ocean-front setting. But since most attenders were college graduates, the campus setting had its own nostalgic affects of youth's freedom and open horizons. It did, however, bring some sexual issues out into the open. Unmarried heterosexual and homosexual couples could no longer make reservations in a Cape May hotel with no questions asked but had to be countenanced by FGC personnel and policies when assigned campus housing.

More generally, the displacement of Conferences from Cape May and "the neighborhood of Philadelphia" put FGC on a much larger map. Friends from other parts of the country who had always been relatively marginal experienced greater parity. But the geographical changes also interacted with the other changes we have sketched here. The second half of the twentieth century accomplished multiple decenterings of FGC Quakerism: Eurocentric, androcentric, and Christocentric norms of the first half of the century were dispersed in various directions and at different rates in different places.

These of course are all aspects of postmodernity: interfaith universalism, the reanimation of the universe in earth-centered spiritualities, the multiculturalism of identity politics, the feminist contestation of male prerogatives, the multiple centers of a globalized economy, the dispersion of "truth" to various social identities and their respective life experiences (from *the* truth to *our* truth), and so on. One effect of these major, tectonic shifts has been for the sense of *time* to be at least partially eclipsed by the experience of *space*. All these religions, spiritual techniques, identities, and cultural inheritances exist on an enlarged map. In this situation, *progress* is eclipsed by *process*. Hence, the pragmatic activism of the heroic period in our study, aiming to further human progress (albeit a progress reckoned from certain privileged perspectives of race, class, religion, and gender) is displaced by a growing concern for appropriate processes whereby multiple positions can interact equitably and peaceably. For all that we heard about "progress," we heard nothing of "Quaker process." By the end of the twentieth century, one heard little mention of progress and quite a lot about "good process."

Another aspect of these profound changes is the demise of "the great man," the totem of the heroic era. There would be no more Rufus Joneses coming down the pike. Jones's greatness still speaks for itself. But it was founded in part upon the selfless devotion of family members, graduate students, and domestic help who would more likely pursue their own interests and concerns in the second half of the century. We heard a Friend describe Patrick Murphy Malin in 1948 as the next Rufus Jones. But Malin left Swarthmore College in 1950 to become the national director for the American Civil Liberties Union for the next 12 years. That was important work to pursue in the McCarthy era and beyond. But it was more administrative than heroic. Postmodern FGC Quakerism might be termed "anti-heroic," not necessarily to suggest a shortage of courageous individuals and selfless actions. But there has been a shift from the romantic idealism of the heroic to a more ironic sense of multiple perspectives, none of which can claim to be final. It is a shift from the upward gaze and stair-step ascent of the figures in those 1940s posters and program covers, to more circumspect glances and tentative, lateral footwork.

CONCLUSION

We heard Bliss Forbush make reference to "our Discipline" in his address to the 1940 Conference. He referred to Uniform Discipline that FGC Friends had crafted and approved in the 1920s. There was an initiative for a revision in 1941, but that quickly stalled. The Uniform Discipline slowly faded into obscurity, gradually "overcome by events" of the 1960s, Chuck Fager surmises. By the time Fager rediscovered it in the late 1990s, it had been completely forgotten by FGC Friends.[249] FGC yearly meetings proceeded to revise their books of discipline by their own lights and at their own pace. The Uniform Discipline appears to be a casualty of the trend-driven focus of an organization that exists for many Friends for one cathartic week per year.

In 1978 the Conferences were renamed Gatherings, to differentiate them from the other, year-round work of Friends General Conference. "Gathering" also connoted feeling tones more than the formal, institutional associations of "Conference." The affective registers of Gatherings remain powerful to this day. The élan of Gatherings has influenced the style of the annual sessions of various liberal yearly meetings in North America and Britain.

These broad-strokes observations about FGC Quakerism and its Conferences/Gatherings after 1950 are hopefully accurate as far as they go. A researched study of this latter period would be a real contribution. I hope someone will undertake it.

APPENDIX 1

A Quaker Moral Compass

The overall social vision we find in Friends General Conferences operates along two moral axes. These may be universal coordinates of personal and social morality. But they correspond to two different codes in the Torah of ancient Israel,[250] which can help us recognize how they operate in the FGC case.

One axis represents the *purity/pollution* code of the Torah, which predominates in the book of Leviticus, rooted in the priestly traditions of ancient Israel. This code addresses issues of sexual morality, kinship relations, food, cultic ceremonies, and so on. Examples include incest taboos, kosher foods, clothing, sacrificial rituals, and care of the land. While this code of the Torah has traditionally had little appeal to Christians and modernists, it does deal with certain vital aspects of life: sexual boundaries, healthy and unhealthy foods, and a sustainable relationship with the land. It seeks to limit violence/violation as it protects moral and material purity against activities that compromise, or pollute it. Leviticus warns Israel that the land will "vomit you out" if it pollutes the land with immoral behavior. As such, this code manifests the irreducible particularity of viable health versus disease, degradation and death. It operates by the principle of limitation, exclusion. According to this code, transgression is typically experienced as shame.

The other axis represents the *gift/debt* code of the Torah, which predominates in the book of Deuteronomy, a later restatement of the laws of Moses. Deuteronomy dates from the seventh century BCE and draws from the priestly and prophetic traditions of Northern Israel. The gift/debt code emphasizes that Israel's life on the land is God's gift. To know this truth requires remembering the story of Israel's redemption from slavery in Egypt. This memory trains the heart to maintain a sense of gratitude, which in turn engenders sympathy and generosity. Thus, because Israel was once a slave and a stranger in Egypt, it should treat the slave and the stranger within its borders with justice and compassion. The gift/debt code aims to limit the violence of social injustice, inequity, and war. It includes the periodic forgiveness of debts and freeing of slaves, care for widows and orphans, the ethics of hospitality, and so on. It thereby manifests those ethical realms that are reducible to universal principles. It thus operates by the principle of extension, the extension of Israel's blessing/giftedness to others. When Israel forsakes its sense of giftedness and thereby loses its motivation for generosity, it falls into debt toward the God who has blessed so richly. Here, sin is typically experienced as guilt.

We can see these two codes, or moral sensibilities, interacting dynamically over time in the history we have been following. In Chapter 1, we traced the Hicksite trajectory through the nineteenth century, a series of rapid changes that generally shifted away from particularity to universality. The unique revelation of the Bible was re-examined according to universal ethical principles. The highly particular observance of the traditional Quaker testimonies in terms of dress, speech, and lifestyle was dropped in favor of more mainstream behaviors, while still upholding general ethical principles of simplicity, peace, and equity. Meanwhile, the Quaker experience of material and spiritual giftedness activated the principle of extension into work for the abolition of slavery, prison reform, and other manifestations of the gift/debt code. We find those shifts continuing into the twentieth century in the addresses we have reviewed in early FGC Conferences.

Still, the purity/pollution code was by no means abandoned. Quaker participation in the wider progressive purity campaigns for temperance and against various vices expressed a concern for the polluting potentials, both material and moral, of an increasingly prosperous society. From their beginnings in seventeenth-century England, Friends had manifested a strong domestic ethic, together with vigorous critiques of alehouses, "vain pastimes," and conspicuous consumption.[251] This traditional domestic ethic readily melded with the wider progressive movement's ideal of family life as the foundation of a just society and a prosperous nation. Note the role of

Aaron Powell, Henry Wilbur and others in the founding and promotion of the wider purity movement.

A broader environmental ethic is not yet audible in the FGC addresses in our period of study. So we find Quaker witness weighted toward the personal pole of the horizontal, purity/pollution axis. Environmental concern begins to appear, however, in the work of President Theodore Roosevelt and Gifford Pinchot, head of the government's forestry division, to create national parks and national forest preserves. But without much support from the progressive movement (or from Friends) to push Congress toward conservation, Roosevelt had to rely exclusively upon his executive powers, which had limits and entailed political costs.

The women's movement, in particular the suffrage campaign, marks a powerful synthesis of the purity/pollution and gift/debt codes. The traditional two-spheres norm in American society had maintained domestic life as the woman's sphere with public and economic life as the man's. With the end of couverture in the nineteenth century, women came out from the economic and legal protection/captivity of men into fuller citizenship, as we heard Mariana Chapman mention. Full citizenship demanded voting rights. The remarks we have heard by both female and male speakers indicate that this extension of full rights (gift/debt) carried with it ambitions to rein in the propensity of men toward vice away from the home, and to make society more "homelike" (purity/pollution). As suffrage became imminent, the rising tide of women's voices finally helped achieve the temperance goal of Prohibition (purity/pollution). It also strengthened the peace movement (gift/debt).

Regarding race, the endemic racism of American society tended toward the purity/pollution code, with its concern to protect kinship systems. European Americans often viewed African Americans as somehow "unclean" and black men as sexually transgressive. For their part, their historic experiences of persecution and marginalization engendered in Friends a predisposition to identify with other victims of prejudice and violence (the principle of extension that animates the gift/debt code). While the Quaker history of racial justice and inclusion is by no means perfect, this dynamic thrust Friends ahead of the progressive mainstream in advocacy for racial

APPENDIX 1   A Quaker Moral Compass

justice. Nevertheless, already in the early decades of the new century, we heard Friends express concern that they have less contact with African Americans than in the past. This trend was probably attributable to the new wave of racial segregation and the racist affects it encouraged generally in society. In the course of this study, we found Friends continuing to push against these dominant affects, slowly progressing from paternalistic assumptions toward an actual dialogue of equals.

These observations, based on the two codes of the ancient Hebrew Torah, which may also be universal moral sensibilities, are useful in detecting the patterns and logic of historic Quaker social testimony.

APPENDIX 2

Chapter Notes

INTRODUCTION

1. Walter Benjamin, Thesis II, "Theses on the Philosophy of History" (1940), in *Illuminations: Essays and Reflections* (New York: Schocken, 2007), p. 254; and Benjamin, "On the Concept of History," as quoted in Jonathan Flatley, *Affective Mapping: Melancholia and the Politics of Modernism* (Cambridge: Harvard University Press, 2008), p. 145.
2. See Jonathan Flatley, *Affective Mapping: Melancholia and the Politics of Modernism* (Cambridge: Harvard University Press, 2008).
3. Walter Benjamin, "Left-Wing Melancholy," quoted in Flatley, p. 64.
4. There is a flood of books and articles in affect theory, not all of them very useful, at least to me. I will draw primarily upon treatments in Jonathan Flatley, *Affective Mapping*; Fredric Jameson, *Antinomies of Realism* (London: Verso, 2013); *The Affective Theory Reader*, Melissa Gregg and Gregory J Seigworth, eds. (Durham: Duke University Press, 2010); Thandeka, *The Embodied Self: Friedrich Schleiermacher's Solution to Kant's Problem of the Empirical Self* (Abany: State University of New York Press, 1995); and *Ecologies of Affect: Placing Nostalgia, Desire, and Hope*, Tonya K Davidson, Ondine Park, and Rob Shields, eds. (Waterloo, Ontario: Wilfrid Laurier University Press, 2011).
5. I draw this perspective from Fredric Jameson's *The Political Unconscious: Narrative as a Socially Symbolic Ac*t (Ithaca: Cornell University Press, 1981) which argues that the capitalist mode of production is the final, unconscious horizon of interpretation for all literary productions, affecting not just content but also genre and structure.

CHAPTER 1: Pilgrims of Progress

6. From *The Hopedale Collection of Hymns and Songs: For the Use of Practical Christians*, quoted in *Angels of Progress: A Documentary History of the Progressive Friends: Radical Quakers in a Turbulent America*, compiled, edited, and introduced by Chuck Fager (Durham, NC: Kimo Press, n.d. [2014]), p. 6.
7. See my early Quaker trilogy, *Apocalypse of the Word: The Life and Message of George Fox* (Richmond, IN: Friends United Press, 1986; second edition, 2014); *The Covenant Crucified: Quakers and the Rise of Capitalism* (Wallingford, PA: Pendle Hill, 1995; reprinted London: Quaker Books, 2006); and *Seekers Found: Atonement in Early Quaker Experience* (Wallingford, PA: Pendle Hill, 2000).

APPENDIX 2   Chapter Notes

8. See Gwyn, *Seekers Found*, Chapter 4.
9. See Jane Calvert, *Quaker Constitutionalism and the Political Thought of John Dickinson* (Cambridge: Cambridge University Press, 2009); for a broader account of Penn's life and thought, see Melvin B. Endy, Jr., *William Penn and Early Quakerism* (Princeton: Princeton University Press, 1973).
10. *Some Account of the Life of Elizabeth Ashbridge*, reprinted in *The Friends' Library*, vol. 4 (Philadelphia, 1840), pp. 10-24.
11. See John Woolman, *The Journal and Major Essays of John Woolman*, Phillips P. Moulton, ed. (New York: Oxford University Press, 1971).
12. See Jack Marietta, *The Reformation of American Quakerism, 1748-1783* (Philadelphia: University of Pennsylvania Press, 1984) for a positive interpretation of these changes.
13. See Job Scott's *Essays on Salvation by Christ, and the Debate Following Their Publication* (Glenside, PA: Quaker Heritage Press, 1993); also online at qhpress.org. Also see treatment of the early nineteenth-century controversies over the essays in H. Larry Ingle, *Quakers in Conflict: The Hicksite Reformation* (Knoxville, University of Tennessee Press, 1986), pp. 13, 15, 42, 68-70, 133-35.
14. For more on Elias Hicks, see the scholarly edition of his *Journal*, Paul Buckley ed. (San Francisco: Inner Light Books, 2009); also *Dear Friend: Letters and Essays of Elias Hicks*, Buckley, ed. (Inner Light, 2011); and a thematic anthology, *The Essential Elias Hicks*, Buckley, ed. (Inner Light, 2013).
15. Richard Hubberthorne, *A Collection of the Several Books and Writings* (London, 1663), p. 271.
16. For some examples, see Hamm, "Hicksite Friends" (unpublished manuscript in the author's possession).
17. See Hamm, "Hicksite Friends."
18. Sigmund Freud, 'Mourning and Melancholia" (1895), p. 247, as quoted in Jonathan Flatley, *Affective Mapping: Melancholia and the Politics of Modernism* (Cambridge: Harvard University Press, 2008), p. 45.
19. John William Graham notes this in *Psychical Experiences of Quaker Ministers* (London: Friends Historical Society, 1933), p. 9, from his reading of *The Journal of Joseph Hoag* (Philadelphia: 1909). Journal references to discerned conditions end at about 1820. Hoag was very involved on the Orthodox side of the controversy, and later on the Wiburite side of the Gurneyite controversy.
20. For extensive studies of the religious and socio-economic dimensions of the Separation, see H. Larry Ingle, *Quakers in Conflict: The Hicksite Reformation* (Knoxville, University of Tennessee Press, 1986); Robert W. Doherty, *The Hicksite Separation: A Sociological Analysis of Religious Schism in Early Nineteenth Century America* (New Brunswick, NJ: Rutgers University Press, 1967); Thomas D. Hamm, *The Transformation of American Quakerism: Orthodox Friends, 1800-1907* (Bloomington, IN: Indiana University Press, 1988); and Hamm, "Hicksite Friends." A good, narrowly focused study is Paul Buckley's 2001 Master's thesis (Earlham School of Religion), *Thy Affectionate Friend: The Letters of Elias Hicks and William Poole*. Reproducing and

analyzing their correspondence, Buckley finds Hicks to be a charismatic leader, led by a few guiding principles, not overly concerned with details. In correspondence with Hicks, Poole drew out certain implications in Hicks's ideas, leading to conclusions Hicks did not reach on his own. According to Ingle (p. 142), Poole was the chief strategist among the Hicksite faction, providing tactical leadership in dealing with the controversy. Hicks was a Long Island farmer and primitivist Friend, while Poole was a prosperous miller in Wilmington, Delaware, active not only in Quaker leadership but also in civic and political affairs. Both men died soon after the separations, Poole in 1829 and Hicks in 1830.

21. See Thomas D. Hamm's classic study, *The Transformation of American Quakerism: Orthodox Friends, 1800-1907*. For a study making the case for the Holiness renewal as integral to historic Quaker spirituality, see Carole D. Spencer, *Holiness: The Soul of Quakerism: A Historical Analysis of the Theology of Holiness in the Quaker Tradition* (Milton Keynes: Paternoster, 2007).
22. Amos Peaslee, as quoted in Hamm, "Hicksite Friends."
23. Phebe Johnson, as quoted in Hamm, "Hicksite Friends."
24. Richard Price, letter to Edward Hicks, 1845, as quoted in Hamm, "Hicksite Friends."
25. *See Fager, Remaking Friends: How Progressive Friends Changed Quakerism & Helped Save America, 1822-1940* (Durham, NC: Kimo Press, 2014), pp. 12-13; Hamm, "Hicksite Friends"; and Hamm, *The Road to ESR: or the Long, Tangled, and Often Confusing story of How Friends Came to Embrace Theological Education*, 2010 Willson Lecture (Richmond, IN: Earlham School of Religion, 2010), pp. 22-5.
26. See Hamm, "Hicksite Friends" for similar views.
27. See Hamm, "Hicksite Friends."
28. See Fager, *Remaking Friends*, Chapter 1.
29. "The Law of Progress," in Fager, *Angels of Progress*, pp. 11-13; complete text in *Lucretia Mott: Her Complete Speeches and Sermons*, Dana Greene, ed. (New York: Edwin Mellen Press, 1980), pp. 71-79.
30. Elizabeth Cady Stanton, as quoted in Carol Faulkner, *Lucretia Mott's Heresy: Abolition and Women's Rights in Nineteenth-Century America* (Philadelphia: University of Pennsylvania Press, 2011), pp. 93-4.
31. Hamm, "Hicksite Friends."
32. Lucretia Mott in 1846 correspondence, as quoted in Hamm, "Hicksite Friends."
33. Chuck Fager, *Angels of Progress*; and *Remaking Friends*; and Hamm, "Hicksite Friends."
34. Waterloo Yearly Meeting, "The Basis of Religious Association," (1848), as quoted in Hamm, "Hicksite Friends."
35. Lucretia Mott, 1848 letter, as quoted in Fager, *Angels of Progress*, p. 138.
36. For more on Dugdale, see Fager, *Remaking Friends, passim*.
37. Green Plain Yearly Meeting, 1848 minute, as quoted in Hamm, "Hicksite Friends."

38. Joseph Dugdale, 1850 sermon, as quoted in Hamm, "Hicksite Friends."
39. Waterloo Yearly Meeting Minute, 1854, as quoted in Hamm, "Hicksite Friends."
40. For a larger summary, see Fager, *Remaking Friends*, pp. 45-50.
41. Salem, Ohio newspaper article, 1857, as quoted in Hamm, "Hicksite Friends."
42. Joseph Foulke, 1846, as quoted in Hamm, "Hicksite Friends."
43. Hamm, "Hicksite Friends."
44. Fager, *Angels of Progress*, pp. 138-39.
45. Hamm, "Hicksite Friends."
46. See Fager, *Remaking Friends*, Chapter 5; and Hamm, "Hicksite Friends." For a wider study of the spiritualist movement, see Ann Braude, *Radical Spirits: Spiritualism and Women's Rights in Nineteenth-Century America*, 2nd ed. (Bloomington: Indiana University Press, 2001).
47. For more on this background, see Gwyn, *Seekers Found*, especially Chapter 2.
48. In Chapter 2 of *Affective Mapping*, Jonathan Flatley explores Henry James' gothic spiritualist tale, *The Turn of the Screw*, in relation to the trial of Oscar Wilde for homosexual activity, which was a sensational event at the time of James's writing.
49. This analysis builds on previous work on Quaker understandings of truth, beginning with the final chapters of *Seekers Found*, and further developed in "Enacting Truth: The Dynamics of Quaker Practice, *Quaker Theology* #17 (Spring-Summer 2010), pp. 15-46; reprinted in *Befriending Truth: Quaker Perspectives*, Jeffrey Dudiak, ed. (Philadelphia: Friends Association for Higher Education, 2016), pp. 136-63.
50. See Fager, *Remaking Friends*, Chapter 7, for a good summary of these degenerating politics.
51. Lucretia Mott, as quoted in Fager, *Remaking Friends*, p. 73.
52. Lydia Foulke, 1861 letter, as quoted in Hamm, "Hicksite Friends."
53. Cited by Fager, *Remaking Friends*, p. 87.
54. Hamm, "Hicksite Friends."
55. Fager, *Remaking Friends*, p. 89.
56. See Hamm, "Hicksite Friends."
57. Hamm, "Hicksite Friends."
58. For more on Martha Schofield, see Mary S. Patterson, "Martha Schofield," in *Quaker Torch Bearers* (Philadelphia: Friends General Conference, 1943), pp. 116-35.
59. William Tallack, as quoted in Hamm, "Hicksite Friends."
60. Deborah Haines, "Friends General Conference: A Brief Historical Overview," *Quaker History*, Vol. 89, No. 2 (Fall 2000): 1.
61. Mott, 1876 speech, as quoted in Fager, *Remaking Friends*, p. 123.
62. Hamm, "Hicksite Friends."
63. Hamm, "Hicksite Friends."
64. *The Friend*, December 1867, as quoted in Hamm, "Hicksite Friends."

65. Hamm, "Hicksite Friends."
66. Hugh Barbour and J. William Frost, *The Quakers* (Westport, CT: Greenwood, 1988), p. 220.
67. Lucretia Mott, as quoted in Hamm, "Hicksite Friends."
68. Barbour and Frost, *The Quakers*, p. 223.
69. See Thomas C. Kennedy's excellent study, *British Quakerism 1860-1920: The Transformation of a Religious Community* (Oxford: Oxford University Press, 2001).
70. For more on Plummer, see Roger Hansen, "Jonathan Plummer and Hicksite Quaker Participation in the World's Parliament of Religions, Chicago, 1893," *Quaker History*, vol. 92, no. 1 (Spring 2003): 34-45.
71. Jonathan Plummer, 1878 correspondence, as quoted in Hamm, "Hicksite Friends."
72. Illinois Yearly Meeting minutes, 1877, as quoted in Fager, *Remaking Friends*, p. 127.
73. Illinois Yearly Meeting minutes, 1879, as quoted in Fager, *Remaking Friends*, p. 128.
74. Hannah Plummer, 1879 letter, as quoted in Hamm, "Hicksite Friends."
75. *Friends General Conference: Its History, Organization, and Program* (n.d., n.p., FGC, 1957); and Haines, "Friends General Conference," p. 4.
76. Fager, *Remaking Friends*, p. 129.
77. Friends General Conference Papers at Friends Historical Library, Swarthmore College, Box 68, documents from the 1930 Conference at Cape May; an anonymous, handwritten history of the formation of FGC, probably used in preparation for a FGC historical pageant that year.
78. Plummer, "Opening Address," *Friends Presentation of Their Faith, Works and Hopes in the World's Parliament of Religions and Proceedings in Their Denominational Congress* (Chicago: Conkey and Co., 1893), p. 12; as quoted in Hansen, "Jonathan Plummer," p. 34.
79. Quoted in Hansen, "Jonathan Plummer," p. 41.
80. Karl Mannheim, *Essays on the Sociology of Knowledge* (London: Routledge & Kegan Paul, 1952), pp. 301-02.
81. Indiana Yearly Meeting epistle, 1894, as quoted in Hamm, "Hicksite Friends."
82. For a statistical table of Orthodox and Gurneyite membership, see Hamm, *Transformation*, p. 175.

CHAPTER 2: A Quaker Chautauqua

83. Aaron Powell, Opening Remarks at the Friends' Religious Conference, *Proceedings of the Swarthmore Conferences* (Philadelphia: Friends' Intelligencer Association, 1896), p. 14.
84. Michael McGerr, *A Fierce Discontent: The Rise and Fall of the Progressive Movement in America, 1870-1920* (New York: Oxford University Press, 2003).
85. As quoted in McGerr, pp. 53, 73.

APPENDIX 2   Chapter Notes

86. McGerr, Chapter 6.
87. Hamm, "Hicksite Friends."
88. As quoted in McGerr, p. 52.
89. See Albert J. Wahl, *Jesse Herman Holmes: A Quaker's Affirmation for Man* (Richmond, IN: Friends United Press, 1979), pp. 95-108.
90. William James, as quoted in McGerr, pp. 69-70.
91. William James, quoted by Jacques Barzun in the Foreword to *The Varieties of Religious Experience* (New York: Mentor Books, 1958).
92. Andrew C. Rieser, *The Chautauqua Moment: Protestants, Progressives, and the Culture of Modern Liberalism* (New York: Columbia University Press, 2003), p. 2.
93. *Report of the Proceedings of the Conference of Members of the Society of Friends, held, by Direction of the Yearly Meeting, in Manchester from Eleventh to Fifteenth of Eleventh Month, 1895* (London: Headley Brothers, 1896), p. 241.
94. Graham, "Adult Schools in England," First-Day School General Conferences, *Proceedings of the Swarthmore Conferences* (Philadelphia: Friends' Intelligencer Association, 1896), pp. 82-89.
95. Jackson, report on "Work with the Colored People," Friends Union for Philanthropic Labor, *Proceedings*, pp. 188-92.
96. Holmes, "How Shall We Make Quakerism Reach the Masses?," Friends' Religious Conference, *Proceedings*, pp. 49-57.
97. Graham, "Three Needs of the Church," Friends' Religious Conference, *Proceedings*, pp. 119-28.
98. Clement Biddle, impromptu comment during session of Friends Union for Philanthropic Concerns, *Proceedings*, pp. 235-37.
99. William Dudley Foulke, Opening Session, *Proceedings of the Friends' General Conference: First-day School, Philanthropic, Educational, Religious [at] Richmond, Indiana, 1898* (Philadelphia: Friends' Intelligencer Association, 1898), pp. 5-8.
100. Albert Beveridge and George Hoar, January 9, 1900, as quoted in Sidney E. Mead, *The Lively Experiment: The Shaping of Christianity in America* (New York: Harper & Row, 1963), pp. 153-54.
101. "Memorial" to President McKinley, *Proceedings*, pp. 212-14.
102. Susan Gaskill, "Military Training," *Proceedings*, pp. 191-96.
103. Aaron Powell letter, *Proceedings*, pp. 306-07.
104. Henry Wilbur, comments at closing session, *Proceedings*, pp. 366-67.
105. For more on Henry Wilbur, see Roger Hansen, "'Hungering and Thirsting for the Contact with Kindred Spirits': Henry Wilbur and the Committee for the Advancement of Friends' Principles, 1900-1914," *Quaker History*, vol. 94, no. 2 (Fall 2005): 44-55.
106. Introduction, *Proceedings of the Friends' General Conference . . . Held at Chautauqua, N. Y., 1900* (Philadelphia: for the Conference, 1900), pp. v-vi.
107. William Birdsall, "What Quakerism Stands for," *Proceedings*, pp. 9-19.

108. See Jonathan Flatley's treatment of DuBois in relation to more recent social thought, in *Affective Mapping: Melancholia and the Politics of Modernism* (Cambridge: Harvard University Press, 2008), pp. 128-29.
109. Howard Jenkins, "Address of the Chairman," *Proceedings*, pp. 4-9.
110. John Wilhelm Rowntree, "The Personal Element in Religion," *Proceedings*, pp. 27-35.
111. Henry Wilbur, "The Duty of Friends to Social Reform," *Proceedings*, pp. 151-64.
112. Mariana Chapman, "Woman as Citizen," *Proceedings*, pp. 160-64.
113. Martha Schofield, "The Womanhood of the Negro Race," *Proceedings*, pp. 216-21.
114. I am helped in this perspective by recent correspondence with Chuck Fager.
115. Edward Janney, "Personal Purity and Its Influence upon Character," *Proceedings*, pp. 56-63.
116. Howard Jenkins, "The Outlook for Peace," *Proceedings*, pp. 103-09.
117. For a record of proceedings, see *The American Friends' Peace Conference: Philadelphia, 1901* (Philadelphia: by the Conference, 1902).
118. Epistle to Friends, *Peace Conference*, pp. 4-5.
119. Rufus Jones, "Response," *Peace Conference*, pp. 29-30.
120. Anna Braithwaite Thomas, "Response," *Peace Conference*, pp. 32-33.
121. Recommendation of the Reorganization Committee, *Proceedings*, pp. 343-44.
122. Report of the Central Committee, *Proceedings*, pp. 342-45.
123. Deborah Haines, "Friends General Conference: A Brief Historical Overview," *Quaker History*, Vol. 89, No. 2 (Fall 2000): 7.
124. See McGerr, pp. 3, 39.
125. Anna Cooper, "Ethics of the Negro Question," *Proceedings of the Friends' General Conference ... Held at Asbury Park, N. J. 1902* (Asbury Park: for the Conference, 1902), pp. 112-24.
126. Mariana Chapman, "Equal Rights of Women," *Proceedings*, pp. 127-31.
127. "The Greatest Need of the Society of Friends," nine panelists plus responses, *Proceedings*, pp. 143-56.
128. John William Graham, "Isaac Penington, a Quaker Mystic," *Proceedings*, pp. 281-91.
129. For more on Rufus Jones in the wider context of American liberal religion, see Gary Dorrien, *The Making of American Liberal Theology, Vol. II: Idealism, Realism, and Modernity, 1900-1950* (Louisville: Westminster John Knox, 2003), pp. 364-71.
130. Anna Jackson, "The Race Problem in the United States," *Proceedings of the Friends' General Conference ... Held at Toronto, Canada 1904* (Philadelphia: for the Conference, 1904), pp. 121-40.
131. Henry Wilbur, "The Problem and Its Solution," *Proceedings*, pp. 150-59.
132. Rufus Jones, "Teaching the Bible," *Proceedings*, pp. 245-57.
133. Haines, "Friends General Conference, p. 7.

APPENDIX 2   Chapter Notes

134. Fager, *Remaking Friends*, p. 157.

CHAPTER 3: The New Normal

135. William Birdsall, opening statement, *Proceedings of the Friends' General Conference . . . Held at Mountain Lake Park, Maryland 1906* (Supplement to Friends' Intelligencer), p. 4.
136. Birdsall, opening statement, *Proceedings*, p. 3.
137. Joseph Walton, "Quakerism: A Normal Religion," *Proceedings*, pp. 4-9.
138. For more on personalism and its influence on Jones and the first half of Pendle Hill's history, see Gwyn, *Personality and Place: The Life and Times of Pendle Hill* (Philadelphia: Plain Press, 2014). But while personalism is a striking, sustained influence at Pendle Hill, I do not find it significantly in my research of FGC Conferences.
139. Lavinia Hoopes, response to Walton, *Proceedings*, p. 11.
140. William Jackson, "Ignorance of the Bible a Loss to Society," *Proceedings*, pp. 11-15.
141. Various speakers, "A Young Man's Religion," *Proceedings*, pp. 32-34.
142. "Report on Week-End Conferences," *Proceedings*, p. 38.
143. Charles Burleigh Galbreath, "Shall the State Kill?," *Proceedings*, pp. 50-55.
144. J. Russell Smith, "Applied Religion," *Proceedings*, p. 59.
145. Henry Wilbur, "Speaking to Twentieth Century Conditions," *Proceedings of the Friends' General Conference . . . Held at Winona Lake, Indiana 1908* (Supplement to Friends' Intelligencer), pp. 20-25.
146. Henry Wilbur, proposal for "Friendly Propaganda," *Proceedings*, p. 13.
147. Report from representatives to International Congress of Religious Liberals, *Proceedings*, p. 11.
148. Joseph Janney, "Report on the Indian Question to Date, *Proceedings*, pp. 99-100.
149. For a critical appraisal of Quaker Indian work under the Grant Administration, see Clyde Milner, *With Good Intentions: Quaker Work among the Pawnees, Otos, and Omahas in the 1870s* (Lincoln: University of Nebraska Press, 1982).
150. Marianna Burgess, response to Janney, *Proceedings*, p. 100.
151. Anna Jackson, Report on the Education of Colored People, *Proceedings*, pp. 100-01.
152. Edward Janney, opening remarks, *Proceedings of the Friends' General Conference Held at Ocean Grove, N. J. 1910* (Supplement to *Friends' Intelligencer*), p. 3.
153. Jesse Holmes, "The Sense of a Larger Fellowship," *Proceedings*, pp. 3-9.
154. Scott Nearing, "Social Religion," *Proceedings*, pp. 13-21.
155. Arthur McGiffert, "The Present Trend of Religious Thought," *Proceedings*, pp. 49-55.
156. Henry Wilbur, "The Society of Friends and the Present Trend of Religious Thought, *Proceedings*, pp. 58-61.

157. Edward Clarkson Wilson, "Conditions That Make for War," *Proceedings*, pp. 71-76.
158. Hansen, "Henry Wilbur," pp. 49-51.
159. Quoted in Michael McGerr, *A Fierce Discontent: The Rise and Fall of the Progressive Movement in America, 1870-1920* (New York: Oxford University Press, 2003), p. 280.
160. Edward Janney, opening remarks, *Proceedings of the Friends' General Conference Held at Chautauqua, N. Y. 1912* (Supplement to *Friends' Intelligencer*), pp. 4-5.
161. Jesse Holmes, "The Modern Message of Quakerism," *Proceedings*, pp. 5-12.
162. John William Graham, "What Is Worth While and Why," *Proceedings*, pp. 14-20.
163. Arabella Carter, Charles McDowell, Leander Williams, John William Graham, et. al, session on prospects for peace, *Proceedings*, pp. 35-43.
164. William Walter Jackson, "Industrial Conditions," *Proceedings*, pp. 76-83.
165. Handwritten notes from 1930 Conference archives, FGC Papers, Box 68.
166. Discussion at close of opening session, *Proceedings of the Friends' General Conference Held at Saratoga Springs, N. Y. 1914* (Supplement to *Friends' Intelligencer*), pp. 10-12.
167. Jesse Holmes, "Experiential Religion as a Motive Force," *Proceedings*, pp. 135-39.
168. Carrie Chapman Catt, "Woman Suffrage," *Proceedings*, pp. 122-28.
169. David Snedden, "The Relation of Education to Morals," *Proceedings*, pp. 145ff.
170. Death of Henry Wilbur and comments, *Proceedings*, pp. 99-100, 143.
171. Elizabeth Gray Vining, *Friend of Life: The Biography of Rufus M. Jones* (Philadelphia: Lippincott, 1958), p. 148.
172. Fredric Jameson, *The Hegel Variations: On the Phenomenology of Spirit* (London: Verso, 2010), p. 20.
173. Rufus Jones, *The Trail of Life in the Middle Years* (New York: Macmillan, 1934), p. 222.
174. Gary Dorrien, *The Making of American Liberal Theology: Volume 2, Idealism, Realism, and Modernity, 1900-1950* (Louisville: Westminster John Knox Press, 2003), pp. 364-65.
175. Dorrien, *American Liberal Theology*, pp. 1-3.

CHAPTER 4: Progress Revised

176. Brian Phillips, "Apocalypse Without Tears: Hubris and Folly among Late Victorian and Edwardian British Friends," in Dandelion, Gwyn, Muers, Phillips, and Sturm, *Towards Tragedy/Reclaiming Hope: Literature, Theology and Sociology in Conversation* (Aldershot, Hampshire: Ashgate, 2004), pp. 57-76.
177. Corder Catchpool, *Letters of a Prisoner for Conscience Sake* (London: George Allen and Unwin, 1941), p. 161.
178. For more on the John Woolman School, see Carol R. Murphy, *The Roots of Pendle Hill*, Pendle Hill Pamphlet #223 (Wallingford, PA: Pendle Hill Publications, 1979). Also see Gwyn, *Personality and Place: The Life and Times of Pendle Hill* (Philadelphia: Plain Press, 2014), pp. 32-33.

APPENDIX 2 Chapter Notes

179. George Walton, "The Development of the Religious Life, Part I," *Proceedings of the Friends' General Conference Held at Cape May, N. J. Seventh Month 6th to 13th 1916* (Supplement to *Friends' Intelligencer*), pp. 3-6.
180. Wilson and Addams as quoted in Michael McGerr, *A Fierce Discontent: The Rise and Fall of the Progressive Movement in America, 1870-1920* (New York: Oxford University Press, 2003), pp. 281-82.
181. Rufus M. Jones, *A Service of Love in War Time: American Friends Relief Work in Europe, 1916-1919* (New York: Macmillan, 1920), p. 3.
182. Central Committee minutes (9/17) as quoted in Roger Hansen, "'The Blessed Community': The Mutual Influences of Friends General Conference and the New Meetings Movement, 1915-1945," *Quaker History* vol. 97, no. 2 (Fall 2008): 41-50.
183. See the Jane Addams Papers, microfilm reel #48, at the Peace Collection of the Swarthmore College Library.
184. See McGerr, Chapter 8.
185. For several case histories of young Puritans and Seekers becoming Quakers in the 1650s, see Gwyn, *Seekers Found: Atonement in Early Quaker Experience* (Wallingford, PA: Pendle Hill, 2000).
186. For more on these early Quaker politics, see Gwyn, *The Covenant Crucified: Quakers and the Rise of Capitalism* (Wallingford, PA: Pendle Hill, 1995).
187. Fosdick became a leading popularizer of Rufus Jones' work. See his *Rufus Jones Speaks to Our Time: An Anthology* (New York: Macmillan, 1950).
188. Fosdick, as quoted in Gary Dorrien, *The Making of American Liberal Theology: Volume 2, Idealism, Realism, and Modernity, 1900-1950* (Louisville: Westminster John Knox Press, 2003), pp. 371-74.
189. For more on this wider pacifist phenomenon and its subsequent marginalization, see Patricia Appelbaum, *Kingdom to Commune: Protestant Pacifist Culture between World War I and the Vietnam Era* (Chapel Hill: University of North Carolina Press, 2009), Chapters 2 and 3.
190. For an appraisal of Frank Aydelotte's leadership at Swarthmore, see the relevant chapter in Burton R. Clark, *The Distinctive College: Antioch, Reed, and Swarthmore* (Chicago: Aldine, 1970).
191. For more detail, see Chuck Fager, *Remaking Friends: How Progressive Friends Changed Quakerism & Helped Save America, 1822-1940* (Durham, NC: Kimo Press, 2014), pp. 181-84.
192. FGC Papers, Box 68. Planning Committee minutes appear only sporadically among other materials from these early Conferences.
193. For more on Crystal Bird, see Donna McDaniel and Vanessa Julye, *Fit for Freedom, Not for Friendship: Quakers, African Americans, and the Myth of Racial Justice* (Philadelphia: Quaker Press, 2009), pp. 210, 215-16, 320, n.470.
194. Also see Chuck Fager, *Shaggy Locks & Birkenstocks: Early Explorations in American Liberal Quaker Theology and Religious Thought* (Fayetteville, NC: Kimo, 2003), particularly the essay, "Shaggy Locks & Birkenstocks: Liberal Friends Discover Fox." in his unpublished paper, "Shaggy Locks & Birkenstocks- Liberal Friends Discover Fox" (2002).

195. Matthew S. Hedstrom, *The Rise of Liberal Religion: Book Culture and American Spirituality in the Twentieth Century* (New York: Oxford University Press, 2013; also see Hedstrom, "Rufus Jones and Mysticism for the Masses," *Cross Currents*, vol. 54, issue 2 (Summer 2004): 31-45.
196. Hedstrom, "Rufus Jones," p. 32.
197. Hedstrom, *Liberal Religion*, p. 9.

CHAPTER 5: An Expansive Depression

198. FGC papers at Friends Historical Library, RG4/025, Box 68, Conference materials for 1930.
199. Isaac Barnes May, "A Peculiar People and a Protestant President: Herbert Hoover and the Question of Quaker Citizenship," in *An Early Assessment of U. S. Quakerism in the 20th Century: Papers from the Quaker History Roundtable June 8-11, 2017*, Chuck Fager, ed. (Durham, NC: Kimo Press, n.d. [2017]), pp. 204-16 traces support for Hoover among Five Years Meeting Friends.
200. See columnist Walter Lippmann's insightful comments in David M. Kennedy's balanced treatment of Hoover in *Freedom from Fear: The American People in Depression and War, 1929-1945* (New York: Oxford University Press, 1999), p. 50.
201. Rufus Jones, as quoted in Elizabeth Gray Vining, *Friend of Life: The Biography of Rufus M. Jones* (Philadelphia: Lippincott, 1958), p. 224.
202. For more on the Independent Meetings in this period, see Elizabeth Cazden, "'Wicked Hard to Herd up': Independent Meetings and the Friends Fellowship Council," *Quaker History*, Vol. 90, No. 2 (Fall 2001): 1-14; and Roger Hansen, "'The Blessed Community': The Mutual Influences of Friends General Conference and the New Meetings Movement, 1915-1945," *Quaker History*, vol. 97, no. 2 (Fall 2008): 41-50.
203. Gregory A. Barnes, *A Centennial History of the American Friends Service Committee* (Philadelphia: FriendsPress, 2016), p. 101.
204. Friends Historical Library, Swarthmore College, Friends General Conference Papers RF 4/025, Box 54. For more on on singing at Conferences and among liberal Friends more generally, see Peter Blood Patterson's essay, "Singing Among FGC Friends" (2002), at www.riseupandsing.org.
205. See Patricia Appelbaum, *Kingdom to Commune: Protestant Pacifist Culture between World War I and the Vietnam Era* (Chapel Hill: University of North Carolina Press, 2009), p. 56.
206. For the full text and background, see *Angels of Progress: A Documentary History of the Progressive Friends: Radical Quakers in a Turbulent America*, compiled, edited, and introduced by Chuck Fager (Durham, NC: Kimo Press, n.d. [2014]), pp. 353, 377-79.
207. For more on Richard Gregg, including his two years at Pendle Hill, see Gwyn, *Personality and Place: The Life and Times of Pendle Hill* (Philadelphia: Plain Press, 2014), pp 67-81; for more on the impact of Gregg's work on the FOR and wider pacifist movement, see Leilah C. Danielson, "'In My Extremity I Turned to Gandhi': American Pacifists, Christianity, and Gandhian Nonviolence, 1915-1941," *Church History*, Vol. 73 No. 2 (June 2003): 361-88.

APPENDIX 2   Chapter Notes

208. See Barnes, *Centennial History*, pp. 90, 92, 155.
209. See Howard H. Brinton, *A Religious Solution to the Social Problem*, Pendle Hill Pamphlet #2 (Wallingford, PA: Pendle Hill, 1934). For more on Brinton's pamphlet and his early engagement with Pendle Hill, see Gwyn, *Personality and Place*, pp. 62-67.
210. See Gary Dorrien, *The Making of American Liberal Theology: Volume II: Idealism, Realism, and Modernity, 1900-1950* (Louisville: Westminster John Knox Press, 2003), pp. 448-51.
211. Rufus M. Jones, *Re-thinking Religious Liberalism* (Boston: Beacon Press, 1935).
212. Dorrien, *American Liberal Theology*, p. 452.
213. See FGC Papers, Box 64. The same box also contains twenty-seven mimeographed letters on a variety of social and economic issues sent by the Industrial Relations Committee to "Minute Men" who had volunteered to use the letters to stimulate discussion in their local meetings. The letters are dated from March 1933 to June 1936.
214. Deborah Haines, "Friends General Conference: A Brief Historical Overview," *Quaker History*, Vol. 89, No. 2 (Fall 2000): 10.
215. David M. Kennedy, *Freedom from Fear: The American People in Depression and War, 1929-1945* (New York: Oxford University Press, 1999), p. 380.
216. Haines, "Historical Overview," p. 9. Haines mentions that the Social Service Section actually did continue in various fading forms until it finally lapsed around 1968.
217. Barnes, *Centennial History*, p. 107.
218. The furniture included rush-seat chairs that can still be seen in various rooms around Pendle Hill. They were made from mountain hickory wood by unemployed coalminers in a program created by the AFSC. Local furniture maker Bud Godlove was hired to teach miners how to make chairs and other furniture. The resulting Mountaineer Craftsmen's Cooperative Association in Morgantown, West Virginia retrained miners for new work. For more on this innovative program, see Paul Moke, "Quakers in the Coalfields: Economic Justice and the American Friends Service Committee, 1920-Present," in *The Political Economy of Quakerism*, forthcoming publication of the Friends Association for Higher Education.
219. For more on Cadbury and this statement, see Gwyn, *Personality and Place: The Life and Times of Pendle Hill* (Philadelphia: Plain Press, 2014), pp. 115-21. For a full biography of Cadbury, see Margaret Hope Bacon, *Let This Life Speak: The Legacy of Henry Joel Cadbury* (Philadelphia: University of Pennsylvania Press, 1987). In place of mysticism, Cadbury offered a more rational and ethical commitment to following the teachings of Jesus. Among British Friends, William Littleboy had already broached this awkward subject in 1916, with the essay, "The Appeal of Quakerism to the Non-Mystic" (reprinted by Friends Home Service Committee, London in 1964). Differently from Cadbury, Littleboy suggested that the inward compulsion to do good in the world is itself a form of divine revelation.
220. Henry Cadbury, as quoted in Gwyn, *Personality and Place*, p. 83.

221. Herbert Hadley, *Quakers Worldwide: A History of the Friends World Committee for Consultation* (York, England: Sessions, 1991), p. 12.
222. Rufus Jones letter to Violet Holdsworth, July 1937, quoted in Vining, *Friend of Life*, p. 269.
223. From The Official Report of the Friends World Conference (n.p., n.d.), in the Friends Historical Library, Swarthmore College.

CHAPTER 6: War Without, Reassessment Within

224. For more on Lewis Benson, see T. H. S. Wallace, ed., *None Were So Clear: Prophetic Faith and the Ministry of Lewis Benson* (Camp Hill, PA: New Foundation Publications, 1996); and Gwyn, *Personality and Place: The Life and Times of Pendle Hill* (Philadelphia: Plain Press, 2014), pp. 139-44.
225. Publicity and other materials from the 1938 Conference in Box 70, Friends General Conference Papers (RG4/025) at the Friends Historical Library, Swarthmore College.
226. Patricia Appelbaum, in *Kingdom to Commune: Protestant Pacifist Culture between World War I and the Vietnam Era* (Chapel Hill: University of North Carolina Press, 2009).
227. Appelbaum, *Commune*, p. 37. For more on Quaker CPS work, see the AFSC's *An Introduction to Friends Civilian Public Service* (Philadelphia: AFSC, 1945); and Pendle Hill, *Friends in Civilian Public Service: Quaker Conscientious Objectors in World War II Look Back and Look Ahead* (Wallingford, PA: Pendle Hill, 1998).
228. Gregory A. Barnes, *A Centennial History of the American Friends Service Committee* (Philadelphia: FriendsPress, 2016), pp. 114, 120.
229. FGC Papers, RG4/025, at the Friends Historical Library, Swarthmore College, Box 70, 1942 Conference materials folder.
230. For more on Turner's work at Pendle Hill, see Gwyn, *Personality and Place*, pp. 126-29.
231. See Gwyn, *Personality and Place*, Chapter 5.
232. For these and other demographic statistics regarding the war, see David M. Kennedy, *Freedom from Fear: The American People in Depression and War, 1929-1945* (New York: Oxford University Press, 1999), pp. 748-80.
233. Kennedy, *Freedom from Fear*, p. 747.
234. An introduction to this useful concept is found in John Field, *Social Capital*, 2nd ed. (New York: Routledge, 2008).

CHAPTER 7: Pax Americana and the End of FGC's Heroic Era

235. Giovanni Arrighi, *The Long Twentieth Century: Money, Power, and the Origins of Our Times* (London: Verso, 1994), p. 298.
236. Peter Brock and Nigel Young, *Pacifism in the Twentieth Century* (Syracuse, NY: Syracuse University Press, 1999), pp. 246-47.
237. Patricia Appelbaum, *Kingdom to Commune: Protestant Pacifist Culture between World War I and the Vietnam Era* (Chapel Hill: University of North

Carolina Press, 2009), p. 40. However, some of that growth is attributable to independent meetings finding their way into affiliation with FGC yearly meetings, and to the uniting of Hicksite and Orthodox yearly meetings in 1955.

238. Gregory A. Barnes, *A Centennial History of the American Friends Service Committee* (Philadelphia: FriendsPress, 2016), p. 157.

239. James T. Patterson, *Grand Expectations: The United States, 1945-1974* (Oxford: Oxford University Press, 1996), p. 341.

240. For more on Eichenberg and on the growth of the artistic expression at Pendle Hill, see Douglas Gwyn, *Personality and Place: The Life and Times of Pendle Hill* (Philadelphia: Plain Press, 2014), pp. 179-84.

241. For more on this remarkable Friend's life, see her autobiography, *All This and Something More: Pioneering in Intercultural Education* (Bryn Mawr, PA: Dorrance, 1984). For excerpts from her writings, see *Nine Contemporary Quaker Women Speak*, Leonard S. Kenworthy, ed. (Kennett Square, PA: Quaker Publications, 1989), pp. 21-ff.

242. Barnes, *Centennial History*, pp. 171, 149.

243. For more on Bayard Rustin, see *Black Fire: African American Quakers on Spirituality and Human Rights*, Weaver, Kriese, and Angell, eds. (Philadelphia: FGC Quaker Press, 2011), pp. 151-78.

244. A documentary history of that ecumenical dialogue may be found in *On Earth Peace: Discussions on War/Peace Issues between Friends, Mennonites, Brethren and European Churches, 1935-1975*, Donald F. Durnbaugh, ed. (Elgin, IL: Brethren Press, 1978); more recent attempts at this outreach may be found in Gwyn, Hunsinger, Roop, and Yoder, *A Declaration on Peace: In God's People the World's Renewal Has Begun* (Scottdale, PA: Herald Press, 1991); and *Seeking Cultures of Peace: A Peace Church Conversation*, Enns, Holland, and Riggs, eds. (Telford, PA: Cascadia, 2004) (a response to the WCC's Decade to End Violence).

245. Reinhold Neibuhr, *The Nature and Destiny of Man*, vol. 1 (New York: Scribner's, 1941), p. 145.

246. Barnes, *Centennial History*, p. 171.

CONCLUSION

247. George Fox, *Works* (Philadelphia: Gould, 1831), vol. 7, p. 19.

248. This shift in consciousness is traced in Gwyn, *The Covenant Crucified: Quakers and the Rise of Capitalism* (Wallingford, PA: Pendle Hill, 1995; reprinted by London: Quaker Books, 2004).

249. See Chuck Fager, "FGC's 'Uniform Discipline' Rediscovered," *Quaker History* Vol. 89, No. 2 (Fall 2000): 51-59.

APPENDIX 1: A Quaker Moral Compass

250. I draw primarily here on Fernando Belo, *A Materialist Reading of the Gospel of Mark* (Maryknoll, NY: Orbis, 1981), "The Symbolic Order of Ancient Israel," pp. 37-59.

251. For more on Quakers and the family, see Barry Levy, *Quakers and the American Family: British Settlement in the Delaware Valley* (Oxford: Oxford University Press, 1988); and J. William Frost, *The Quaker Family in Colonial America* (New York: St. Martin's, 1973).

INDEX

(page numbers in italics indicate a photograph of the subject)

Abolition, anti-slavery, 5, 12-13, 15, 18-19, 23-24, 48, 52, 56, 64, 88, 118, 124, 134, 160, 166, 177, 254, 267

Addams, Jane, 105, 111, 113-*114*, 117, 139, 279

Affect, ix, xi-xv, xviii, xx, 1, 3, 9-10, 12, 14, 16, 22, 31-33, 52, 55, 72, 75, 87, 91, 98, 111, 116, 125, 137, 138, 143-44, 152, 157, 160, 162, 170, 182, 186, 199, 212, 218, 222, 236, 238, 243-44, 255-65, 269, 270

African Americans, x, xviii, 5, 10, 24, 29, 35-37, 42-43, 58, 64-68, 79, 85, 108-09, 115, 116, 118, 124-25, 127, 129, 133-34, 138-39, 144, 147, 154, 157, 165-66, 177-78, 180, 196, 204, 211, 214, 226, 231-32, 235, 256, 261-62, 268-69, 279, 283

Alexander, Will, 146-47

All-Friends Gathering (1920), 111, 176

American Friends Fellowship Council (AFFC), 169, 206-07, 237-38, 280

American Friends Service Committee (AFSC), xviii-xix, 106-08, 113, 118, 127, 130, 133-34, 140-41, 148-49, 152-55, 160-61, 169, 171, 175-76, 178, 185, 187, 194-95, 200, 201, 207, 211, 221, 223, 226, 229, 241, 245, 250-52, 257, 260-63

Anderson, Matthew, 64-65

Appelbaum, Patricia, 188, 193, 279

Ashbridge, Elizabeth, 5-6, 271

Ashelman, Samuel, 205

Aydelotte, Frank, 121-*122*, 124, 128, 134, 185, 192, 224-25, 279

Baltimore Yearly Meeting, Hicksite, 13, 28, 30, 64, 83, 171

Barnes, Gregory, 141, 169, 194, 241, 252, 280

Bartlett, Elizabeth 198

Benjamin, Walter, xi, xiii, 270

Bible, xiv-xv, 6-9, 21-22, 30, 41, 45, 69-70, 75-76, 94, 101, 102, 104, 134, 154, 165, 197, 228, 234, 254, 255, 267

Biddle, Clement, 45-47

Biddle, William, 236

Bird, Crystal (later Fauset), 133-34, 154, 279

Birdsall, William, 32, *53*-54, 72, 97

Blackmar, Mary, 249

Blanshard, Brand, 136, 171, 205-*06*

Blood Patterson, Peter, 280

Bond, Eleanor Powell, 109

Branson, Anna Jackson, 124-25

Brinton, Howard and Anna, 161, 175, 213, 245

Brock, Peter, 218

Bruere, Martha Bensley, 133

British Friends, London Yearly Meeting, xvi, xvii, 27, 41, 76, 88, 100, 103, 106, 108, 127, 176, 180, 278

Brooke, Gladys, 112

Brown, John, 23

Buck, Pearl, 246

Buckley, Paul, 271-72

Burgess, Marianna, 78-79

Burke, Frances Hart, 191, 198

Cadbury, Henry, 141, 154, 174-78, *175*, 196, 227, 234-35, 281

Calvert, Jane, 271

Carter, Arabella, 88, 126

Carver, George Washington, 129

Catchpool, Corder, 101

Catt, Carrie Chapman, 37, 65, 95
Chapman, Marianna, 43, 57-58, 65, 268
Chautauqua (Assemblies and Associations), xvii, xviii, 37-38, 52-61, 72, 77, 85-92, 106, 143, 258, 275
Christ, Christian, Jesus, xiv, xix, xx, 2-3, 6-9 17, 18, 20-21, 30, 33, 43-45, 51, 54, 55, 60-61, 64, 66, 69, 70, 75, 77, 79, 80-81, 85-87, 90, 93, 103, 114, 124, 126, 134-36, 144, 145, 148, 155, 163, 165-66, 179, 180-82, 186, 188, 195-96, 201, 210, 212, 219, 222-23, 229, 238, 244-45, 248-51, 253-54, 257, 260, 263, 266
Civilian Public Service (CPS), 188, 204, 210, 214, 282
Class, socio-economic, xvi, 3, 35-38, 42, 54, 55, 59, 87-88, 90-91, 95-96, 109, 113, 133-34, 136-37, 149, 152, 195-96, 198, 212, 218, 225, 243, 255-56, 258, 264
Committee for the Advancement of Friends' Principles, 62, 67, 275
Congregational (Progressive) Friends, 16-19, 21, 131
Conservative and Wilburite Friends, 11, 34, 238, 241
Constitution, 4, 19, 22, 29, 45, 61-62, 125, 192, 216, 238, 255, 271
Cooper, Anna, 64, 68
Cooperatives, 167, 171, 205, 232, 243, 281
Covenant, 4, 19, 22, 45, 254-55, 279
Curtis, Anna, 133, 143-44, 152, 154, 158, 171, 184, 191

Dandelion, Ben Pink, xvi, 53
Davis, Preston, 153
Dorrien, Gary, 98, 164-65, 276
DuBois, Rachel Davis, xviii, 115, 128, *129*-30, 133-34, 147, 175, 178, 204, 211, 237, 256
DuBois, W. E. B., 55, 65, 124, 129
Dugdale, Joseph, 11, 17-18, 272

Eby, Kermit, 225
Eddy, Sherwood, 119, 134

Einstein, Albert, 152, 179
Endy, Melvin, 271
Environment, xii, 88, 94, 108, 146, 261, 268
Evangelicalism, evangelical Friends, 7, 9, 12, 20-22, 25, 33-34, 48, 61, 100-01, 136, 241, 248-49, 252, 254
Evolution (theory and ideology), xviii, 1, 22, 27, 30, 37, 55-57, 59, 60, 66, 75, 82, 87, 91, 98, 145, 163, 191

Fager, Chuck, 16-17, 19, 23, 30, 70, 130-31, 265, 270
Federal Council of Churches (FCC), 80, 238
Fellowship of Reconciliation (FOR), xix, 101, 118, 128, 138, 148, 229
Feminism, women's movement, 59, 69, 261-62, 264, 268
Ferris, Benjamin, 12-13
First-Day Schools (and Conference), 29-30, 39-40, 47, 61, 65, 69, 126, 143, 144, 172, 248
Five Years Meeting, 61-62, 120, 141, 158, 170, 176, 186-87, 229
Flatley, Jonathan, xii, 270
Forbush, Bliss, xv, xix, 186-88, *194*-98, 203, 210-11, 215, 217, 222-23, 234, 238-39, 250, 257, 210, 265
Fosdick, Harry Emerson, 118, 134, 137
Foulke, Dudley, 48
Foulke, Joseph, 18-19
Foulke, Lydia, 23
Fox, George, xiv-xv, 2-3, 15, 16, 19, 21, 55, 79, 83, 87, 100, 123, 148, 182, 210, 228, 250-51, 253, 255, 270
Freelon, Allan, 235
Freud, Sigmund, 9-10, 271
Friends Council on Education, 198
Friends, early (see Quakers, early)
Friends (General) Education Conference, 47, 61, 198
Friends General Conference (FGC), formal organization, 61-62
Friends General Conference (FGC), Central Committee, 32, 39, 56, 61, 63, 64, 67, 84, 91, 92, 96, 103,

INDEX

107-09, 111, 119-120, 123, 125-26, 130-31, 141, 143, 153-54, 157, 166, 168, 170, 183, 186-87, 206, 215, 219, 227-32, 238, 240, 245, 249-50
Friends General Conference (FGC), Executive Committee, 40, 62, 120, 166, 167-70, 183, 186-87, 199, 206, 238, 240, 286
Friends General Conference (FGC) Planning Committee, 108, 12, 131, 201, 230, 232-33, 279
Friends Hymnal, 144, 201, 280
Friends Religious Conference, 31, 39, 43, 46, 51, 62
Friends Union for Philanthropic Labor (FUPL), 29-30, 41, 43, 45, 172
Friends World Committee for Consultation (FWCC), 176, 282
Friends World Conference (1937), 169, 171, 174, 176-77, 183-85, 282
Furnas, Elizabeth, 167-70, 172, 180, 182, 209

Galbreath, Charles Burleigh, 76
Gandhi, Mohandras, 121, 130, 157
Genesee Yearly Meeting, 16, 30, 40, 62, 67
George School, 31, 43, 73, 104, 107-09, 127, 171, 185, 246, 286, 287
Gilkey, James Gordon, 212
Graham, John William, xvii, *40-41*, 44-45, 56, 66, 67, 87-88, 90-91, 100, 120, 271
Gramm, Hans, 127
Green Plain Yearly Meeting, 17
Gregg, Richard, 157-58, 183, 188, 280
Gurney, Joseph John, 11
Gurneyite Friends, xvii, xx, 11, 20-21, 27, 28, 33-34, 41, 48, 61, 120, 138, 139, 141, 163, 196, 238, 241

Haines, Deborah, 62, 166, 169, 273
Haines, Vesta, 144, 240
Hamm, Thomas, 16, 19, 23, 25, 41, 271
Hansen, Roger, 85, 274-75, 278-80
Hayes, Russell, 43, 143
Hedstrom, Matthew, 136-37, 280

Hicks, Elias, 7, *8*, 10-12, 19, 31, 83, 84, 222, 234, 250, 257, 271-72
Hicks, Edward, 19-20
Hicksite Friends, xi, xiv-xv, 1, 7-34, 39, 41, 47, 48, 53-54, 56, 61, 66, 71, 98, 102, 105, 107, 111, 120, 148, 199, 271, 228, 254-55, 267, 271
High School Section, 183, 190-91, 199, 210, 211, 237, 243, 257
Hillman, Sidney, 127
Hoag, Joseph, 10
Hodgkin, Henry, 101, 148, 149, 150, 229
Holmes, Jesse, xviii, xix, 31, 32, 38, 43, *44*, 52, 56, 67, 69, 80-81, 83, 85-88, 91, 93-94, 102, 105, 107-08, 111, 115, 118, 128, 131, 134, *135*-36, 145-46, 150, 155, 265, 171, 185, 186, 197, 223, 257, 259, 275
Hoopes, Lavinia, 75
Hoover, Herbert, 117, 139-41, 280
Hubben, William, 187, 209, 214, 226, 228, 234, 244-48
Hubberthorne, Richard, 7
Hull, Hannah Clothier, 169
Hull, William, 105, 109

Illinois Yearly Meeting, 24, 26, 28-29, 40, 62, 130, 210
Indiana Yearly Meeting, Hicksite, 17, 32-33
International Association for Liberal Christianity and Religious Freedom, 186, 238
International and National Congresses of Religious Liberals, 78, 85, 164

Jackson, Anna, 42-43, 58, 67-68, 79, 115, 124, 261
Jackson, Arthur, 120, 124, 127, 152, 163, 171, 185-87, 191
Jackson, William, 75-76, 90-91, 93
James, William, 38, 82, 86, 98, 137, 182, 258
Jameson, Fredric, 98
Janney, Edward, 59, 62-*63*, 65, 91, 85-86, 91, 103, 112, 134, 136
Janney, Joseph, 78

287

Janney, Samuel, 30
Japanese Americans, 129, 204, 235
Jenkins, Howard, 26, 31, *55*, 59-60
Jenkins, Marie, 76
Jenkins, Thomas, 109
John Woolman School, 101-02, 105, 115, 127, 148, 198, 278
Johnson, Phebe, 12
Jones, Esther Holmes, 198, 225, 248
Jones, Rufus, xix, 46, 56, 60, 66, 69-70, 74, 87, 97-98, 101-02, 206-07, 112, 118, 136-37, 140-41, 148, 157, 159, 161, *162*-63, 165, 176-77, 180, 196, 228-29, 234-35, 241, 257-58, 264
Jones, Thomas, 203

Kennedy, David, 167, 215
Kilpack, Gilbert, 236, 245
King, Martin Luther, Jr., 237, 247, 262
Knight, Rachel, 93
Krusé, Cornelius, 245-46

Labor relations, unions, 19, 35, 36, 49, 65, 90-92, 94, 106, 117, 124, 134, 205, 213-14, 218, 225, 241, 247-48
Laing School, 24, 42, 79
Lamb, Eli, 28
League of Nations, 109, 111, 113, 116, 124, 160, 230
Lenroot, Katherine, 213
Libby, Frederick, 128, 158, *206*
Liberal Friends, Quakerism, ix, xi, xiii-xx, 2, 4, 7, 9, 19, 22, 27, 31, 33, 41, 43, 44, 46, 52, 53, 56, 67, 70, 84, 86, 99, 100, 112, 113, 120-21, 136-37, 145, 158, 166-68, 174, 180-82, 188, 195-99, 205, 215, 218, 227, 236, 242, 244, 248-49
Liberal Protestantism, 33-34, 37, 38, 66, 98, 163-65
Light, inward/inner, xiv-xv, xviii, 3-4, 7, 13, 31, 33, 54, 67, 86, 109, 131, 148-50, 158, 161, 164, 173, 185, 199, 205, 207, 234, 236, 253-55

Magill, Edward, 31, 47

Malin, Patrick Murphy, 165, 171, 192, 201-*02*, 235, 264
Mannheim, Karl, 31, 274
Mazumdar, Haridas, 121
McGerr, Michael, 35, 116, 274
McGiffert, Arthur, 82
Melancholy, mourning, xii-xiii, 1-3, 5-6, 9-11, 20, 25, 52, 84, 186, 227, 234, 256, 270, 271
Methodists, xvi, 11, 33, 37, 52, 63, 72, 79, 85, 120, 122, 188, 203
Military conscription, draft, xix, 23m 107, 101, 109, 187, 212, 218, 225, 229-30, 247
Miller, George, 96-97
Modernity, modernism, xii, 66, 87, 191, 199, 221, 256, 266, 270
Morgan, Arthur, 128, 158
Mott, Lucretia, 11, *14*-17, 19, 20, 23, 25-27, 43, 58, 272-73
Muste, A. J., 119, 188
Mysticism, 46, 66, 87-88, 98, 112, 137, 148, 173-74, 177, 222, 226, 249, 253

Nasmyth, George, 105
Native Americans, 5, 10, 24, 35, 37, 42, 78, 129, 152, 154, 204, 260-61.
Nearing, Scott, 81-82
Neo-orthodox theology, movement, 164-65, 180, 257
New England Yearly Meeting, 228, 238, 287
New York Yearly Meeting, Hicksite, 26, 30, 40, 48, 62, 103, 131, 133, 228
Newton, Ray, 134
Nicholson, Vincent, 100, 107, 113, 140
Niebuhr, Reinhold, xx, 119, 131-32, 163, 165, 249, 257
Nonviolence, 121, 157, 256, 280
Norment, Caroline, 127, 148

Ohio Yearly Meeting, Hicksite, 17, 40, 61, 62, 186
Orthodox Friends, Quakerism, xiv, xvii, xix, xx, 7, 9-12, 15, 24, 26, 29, 30, 33, 41, 45, 46, 61, 102, 105, 111,

INDEX

120, 133, 141, 148, 152, 158, 163, 168-70, 187, 199, 227-28, 238, 254, 271, 274

Page, Kirby, 119, 188
Palmer, Edward, 112
Patterson, James T., 233, 283
Paul, Alice, 37, 106
Paxson, Margaret, 153
Peace, Quaker peace testimony, pacifism, xii, xviii-xix, 4, 8, 22, 24-25, 29, 42, 50-51, 58-61, 69, 89-90, 93, 100-01, 103, 118, 128, 147, 154, 160, 162-63, 175, 182, 185, 192, 196, 223, 267
Peace Caravans, 134, 140, 147, 153
Peace Churches, Historic, 107, 188, 230, 248
Peace movement, mainstream, xviii, 15, 25, 89, 100, 105, 118-19, 121, 124, 129, 134, 147, 157, 160, 163, 188-89, 218, 256, 268
Peace Prize, Nobel, 227, 241
Pendle Hill, ix, xiii, xx, 148-50, 157, 161, 175-76, 180, 188, 198, 200, 205, 207, 213, 232, 236-37, 241, 245, 248, 277-78, 281, 282, 287, 289
Penn, William, 3-5, 10, 22, 61, 100, 105, 109, 113, 201, 216, 255, 271
Pennsylvania, xvii, 4, 10, 128, 149, 154, 161, 170
Pennsylvania/Longwood Yearly Meeting, 18-19, 199
Philadelphia Yearly Meeting, Hicksite, 18, 19, 23, 26, 30, 73, 75, 107, 130-31, 141, 143, 158, 169, 170, 172, 174, 183, 187, 227
Philadelphia Yearly Meeting, Orthodox, 33, 107, 227, 238
Phillips, Brian, 100, 278
Pickett, Clarence, xv, xix, 140-41, *146*-47, 149-50, 154-56, 159-61, 163, 174, 179, 192-96, 203, 212-13, 215, 216, 219, 223-24, *240*-41, 252, 257, 258, 262
Plummer, Hannah, 26, *28*-30

Plummer, Jonathan, 11, 26, *28*-30, 35, 46, 274
Poole, William, 13, 271-72
Post, Isaac, 19-20
Postmodernity, postmodernism, 263-64
Powell, Aaron, 26, 31, 35, 43, 46-47, *50*, 51, 56, 64, 268
Progress, xii, xiii, xv, xviii, xx, 1, 7-9, 13, 15, 18, 20-21, 23, 27, 49, 51, 54, 59, 68, 70, 77, 82, 87-88, 91-98, 105, 112, 115, 145, 154, 191, 199, 201, 202, 221, 256, 264
Progressive Friends, Quakerism, xi, xiii, xiv, xvi-vii, xx, 1, 13, 15-24, 26, 28, 44-46, 52, 54, 87, 101, 131, 140, 145, 150, 155, 178, 182, 197, 199, 216, 222, 234, 244, 256, 258, 261, 267, 270, 272, 274, 275, 287
Progressive movement (religious and political), xvi, xviii, 30, 33, 35-38, 42, 52-54, 58, 62, 64, 66, 68, 77, 85, 87, 98, 105, 116-19, 124, 138, 140, 178, 218, 236, 257, 258, 261, 267, 268
Progressive Party, 85, 90, 167, 192
Progressive revelation, 85, 90, 167, 192
Prohibition, xvi, 106, 111, 124, 133, 153, 170, 232, 261, 268
Purdy, Alexander, 165, 185, 191-92
Purity, xvi, xviii, 29, 36, 42-43, 54, 56, 57, 59, 64, 68-69, 71, 81, 84, 105, 106, 111, 118, 144, 170, 232, 253, 255, 261, 262, 266-68

Quakers, early, xv, xvii, 1-5, 7-8, 20-21, 33, 54, 73, 99, 117, 121, 123, 174, 180, 182, 196, 203, 228, 253-54, 270
Quietism, 11, 109, 197, 222, 234, 254

Racial justice, xix, 67, 71, 99, 255, 257, 262, 268
Rieser, Andrew, 38, 275
Roberts, Isaac, 56
Roberts, Preston, 251-52
Robbins, Raymond, 124

289

Robinson, Alice, 93
Roosevelt, Franklin, 159, 167, 179, 192, 214, 217-18, 221
Roosevelt, Theodore, 37, 42, 62, 78-79, 85, 92, 268
Rowntree, John Wilhelm, 56
Rural America, 34, 116, 138-39, 147, 195, 213, 221, 225, 228-29, 236-37, 241, 251
Rushmore, Jane, xviii, 31, 32, 131, *172*-74, 198, 257, 261
Russell, Elbert, 102-05, 109, 115, 127
Rustin, Bayard, 201, 204, 211, 225, 243, 246, *247*, 256, 262, 283

Sayre, John Nevin, 128
Schofield, Martha and Schofield School, 24, 42, *58*-59, 79, 273
Scott, Job, 6
Seekers, early and modern, xvii, 1-4, 9, 21, 33, 75, 112, 141, 182, 198, 199, 210, 214, 221, 226, 236, 249, 253-55, 260, 270
Silver, Hillel, 158
Simkin, William, 247-48
Slavery, 17-18, 20, 22-23, 68, 75, 266
Smith, Russell, 76-77, 113
Snedden, David, 95-96
Solenberger, Edith Reeves, 201, 209-10
Spiritualism, 19-20, 273
Stanton, Elizabeth Cady, 15
Starr, Eleanor, 221, 226, 233-34, 237
Steere, Douglas, 188
Swarthmore College, 27, 30, 31, 38, 39-47, 80, 81, 105, 120-22, 128, 130, 134, 136, 169, 176, 179, 286, 287
Synteresis, 4

Tallack, William, 24
Temperance, xvi, xviii, 15, 19, 29, 36, 42, 43, 52, 78, 144, 170, 255, 267-68
Thomas, Norman, 144-45
Thomas, Wilbur, 130, 140-41
Thurman, Howard, 137, *164*-65
Tilly, Dorothy, 235

Trueblood, D. Elton, 192
Turner, Haines, 205

United Nations, 192, 217, 221, 225, 229

Vining, Elizabeth Gray, 97, 201
Visser 'T Hooft, William, 248

Walton, George, 103-*04*, 108, 171, 185, 249
Walton, J. Barnard, *102*-03, 198-99, *239*-40, 243-44, 250-51
Walton, Joseph, 73-*74*, 97, 102
War (causes, horrors, prevention, etc.), xii, 4, 8, 24, 49, 50, 59, 60, 66, 69, 73, 83, 88-90, 93-94, 96, 111-13, 118-19, 121, 124, 128-30, 144-45, 192, 196, 222, 23, 225, 267
War, American Civil, 11, 19, 22-25, 36, 50, 52, 56, 69, 89, 93
War, English Civil, 1, 117
War, Korean, 218, 235, 246
War, Lamb's, 3, 9, 10, 117, 121
War, Spanish-American, 48-49, 59
Washington, Booker T., 37, 43, 68, 91
Waterloo Yearly Meeting, 16-18
Watson, Frank, 159
Wilbur, John, 11
Wilbur, Henry, 51-52, 56-*57*, 59, 66, 68, 70-71, 76-78, 83-85, 92-93, 96-97, 101, 102, 186, 198, 240, 259, 268, 275
Williams, Leander, 89
Wilson, Edward Clarkson, 83-84
Wilson, Raymond, 246
Wilson, Woodrow, xviii, 85, 90, 92, 100, 105-06, 109, 116, 118, 128, 217
Women's Christian Temperance Union, 36, 153
Women's suffrage, 37, 52, 57-59, 65, 92, 106, 215, 255, 261, 268
Woolman, John, xv, 6, 41, 101, 115, 162, 201, 271
World Council of Churches (WCC), xix, 176, 180, 186-87, 203, 238, 248
World War I, xv, xviii, 27, 88-90, 92, 94, 96-108, 118, 147, 188, 193, 230, 256

World War II, xix, 158, 160, 179, 187-90, 199, 205-06, 212, 214-18, 230
World's Parliament of Religions, 30-32, 274

Yeatman, Lavinia, 31
Yerkes, Sue, 167, 180, 182
Young Friends; Movement, Association, xviii, 30-32, 42, 47, 56, 70, 76, 92, 101, 111, 115, 120, 124, 131, 133, 140, 152, 153, 157, 168, 171-73, 183, 192, 196, 198-99, 207, 208, 211, 214, 221, 222, 229, 232, 236, 27, 243, 244, 251-52, 256-57, 259
Young, Nigel, 218
Zeitgeist, ix

SOURCES

The primary sources I have utilized are mainly the *Conference Proceedings* that were collected in bound volumes published by *The Friends Intelligencer* for the Conferences 1896 to 1916. Starting in 1918, papers and proceedings appeared in print only in *The Friends Intelligencer*. I have cited in the text the specific issues I drew upon. Manuscript resources were mostly the minutes of FGC's Central and Executive Committees. I have referenced specific meetings of these Committees in the text. All of these materials are found in the Friends General Conference Papers archived at the Friends Historical Library of Swarthmore College. FGC's photographic archives for the first half of the twentieth century proved skimpier than I had hoped. I was able to supplement those archives with photographs from the Friends Historical Library's other photo archives, particularly the Swarthmore College archives, as well as the George School archives, the American Friends Service Committee archives, and some other random sources. The sources are credited with the photos and other graphics. I was sorry not to find photos for some important Conference speakers.

ACKNOWLEDGEMENTS

I am grateful to the Friends Historical Library for the Margaret W. and John M. Moore Research Fellowship for 2016 and to the Obadiah Brown Fund of New England Yearly Meeting for the financial assistance that made this project possible. In addition, I thank Pendle Hill, the Quaker study and conference center near Swarthmore College, for inviting me to spend the 2017 year as a Friend in Residence, which afforded me time for the research and writing of this book. Pendle Hill has been a great blessing in my life and work over the past 30 years.

In addition, I am grateful to Patricia O'Donnell, Christopher Densmore, Susanna Morikawa, and Celia Caust-Ellenbogen of the Friends Historical Library, and to Julie Swierczek of the Peace Collection of Swarthmore College for their friendly advice and assistance in my research. Don Davis, American Friends Service Committee's archivist, Dave Long, the George School's archivist, and the Walton family supplied additional photographs.

I am also indebted to Thomas Hamm, Quaker historical archivist at the Lily Library of Earlham College, and to Chuck Fager, a fellow independent scholar, for sharing their writings and insights on Hicksite and Progressive Friends in the nineteenth century. I have relied largely upon their primary research in writing Chapter 1, as the citations there show, though I take responsibility for that chapter's overall interpretation of nineteenth-century developments. Weekly conversations with Chuck Fager about Progressive Friends during his 2013-14 Cadbury Scholarship year at Pendle Hill planted the seeds of my interest in this project. Both Fager and Hamm have offered helpful comments on chapters from this book.

I also want to express my thanks to Brent Bill for taking this manuscript under his wing and giving it such a helpful editing process. And it's a treat to work again with David Botwinik, whose artful layout and cover design are elegant. All remaining blemishes and indiscretions are mine.

Finally, it was a chance conversation with Jerimy Petersen in the 2015 FGC Gathering bookstore that crystalized the concept and approach for this book. I am thankful for the friendship and encouragement of all these friends.

ABOUT THE AUTHOR

Douglas Gwyn was called to ministry in 1968 and has served among Friends variously as a peace educator for the American Friends Service Committee, as a Friends pastoral minister, as a teacher at the Pendle Hill and Woodbrooke Quaker study centers, and as a writer. He has been a student of Quaker history and thought for over forty years. He finds himself drawn to the various streams of Friends and has sought to exercise a ministry of reconciliation among them. His wife, Caroline Jones, is a dharma teacher in the Insight Meditation stream of Buddhism. Guided by the left hand of God, Doug writes songs about fast-food ("Cheeseburger Deluxe"), alienation ("Grandma Was a Klingon"), individuation ("That of Odd in Everyone"), the middle class ("The Parlor of No Return"), and of course Quakers ("Eighty-Weighty Friend," "A Process in the Wind," etc.) He is now retired, living in Richmond, Indiana and looking back with gratitude and wonder. But he's still apocalyptic after all these years.

www.ingramcontent.com/pod-product-compliance
Lightning Source LLC
Chambersburg PA
CBHW051038160426
43193CB00010B/984